AF608236

The Truth Required in the *Preces* for Rescripts

This dissertation was approved by the Rev. John Rogg Schmidt, A.B., J.C.D., LL.B., Professor of Canon Law, as director, and the Very Rev. Clement V. Bastnagel, S.T.L., J.U.D., and the Rev. Frederick R. McManus, A.B., J.C.D., as readers.

THE CATHOLIC UNIVERSITY OF AMERICA
CANON LAW STUDIES
No. 392

The Truth Required in the *Preces* for Rescripts

A HISTORICAL SYNOPSIS AND A COMMENTARY

A DISSERTATION

Submitted to the Faculty of the School of Canon Law of The Catholic University of America in Partial Fulfillment of the Requirements for the Degree of Doctor of Canon Law

BY

DONALD E. ADAMS, A.B., J.C.L.
A Priest of the Diocese of Harrisburg

THE CATHOLIC UNIVERSITY OF AMERICA PRESS
WASHINGTON, D. C.
1960

Nihil Obstat:

JOANNES R. SCHMIDT, A.B., J.C.D., LL.B.
Censor Deputatus

Washingtonii, die 25 martii 1959.

Imprimatur:

✠ GEORGIUS LEO LEECH, D.D., J.C.D.
Episcopus Harrisburgensis

Harrisburgi, die 27 aprilis, 1960.

Printed by
THE WICKERSHAM PRINTING CO.
Lancaster, Pennsylvania

AFFECTIONATELY DEDICATED

TO

MY FATHER AND MOTHER

FOREWORD

It is difficult to overestimate the role which the Roman Law Institute of Rescript plays in regulating the lives and affairs of individual members of the Church. Ever since its introduction into the ecclesiastical governmental mechanism, this written reply has been used with ever-increased frequency by Church authorities not only to vindicate the rights of clergy and faithful alike but also to bestow upon them privileges, faculties, dispensations, benefices, and, in a word, probably any other favor which they receive. The objective value of these concessions, however, always depends upon the validity of the rescripts which convey them to their prospective beneficiaries.

Little wonder it is, then, that the ecclesiastical lawgiver has ever been most careful to ensure the validity of rescripts. His care in this regard has been especially evident from the minute specifications that he has made in reference to the truth that is required in the *preces* for these letters. Indeed, from the very beginning of the use of rescripts in the Church the truth that must be had in the petitions for them has been looked upon as the most fundamental basis for their validity. The legislator himself made this fact clear centuries ago when he prescribed that in all rescripts the essential condition *"si preces veritate nitantur"* was to be at least understood, even when it was not expressed in so many words. This same prescription is still found in his Code of Canon Law. With it are several other norms which propose to specify and to clarify the lawgiver's demand for truthful *preces* as a *conditio sine qua non* for the validity of rescripts.

Unfortunately, however, the general principles that govern the condition *"si preces veritate nitantur"* sometimes lead to practical and perplexing problems for those whose ministry involves the more or less frequent handling of rescripts. Very often these problems arise because the basic significance of these general principles is not fully or clearly appreciated. Such is the case, for instance, when one believes that, so long as the reasons given for a rescript are true, the legislator's demand for truthful *preces* is fulfilled. Therein lies the reason which has provoked the canonical commentary that is presented in this dissertation. Correspondingly the writer's purpose, in offering this commentary, is to enunciate and to explain in a thorough and practical manner the basic principles that regulate the operation of the essential condition *"si preces veritate nitantur."*

Moreover, the desire to accomplish this purpose in as adequate a manner as possible has led the writer to offer also in this work a historical synopsis both of the pre-Code law in this matter and of the copious commentary which was written on that earlier legislation. It is to be noted that the present jurisprudence in reference to the truth that is required in the *preces* for rescripts is an outgrowth of the canonical discipline which developed through the many centuries that preceded the Code of Canon Law. The modern jurisprudence in this regard is, however, a modified and a clarified outgrowth of that previous discipline. So, it is hoped that, if anyone sees the beginnings and the controversy-marked evolution of the general principles which are the subject of this study, he will perhaps be able to appreciate more the clearness and the conciseness of the norms that now govern the legislator's demand for truthful *preces*.

The writer welcomes this occasion to express his sincere gratitude to His Excellency, the Most Reverend George L. Leech, D.D., J.C.D., Bishop of Harrisburg, for the opportunity of graduate study in Canon Law at the Catholic University of America. He also wishes to thank both the members of the Faculty of the School of Canon Law for the learning imparted by them and the Reverend Doctor John Rogg Schmidt, A.B., J.C.D., LL.B., the director of this work, for the patient and scholarly guidance received from him. He wants likewise to make known his gratefulness to his parents, to his classmates at the University, and to all others whose prayers, helpful suggestions, and kind encouragement have helped to make this dissertation a reality.

TABLE OF CONTENTS

PART III

CANONICAL COMMENTARY ON THE PRESENT LAW IN THE CODE OF CANON LAW

PART I

BASIC CONCEPTS

CHAPTER I

BASIC CONCEPTS IN THE LAW ON RESCRIPTS

The Code of Canon Law has eliminated many of the legal complications which developed through the years in the Church's general legislation on rescripts and the truth that is required in the *preces* for them. Nonetheless, the nature of rescripts themselves, as well as the widely diversified uses to which they are put, has prevented even the systematic codifiers of the present law from formulating a single norm to cover all the possible applications of the principle *"si preces veritate nitantur."* [1] In order, therefore, to give the reader some understanding of the more important basic concepts upon which the rest of this study is founded, the writer offers the following considerations.

Section I. Concerning Rescripts

Article 1. The Definition of Rescript

Neither the Roman nor the ecclesiastical lawgiver has ever given an express definition of the term "rescript." [2] Etymologically, the word is derived from the Latin *"re"* and *"scribere,"* meaning to write back.

Accordingly, canonical commentators, writing before the Code of Canon Law, generally defined a rescript as a written reply given by the Pope (or the Emperor) to someone's consultation, report, or petition.[3] It is noteworthy that throughout the entire

[1] The basic norms that govern this principle are stated in canons 39, 40, 41, 42, 45, and 1054 of the Code of Canon Law. *Codex Iuris Canonici Pii X Pontificis Maximi iussu digestus, Benedicti Papae XV auctoritate promulgatus, Praefatione, Fontium Annotatione et Indice Analytico-Alphabetico ab Emo Petro Card. Gasparri Auctus,* Westminster, Md.: The Newman Press, 1949. The abbreviation "can." is hereafter used in the footnotes of this work to designate the individual canons of the Code.

[2] Cf. *infra,* pp. 39-40.

[3] "[Rescriptum] est illud quod ab Apostolico, idest a Papa, seu a Principe rescribitur ad consultationem, relationem, seu intimationem alterius, vel alicui indulgendo."—Hostiensis (d. 1271), *Summa Aurea*

pre-Code period common usage reserved the term "rescript" for the written replies of the Sovereign Pontiffs (or the Emperor). It was standard practice, however, for those replies to be issued through the various Congregations, Offices, and Tribunals of the Roman Curia, as well as through papal legates.[4] Nonetheless, with proper adjustment most of what was said regarding papal rescripts could have been easily and correctly applied to the written replies that were issued by bishops and other ordinaries.[5]

In fact, canon 36, § 1, of the Code of Canon Law has clearly extended the comprehension of the term "rescript" so as to make it include the written replies both of the Apostolic See and of other ordinaries.[6] With this more comprehensive meaning in

(Venetiis, 1570), Lib. I, tit. III, in rubricam, n. 1. "Ita [rescriptum] sumitur praesenti titulo, et definitur, quod sit responsum a papa, imperatore, vel alio principe, praesertim supremo, ad alicujus supplicationem, relationem, vel consultationem in scripto datum. Ita quoad sensum communiter DD."—Schmalzgrueber (1663-1735), *Jus Ecclesiasticum Universum* (5 vols. in 12, Romae, 1843-1845), Lib. I, tit. III, n. 1 (hereafter cited as *Jus Ecclesiasticum*).

The above-delineated concept of a rescript is used in the historical part of this dissertation.—Cf. *infra,* pp. 35-106.

[4] Cf. Reiffenstuel (1642-1703), *Jus Canonicum Universum* (5 vols. in 7, Parisiis, 1864-1870), Lib. I, tit. III, n. 3 (hereafter cited as *Jus Canonicum*); Santi (1830-1885), *Praelectiones Juris Canonici* (cura M. Leitner, 5 vols. in 2, Ratisbonae-Romae-Neo Eboraci-Cincinnati, 1904), I, 29 (hereafter cited as *Praelectiones*).

[5] Wernz (1842-1914), *Ius Decretalium* (6 vols., Vol. I, 2. ed., Romae, 1905), I, n. 150, nota 21.

[6] Can. 36, § 1, states: "Rescripta tum Sedis Apostolicae tum aliorum Ordinariorum impetrari libere possunt ab omnibus qui expresse non prohibentur." Cf. also cans. 43 and 44 for further evidence of this extended comprehension of the term "rescript."

The expression "Apostolic See" is to be understood according to can. 7; the term "ordinaries" is explained in can. 198, § 1, and in can. 488, n. 8.

Notwithstanding this extension of the comprehension of the term "rescript," very often when the word is used without qualification, it signifies replies of the Holy See. Except for those prescriptions which from their tenor can apply only to rescripts of the Apostolic See, the norms set down in *Titulus IV, De rescriptis,* of *Liber I* of the Code of Canon Law are applicable not only to rescripts issued by the Holy See and to those emanating from other ordinaries but also to those granted by other persons who are duly authorized to issue them.—Cf. *infra,* pp. 119-122.

mind, canonists, writing after the promulgation of the Code of Canon Law in 1918, agree substantially in defining a rescript as an authoritative reply of a competent ecclesiastical superior, given in writing to someone's consultation, report, or petition.[7]

Accordingly, the juridic concept of a rescript comprises three distinct elements. First of all, a rescript is a *reply to someone's consultation, report, or petition.* Hence, the very nature of this institute necessarily requires that it has been preceded by another's petition or issued at another person's instance.[8] Moreover, from the fact that the issuance of a rescript is prompted by the consultation, report, or petition of some individual, one can conclude that a rescript is intended for the good only of an individual. Chelodi (1880-1922) made this point by saying:

> . . . rescriptum, privilegium, dispensatio casus vel personas *singulares* respiciunt et sunt fontes iuris *subiectivi.* . . . Et se refert [rescriptum] hodie exclusive ad negotia privatorum, unde ius facit tantum inter partes (can. 17, § 3) aut favorem tribuit impetranti.[9]

[7] Cf., e.g., Michiels who writes: ". . . rescriptum in jure communiter definiri solet: 'responsum principis scripto datum ad alicujus supplicationem vel relationem vel consultationem'."—*Normae Generales Juris Canonici* (2 vols., 2. ed., Parisiis-Tornaci-Romae: Desclée et Socii, 1949), II, 282 (hereafter cited as *Normae Generales*); Rodrigo, who states: "Rescriptum definiri potest in iure ecclesiastico, responsum auctoritativum Principis ecclesiastici scripto datum."—*Praelectiones Theologico-Morales Comillenses,* II, *Tractatus de Legibus* (Santander: Sal Terrae, 1944), p. 522 (hereafter cited as *Tractatus de Legibus*).

This broader concept of a rescript is used in the canonical commentary offered in this dissertation, beginning at p. 109.

[8] This first element differentiates a rescript from other acts by competent ecclesiastical authorities. For instance, a rescript is not, strictly, a *motu proprio* effected enactment. The very expression *"motu proprio"* indicates that the person in authority intends to act spontaneously, as it were, and because of his own liberality and generosity rather than because of any petition which he may have received. A rescript is also not a decree, for a decree is characteristically issued *motu proprio.* Cf. *infra,* p. 9, where the seeming contradiction involved in speaking of a *"motu proprio* granted rescript" is discussed.

[9] *Ius Canonicum de Personis* (3. ed., recognita et aucta a Pio Ciprotti, Vicenza: Società Anonima Tipografica; Trento: A Ardesi, 1942), pp. 125-126.

Secondly, a rescript is a *written* reply. Hence, while the same purposes may be accomplished by a superior's verbal answer to someone's petition, such an oral reply is not a rescript, even though it may afterwards be reduced to writing, for instance, for the sake of proof.[10] Nor is such a verbal reply governed by all the prescriptions which regulate rescripts.[11]

It may be noted here that the Roman Curia issues its rescripts in the form of Bulls, Briefs, and Simple Rescripts. The *Apostolic Bull,* the most solemn form of papal document, is reserved for rescripts of greatest importance. The *Apostolic Brief* is a form of rescript used for matters of minor importance. The *Simple Rescript,* the form most frequently used by the Roman Curia, lacks the formalities of the Bull and the Brief and is issued in a rather simple style on ordinary paper.[12]

Thirdly, a rescript is a written reply *of a competent ecclesiastical superior.* That is to say, in order to have a real rescript, it is essential that the answer be given authoritatively by a legitimate ecclesiastical superior who has either legislative power or the power of jurisdiction in both the internal and the external forum.[13]

Thus a rescript differs from a law, for a law is enacted for the common good of a community. Likewise it differs from a constitution, for a constitution is a papal document in which a law is solemnly enacted. A rescript differs also from a decretal letter, for a decretal "aliquid circa ius commune universaliter resolvebat aut statuebat."—Rodrigo, *Tractatus de Legibus,* p. 522.

[10] O'Neill (1900-1943), *Papal Rescripts of Favor,* The Catholic University of America Canon Law Studies, n. 57 (Washington, D. C., 1930), p. 4.

[11] Van Hove, *Commentarium Lovaniense in Codicem Iuris Canonici,* Vol. I, tom. IV, *De Rescriptis* (Editum a Magistris et Doctoribus Universitatis Lovaniensis, Mechliniae-Romae, 1936), p. 82 (hereafter cited as *De Rescriptis*).

[12] Cf. O'Neill, *op. cit.,* pp. 59-61.

[13] Michiels, *ibid.,* p. 283. According to this author those who can now issue rescripts are the following: a) the Pope and the various dicasteries of the Roman Curia according to their competence; b) all the ordinaries mentioned in can. 198, § 1, and can. 488, n. 8, within the scope of their authority, and c) all to whom the power of granting rescripts has been given by those mentioned under a) and b), "sive a jure sive ab homine legitime fuit concessa [potestas rescribendi]."—*Ibid.,* pp. 283-284.

Article 2. The Parts of a Rescript

A rescript is composed basically of three parts: the narrative part, the motive part, and the dispositive part. The narrative part (*pars narrativa*) is a summary of the petition. That is, in this *pars narrativa* are noted, for instance, the petitioner's name, his diocese or religious order, the object of his petition, and the circumstances of his case as they have been mentioned in his petition. The motive part (*pars motiva*) outlines the reasons for which the rescript is being granted. These reasons are usually those which the petitioner has presented in his *preces*. There are instances, however, in which the superior indicates that he is issuing the requested rescript for reasons other than those offered by the petitioner. The dispositive part (*pars dispositiva*) sets forth the point of law at issue, or grants or denies the requested favor. In this last part also are listed the conditions, if any, which must be observed in connection with the rescript.[14]

In this dissertation the term "superior" is used to signify all those who can lawfully issue rescripts.

[14] Cf. Cicognani, *Canon Law* (2. ed., authorized English version by J. M. O'Hara and F. J. Brennan, Westminster, Md.: The Newman Press, Reprint, 1949), p. 699.

Cf. also Engel (1634-1674), *Collegium Universi Juris Canonici* (Beneventi, 1760), Lib. I, tit. III, n. 6 (hereafter cited as *Collegium*) and Conte a Coronata, *Institutiones Iuris Canonici ad usum utriusque cleri et scholarum,* I (4. ed., Taurini: Marietti, 1950), 70 (hereafter cited as *Institutiones*). In the places just cited, those authors divide a rescript into a) the narration in which the case involved is explained; b) the supplication in which the favor is requested, and c) the conclusion in which the favor is granted and the conditions or clauses to be observed are set forth.

Some present-day canonists combine the narrative and motive parts and, taking them together, call them the expositive part. Cf. Vermeersch-Creusen, *Epitome Iuris Canonici cum Commentariis ad Scholas et ad Usum Privatum* (3 vols., Vol. I, 7. ed., 1949; Vol. II, 6. ed., 1940, Mechliniae-Romae: H. Dessain), I, n. 153. For these canonists, then, a rescript consists of an expositive part and a dispositive part.

Michiels gives the following example of a typical rescript. (One could expect to find this form in use before the format of rescripts was shortened. Reference is made in the text immediately below to the present-day digested format of rescripts.) "(*I. Pars expositiva: a. narrativa*) Beatissime Pater, Gustavus Josephus Waffelaert, Episcopus Brugensis, ad

In times past these three parts were set down with considerably more detail than they are today, for now the internal form or structure of rescripts has been somewhat shortened. The narrative part is often restricted to a statement of the name of the petitioner and his diocese or religious order. The motive part is stated very briefly or omitted entirely. The dispositive part frequently contains only the clause *"iuxta petita,"* together with the conditions to be observed.[15]

Article 3. The Kinds of Rescripts

Canonical commentators have found various bases upon which to distinguish the many rescripts which have been issued by the Holy See and other ordinaries, as well as by their delegates. In this study, however, it is sufficient to note the distinction which is found between rescripts issued *ad instantiam* or *ad preces* and those granted *motu proprio,* between rescripts of justice, rescripts of favor, and mixed rescripts, and between rescripts granted *in forma gratiosa* and such as are issued *in forma commissoria.*

The distinction between rescripts issued *ad instantiam* and

---

pedes S. V. humiliter provolutus, exponit sequentia: N. N. ex . . . et N. N. ex . . . , dioecesis Brugensis subditi, paucis ante matrimonium hebdomadibus, diverterunt in X., ibique, mutato ob certas rationes et ad breve tempus domicilio civili, contractum civilem inierunt; coram parocho de X . . . contraxerunt matrimonium invalidum ob impedimentum clandestinitatis, quum in dicto loco nec domicilium, nec quasi-domicilium acquisissent, ac parochus proprius, tum oratoris tum oratricis, prae inadvertentia, omiserit delegare parochum de X., ut praefato matrimonio assisteret. (*b. motiva*) Quum autem oratores bona fide egerint, et in omnimodo versentur bona fide circa valorem matrimonii, nec de ipsius nullitate, absque gravissimis incommodis, certiorari possint, (*c. supplicatio*) supplex rogat Episcopus orator, ut S. V. matrimonium eorum in radice sanare ac proles exinde natas vel nascituras legitimas declarare dignetur. Et Deus . . . (*II. Pars dispositiva*). Sacra Poenitentiaria de speciali et expressa Apostolica auctoritate, praefatum matrimonium, sic, uti praefertur, nulliter contractum, in radice sanat et convalidat, prolemque susceptam sive suscipiendam legitimam enuntiat. Praesentes autem litterae in Cancellaria Episcopali diligenter custodiantur, ut pro quocumque futuro eventu de matrimonii validitate et prolis legitimitate constare possit. Datum Romae ex S. Poenitentiaria, die 5 Nov. 1906."—*Normae Generales,* II, 285, nota 3.

[15] Cf. Cicognani, *loc. cit.*

rescripts granted *motu proprio* is based upon the *formula concessionis* which indicates the superior's intention in giving his rescripts. Thus, a rescript issued *ad instantiam* is one which the superior, after examining the petitioner's *preces,* intends to and actually does grant on account of the reasons alleged by the petitioner and in view of the circumstances described in his *preces.*[16] A rescript issued *motu proprio* is one which the superior grants independently of the facts and circumstances that he is informed of in the *pars narrativa* of the petition for the letter.[17] That is to say, in giving his written reply, the grantor acts, as it were, spontaneously by prescinding from the aforementioned facts and circumstances of the prospective beneficiary's case as they are set forth in the *preces.* He does not act independently of the motivating reason or reasons which are alleged for the rescript in the petition for it,[18] nor of the petitioner's statement of the concession which he hopes to receive.[19] It should be noted in reference to this type of rescript that the reason it is not a contradiction in terms to designate a rescript as being issued *motu proprio* is that a petition for such a rescript is always presupposed. The phrase *"motu proprio"* merely indicates that the validity of the rescript does not depend upon the truthfulness of the facts and circumstances in the *pars narrativa* of the *preces* for the letter.[20]

As for rescripts of justice, rescripts of favor, and mixed rescripts, they are distinguished from one another by reason of their subject matter. Accordingly, rescripts of justice (*litterae*

[16] Cf. Panormitanus (1386-1453), *Commentaria in Quinque Libros Decretalium* (5 vols. in 7, Venetiis, 1588), Lib. I, tit. III, ad c. 2, X, *de rescriptis,* I, 3, n. 3; Schmalzgrueber, *Jus Ecclesiasticum,* Lib. I, tit. III, n. 3.

[17] For a description of the *pars narrativa* of the *preces,* cf. *infra,* pp. 16-17.

[18] Cf. can. 45, and *infra,* pp. 181-186.

[19] Cf. *infra,* p. 187.

[20] Cf. c. 23, *de praebendis et dignitatibus,* III, 4, in VI° (Boniface VIII: 1294-1303); D'Annibale (1815-1892), *Summula Theologiae Moralis* (4. ed., 3 vols., Romae, 1896-1897), I, 222, nota 1 (hereafter cited as *Summula*); O'Neill, *Papal Rescripts of Favor,* p. 3.

ad lites), on the one hand, are those which contain either statements intended to explain a point of law connected with litigation, or provisions pertaining to legal suits and the administration of justice in judicial and non-judicial procedures. Such provisions may be, for example, the appointment of judges and the conferral of jurisdiction upon them for a given case, or the determination of the mode of procedure to be followed in a given trial, or the decreeing of a *restitutio in integrum*. Rescripts of this kind are *secundum ius commune* and are so called because they refer to matters of justice.[21]

Rescripts of favor (*litterae gratiosae*), on the other hand, are those through which a superior grants favors which are in no way connected with matters of justice. Thus, benefices, privileges, dispensations, permissions, and so forth, are often granted through rescripts of favor. These written replies are called rescripts of favor because they contain things to which the recipient has no legal title. Rather, the favors are granted out of the free choice and generosity of the superior who issues the rescript.[22]

Depending on their content, rescripts of favor are *secundum ius commune* (for example, when they grant permission to erect a *domus religiosa*), *contra ius commune* (for instance, when they convey a dispensation), or *praeter ius commune* (for example, when they concede a privilege which transcends but is not contrary to the common law.[23]

Prior to the Code some canonical authors subdivided rescripts of favor into the *rescriptum beneficiale,* which concerned the matter of benefices, and into the *rescriptum gratiae* which was to be understood in a more restricted sense. The difference between these two types of rescripts lay in the fact that the *re-*

[21] Cf. Schmalzgrueber, *loc. cit.*, and Maroto, *Institutiones Iuris Canonici ad normam novi Codicis* (2 vols., Vol. I, 3. ed., Romae, 1921), I, n. 278, ad B) (hereafter cited as *Institutiones*).

[22] O'Neill, *op. cit.*, p. 2.

[23] Apropos of these examples, one may note in passing that the rescript itself is not the permission, the dispensation, nor the privilege. The rescript is merely the means by which these favors are conveyed to their beneficiary.

scriptum beneficiale was *secundum ius commune,* whereas the *rescriptum gratiae* was either *contra* or *ultra ius.*[24]

Finally, mixed rescripts are those which contain at the same time provisions pertaining both to the administration of justice and to a favor which is in no way connected with matters of justice, and hence the name.[25]

The last distinction among the different kinds of rescripts to be considered in this study is that which is drawn between rescripts granted *in forma gratiosa* and rescripts issued *in forma commissoria.* This distinction is based upon the form in which rescripts are granted. Rescripts *in forma gratiosa,* then, are those in which the superior himself grants the favor *"complete et perfecte, de iure et de facto,"* and applies it directly and immediately to the beneficiary, without using any intermediary as an executor of the grant.[26] Consequently, such rescripts contain

[24] Cf. Suarez (1548-1617), *Opera Omnia* (26 vols. in 28, Parisiis, 1856-1866), Vol. VI, *Tractatus de Legibus et Legislatore Deo* (ed. nova, a Carolo Berton, Parisiis, 1856), Lib. VIII, cap. II, 230, n. 8. The writer has not found any author who since the promulgation of the Code retains this subdivision.

[25] Cf. Felinus Sandeus (1444-1503), *Commentaria in Quinque Libros Decretalium* (3 vols., Venetiis, 1570), Lib. I, tit. III, ad c. 20, X, *de rescriptis,* I, 3, nn. 2-3 (hereafter cited as *Commentaria*); Toso, *Ad Codicem Iuris Canonici Commentaria Minora* (5 vols. in 2, Vol. I, 2. ed., Taurini-Romae: Marietti, 1921), I, 113 (hereafter cited as *Commentaria Minora*).

[26] Van Hove, *De Rescriptis,* pp. 111-112. "Est in forma gratiosa, quando Romanus Pontifex vel Congregatio Romana 'petitam gratiam oratori benigne impertitur,' ut fit in dispensatione super matrimonio rato non consummato et in concessione facultatum habitualium Ordinariis, aut facultatis ad casum in individuo non determinatum, aut ita expedire Sacra Congregatio iudicaverit."—Van Hove, *op. cit.,* p. 113. The following excerpts are examples of the wording found in rescripts granted *in forma gratiosa:* "'S. C. de disciplina Sacramentorum, vigore specialium facultatum Card. Praefecto a SSmo Dno Nostro . . . tributarum, attentis . . . gratiam indulget iuxta petita . . .'; 'Oratori (Ordinario) facultatem benigne indulget iuxta petita'; 'Veniam benigne tribuit permittendi iterationem sacri' in festis quae fidelium concursu ac devotione celebrantur; 'praefatum matrimonium, dummodo prior maritalis consensus perseveret, nullum . . . obstet canonicum impedimentum a quo Sancta Sedes non dispensat, in radice sanat ac revalidat et prolem iam susceptam legitimam nunciat et declarat.'"—Van Hove, *ibid.,* nota 5.

a *gratia iam facta.* Rescripts *in forma commissoria,* however, are those in which the request is granted through the medium of an executor.

It is most important to note that all rescripts issued *in forma commissoria* always require execution before they become effective. The reason for this necessity in reference to the execution of such rescripts is that they convey a *gratia adhuc facienda,* and not a concession that is consummated as it leaves the hands of the grantor.[27] That is to say, when such a letter is issued with a *necessary* executor, it contains a mandate or an order for the executor to apply the grant, intended by the superior for the prospective beneficiary of the rescript, whenever the requirements set forth in the law and in the mandate of the executor's commission are properly fulfilled.[28] When a rescript *in forma commissoria* is issued with a *voluntary* executor, it conveys to the executor from the grantor of the rescript the power or the faculties to concede or deny the favor with which the letter is concerned according to the executor's own prudent judgment and conscience.[29] Thus, Van Hove (1872-1947), speaking of a rescript granted *in forma commissoria* with a *necessary* executor, made this observation: *"Ipse rescribens concedit gratiam de iure, non de facto, per exsecutorem impertiendam de facto, exsequendo mandatum quod recipit (can. 55), seu fulminando rescriptum."* [30] This statement could have been applied also to

[27] Cf. De Smet (1868-1927), *Betrothment and Marriage* (translated from the French edition of 1912 by W. Dobell and A. Owens, 2 vols., St. Louis, 1913), II, 225; Rodrigo, *Tractatus de Legibus,* p. 523.

[28] For a description of the necessary executor, cf. *infra,* pp. 14-15.

[29] For an explanation of the voluntary executor, cf. *infra,* pp. 14-15.

[30] *Op. cit.,* p. 112. The following excerpts are examples of the wording that one can expect to find in rescripts which the Holy See issues *in forma commissoria* with a necessary executor: "'S. C. de disciplina Sacramentorum . . . Ordinario committit ut . . . dispensationem a memorato impedimento oratoribus benigne largiatur, quo nuptias, prout desiderant, contrahere valeant, prolemque susceptam legitimam decernat atque declaret';—'Ordinario committit ut, servatis canonicis praescriptionibus, dispensationem a memorato impedimento oratoribus benigne largiatur, quo contrahere optatas nuptias valeant, contrariis quibuslibet minime ostantibus';—'benigne committit Ordinario . . . ut praefatos coniuges ab impedi-

a rescript that was to be executed, according to the pre-Code commentators, by a *mere* executor.[31] Concerning a rescript issued *in forma commissoria* with a *voluntary* executor, the same author noted: *"Haec commissio continet gratiam faciendam, nullo modo gratiam factam, nec de iure nec de facto."* [32] Rescripts *in forma commissoria* differ from one another, therefore, according to the kind of commission their executors are given.

Pre-Code authors generally listed three types of executorial commissions, namely, that of the *mere* executor, that of the *necessary* or *mixed* executor, and that of the *voluntary* or *free* executor.[33] The *mere* executor was a person who received solely the ministry of executing the rescript involved without jurisdiction and apart from specific knowledge of the case. When such an executor was employed, the case had already been fully in-

---

mento . . . dispenset . . .';—'committit (Ordinario) ut gratiam indulgeat iuxta petita';—'attentis expositis benigne committit . . . Ordinario ut praefatum matrimonium, dummodo prior maritalis consensus perseveret et nullum aliud obstet impedimentum a quo S. Sedes non dispensat, in radice sanet ac revalidet et prolem iam susceptam legitimam nunciet et declaret, cauto pro viribus ne scandalum exinde obveniat, et ut, si quod existat, amoveatur.' "—Van Hove, *op. cit.*, p. 114, nota 2.

31 Cf. *infra*, pp. 13-14.

32 *Op. cit.*, p. 112. "Exsecutor voluntarius constituitur per clausulam quae preces remittit 'arbitrio et conscientiae exsecutoris cum facultatibus necessariis' aut 'arbitrio et voluntati exsecutoris' aut si additur clausula: 'si ita expedire iudicaveris.' "—Van Hove, *op. cit.*, p. 116. "In quibusdam concessionibus ad Ordinarios directis, adduntur verba: 'pro suo arbitrio et conscientia,' aut si agitur de cardinali: 'pro suo arbitrio.' Hanc formulam, qua exsecutor non constituitur voluntarius, inseri mere urbanitatis et reverentiae causa, notat I. d'Annibale."—Van Hove, *op. cit.*, pp. 114-115.

33 Cf. Corradus Pyrrhus (d. 1686), *Praxis Dispensationum Apostolicarum* (Venetiis, 1735), Lib. IX, cap. V, n. 5 (hereafter cited as *Praxis*); D'Annibale, *Summula*, I, 222, nota 5, and I, 72, nota 20; De Justis (d. after 1691), *De Dispensationibus Matrimonialibus* (Lucae, 1726), Lib. I, cap. VI, nn. 286, 505, 506; De Rosa (d. 1695), *De Executoribus Litterarum Apostolicarum* (Aschaffenburgi, 1747), Pars I, cap. VI, nn. 1-2 (hereafter cited as *De Executoribus*); Reiffenstuel, *Jus Canonicum*, Lib. I, tit. III, nn. 257, 258, and Lib. I, tit. XXIX, n. 157; Th. Sanchez (1550-1610), *De Sancto Matrimonii Sacramento* (3 toms., Antverpiae, 1626), Lib. VIII, disp. 27, n. 14, and disp. 28, n. 87 (hereafter cited as *De Matrimonio*); O'Neill, *Papal Rescripts of Favor*, p. 168.

vestigated by the grantor of the rescript. Hence the only thing that remained for the executor to do was to apply the concession in the rescript to the designated recipient. A *necessary* or *mixed* executor was one who was ordered to execute the rescript given to him, if, after a suitable investigation, he found that the *preces* for the letter were true and that all the other conditions required by law for the execution of the letter were fulfilled.[34] The *voluntary* or *free* executor was a person who was not ordered to grant the favor requested by the petitioner by executing the rescript issued by the superior, but was rather given the necessary faculties to grant the concession asked for, if he saw fit to do so. The concession or denial of the favor involved was left to the good judgment and conscience of the executor himself. One of the factors that was of extreme importance to the voluntary executor in making his decision in this regard was the substantial truthfulness or falseness of the *preces* for the rescript in question.

On the basis of canon 54 of the Code of Canon Law modern-day authors have, by and large, abandoned the foregoing threefold designation of the different types of executors.[35] Nonetheless, they sometimes make reference to the different kinds of executors who were spoken of under the pre-Code discipline when they explain the function of the executors who are recognized today.[36] The kinds of executors who are mentioned in canon 54, §§ 1 and 2, respectively, are the *necessary* executor and the *voluntary* executor. The *necessary* executor is described in canon 54, § 1, as one to whom is committed "*merum exsecu-*

[34] An important difference between the *mere* executor and the *necessary* executor lay in the fact, that, while both of them were ordered to execute the rescript transmitted to them, the *mere* executor had no jurisdictional power to investigate the petition, especially as far as its truthfulness was concerned, whereas the *necessary* executor not only had the power to make such an investigation but was actually obliged to do so before performing his ministry of execution.—O'Neill, *op. cit.*, p. 169.

[35] Coronata, however, still distinguishes the *exsecutor commissarius absolutus*, the *exsecutor mixtus*, and the *exsecutor merus* or *necessarius*.—*Institutiones*, I, 71-72.

[36] Cf. O'Neill, *op. cit.*, pp. 169-173; Toso, *Commentaria Minora*, I, 138; Van Hove, *op. cit.*, pp. 235-236.

tionis ministerium." [37] The *voluntary* executor is characterized in the second paragraph of this canon by the words *"ipsius est pro suo prudenti arbitrio et conscientia gratiam concedere vel denegare."* [38]

SECTION II. CONCERNING THE *Preces*

Article 1. The Description of the Preces

In the clause *"si preces veritate nitantur"* the term *"preces"* means a request or an entreaty.[39] Hence the *prèces* are the petition for a rescript. Ordinarily they signify the instrument or letter that is used in request of a rescript.[40] In legal language,

[37] "Illis [exsecutoribus] quibus committitur merum exsecutionis ministerium a scriptoribus vocantur communius exsecutores *necessarii*, quin distinguant exsecutores necessarios meros et mixtos.

"Opinamur in can. 54, § 1, agi solum de exsecutore *mero*, prout illum exsecutorem definiendum censuimus sub iure superiore, de illo cui nulla conceditur iurisdictio ad iudicandum de veritate precum, qui tamen desistere debet ab exsecutione, si manifeste pateat rescriptum esse obreptitium vel subreptitium.

"De exsecutore *mixto*, prout illum definimus [cf. *supra*, p. 14], canon expresse non agit, quia talis non solet deputari a Sancta Sede: conditio communis cuicumque rescripto non est 'si preces veritate niti repereris' sed 'si preces veritate nitantur.' Implicite exsistentia exsecutoris mixti retinetur in iure per canonem 55: 'Exsecutor procedere debet ad mandati sui normam.' Pendet a voluntate rescribentis ut praescribat inquisitionem tamquam conditionem essentialem ad exsecutionem rescripti et proinde constituat exsecutorem mixtum."—Van Hove, *op. cit.*, pp. 235-236. Cf. also Michiels, *Normae Generales*, II, 448, nota 2. For an explanation of the investigation to be made by the *necessary* executor before he decides concerning the presence or the absence of truthful *preces*, cf. *infra*, pp. 220-224.

[38] For an explanation of the phrase *"pro suo prudenti arbitrio et conscientia"* and of the manner in which the *voluntary* executor reaches his decision concerning the veracity of the *preces*, cf. *infra*, pp. 224-225.

[39] The singular form of this word is *prex, precis.* It is used in the singular number, however, only in the dative, accusative, and ablative cases.—*Cassell's Latin Dictionary* (Revised by J. Marchant and J. Charles, New York and London: Funk and Wagnalls Co., 1942), p. 439.

[40] As a general rule, a petition for a rescript is to be made in writing, for when a person puts his request into writing he is more likely to comply with the norms established by the *stylus Curiae* and set forth by the vari-

then, the term "*preces,*" as it is used in this study, is synonymous with *instantia, libellus supplex, supplices litterae,* and *supplices.*[41]

In considering the truth that is required in the *preces* for rescripts, one must keep in mind that a petition for a rescript is composed of three distinct parts. These parts are the *pars narrativa,* the *pars postulativa,* and the *pars motiva* (*persuasiva* or *impulsiva*).[42]

The *pars narrativa* is that part of the petition in which the facts and circumstances about the prospective beneficiary of the rescript and his case are set forth. In other words, this narrative part of the *preces* contains the *species facti* upon which the

---

ous pontifical instructions in the matter of asking for rescripts. Fundamentally (*per se*), however, there is nothing to prevent one from making an oral petition, so long as he does it in a personal manner and not by telephone nor by telegraph. As a general rule, at least, the telephone and telegraph are not to be used in the requesting of rescripts. Michiels, *Normae Generales,* II, 338; Litterae Secretariae Status, 10 dec. 1891—*Collectanea S. Congregationis de Propaganda Fide* (2 vols., Romae, 1907), II, n. 1775 (hereafter cited as *Collectanea*); Pontificia Commissio ad Codicis Canonis Authentice Interpretandos, 12 nov. 1922—*Acta Apostolicae Sedis, Commentarium Officiale* (Romae, 1909-1929; Civitate Vaticana, 1929-), XIV (1922), 662 (hereafter cited as *AAS*). For an English translation of this document, cf. *The Canon Law Digest* (4 vols., Milwaukee: Bruce Publishing Co., Vol. I, 7. printing, 1950; Vol. II, 5. printing, 1949; Vol. III, 1954, edited by T. Lincoln Bouscaren; Vol. IV, 1958, edited by T. Lincoln Bouscaren and James I. O'Connor), I, 502 (hereafter cited as Bouscaren, *The Canon Law Digest*).

41 Vlaming-Bender, *Praelectiones Iuris Matrimonii ad Normam Codicis Iuris Canonici* (4. ed., Bussum in Hollandia: Sumptibus Societatis Editrieis Anonymae Paulus Brand, 1950), p. 285 (hereafter cited as *Praelectiones*).

42 Cf. Gonzalez-Tellez (d. after 1673), *Commentaria Perpetua in Quinque Libros Decretalium* (4 vols., Lugduni, 1673), Lib. I, tit. III, ad c. 2, X, *de rescriptis,* I, 3, n. 15 (hereafter cited as *Commentaria*), and Vecchiotti (d. 1870), *Institutiones Canonicae* (16. ed., 3 vols., Augustae Taurinorum, 1875), I, 103-104.

The petition should include also an appropriate salutation to the superior to whom it is being sent, as well as the mention of the date and place of its making together with the signature or sign of the petitioner. In this connection it must be remembered that the person who is to benefit from a rescript can himself petition it, or someone else may request the rescript for him.—Cf. cans. 36 and 37.

petition is based, together with the recounting of any circumstances which may help or hinder the petitioner in his efforts to obtain the requested rescript.[43]

Apropos of this general description of the content of the *pars narrativa* of the *preces,* the writer wishes to stress the fact that the term *"preces"* in the clause *"si preces veritate nitantur"* signifies only the formal petition that is presented for rescripts. It does not include, therefore, statements which are not part of the formal petition. Hence, in cases in which the petitioner requests a rescript conveying a dispensation from a *ratum et non consummatum* marriage or a dispensation *in favorem fidei,* the acts that are assembled in proof of the petitioner's allegations are not part of the *preces.* Rather the proof that is required in such cases is a condition for the lawful granting of the dispensations in question. It is a condition that must be verified by means of truthful statements in support of the petitioner's allegations in his *preces.*[44] Nonetheless, it is a condition separate and distinct from *"si preces veritate nitantur."* Therefore this principle is not inherently directed to the body of proof submitted for the verification of the *preces.*[45]

[43] Cf. Toso, *Commentaria Minora,* I, 124.

[44] "Ut autem Apostolica Sedes dispensationem largiatur, duo sibi constare necesse est: matrimonium revera non fuisse consummatum et iustam exstare causam pro dispensatione concedenda."—S. C. de Sacramentis, decretum, *De processibus in causis dispensationis super matrimonio rato et non consummato,* 7 maii 1923—*AAS,* XV (1923), 389; cf. Bouscaren, *The Canon Law Digest,* I, 764.

[45] The foregoing conclusion is substantiated by the following texts, the first of which is from the decree issued on May 7, 1923, by the Sacred Congregation of the Sacraments for cases on the non-consummation of marriage: "Alterum dein consequitur, quod alte usque insidere debet in animo iudicum et testium ac praesertim partium dispensationem efflagitantium; videlicet, *si res aliter se habeant ac ab oratoribus asseruntur, id est si matrimonium ratum reapse fuerit consummatum,* et veritas in processu non detegatur, vel ex culpa aut oscitantia tribunalis, vel ex fraude aut desidia partium et testium, *pontificia dispensatio forte obtenta, utpote suo fundamento destituta, nullius est valoris. . . .*"—*AAS,* XV (1923), 390.—The first italics are the writer's. Cf. Bouscaren, *ibid.,* pp. 764-765.

The second text is Rule 12 of the *Regulae Servandae in Processibus super Matrimonio Rato et Non Consummato,* which were issued together

Furthermore, the *cautiones* which are demanded in canon 1061, § 1, and in canon 1071 for the validity of dispensations from the matrimonial impediments of mixed religion and disparity of worship respectively are not part of the *preces* for the rescripts that convey these dispensations.[45a] The following remark made by D. Boyle is apropos: "The *preces* in the application for a dispensation embrace the *cause* for the dispensation and not the *cautiones,* which constitute the condition under which the dispensation is granted."[45b] Accordingly, as essential as the *cautiones* are to the validity of the dispensations in question, they constitute a condition which is not comprehended in *"si preces veritate nitantur."*

The other two parts of the *preces* are the *pars postulativa* and the *pars motiva.* The *pars postulativa* is that part in which the object of the petition is expressed. The *pars motiva* is that sec-

---

with the aforementioned decree: "Si, accepto libello, haec Sacra Congregatio censuerit precibus annuendum esse, solet Ordinario loci, qui oratorem commendavit, dare litteras delegationis pro causa instruenda, iuxta has regulas et cum clausulis opportunis."—*AAS,* XV (1923), 394; cf. Bouscaren, *ibid.,* p. 768.

The third text is Rule 103 of the same *Regulae super Rato:* "Attenta eiusmodi forma [i.e., haec dispensatio expeditur per rescriptum in forma gratiosa—cf. Rule 102], rescriptum effectum habet a temporis momento, quo in die audientiae Summus Pontifex dispensationem concessit, *dummodo tamen eo momento preces veritati nitantur, tum quoad matrimonii inconsummationem, tum quoad dispensationis causas (can. 41).* Quod si unum vel alterum desit, rescriptum, utpote obreptionis vel subreptionis vitio infectum, impetranti minime suffragatur."—*AAS,* XV (1923), 413.—Italics are the writer's. Cf. Bouscaren, *ibid.,* pp. 791-792.

[45a] Canon 1061, § 1, states: "Ecclesia super impedimento mixtae religionis non dispensat, nisi: 1°. . . . ; 2°. Cautionem praestiterit coniux acatholicus de amovendo a coniuge catholico perversionis periculo, et uterque coniux de universa prole catholice tantum baptizanda et educanda; 3°. Moralis habeatur certitudo de cautionum implemento."

Canon 1071 states. "Quae de mixtis nuptiis in canonibus 1060-1064 praescripta sunt, applicari quoque debent matrimoniis quibus obstat impedimentum disparitatis cultus."

[45b] *The Juridic Effects of Moral Certitude on Pre-Nuptial Guarantees,* The Catholic University of America Canon Law Studies, no. 150 (Washington, D. C.: The Catholic University of America Press, 1942), p. 105.

tion of the *preces* in which the petitioner gives the reason or reasons which he hopes will move or dispose the superior to grant his request.[46]

Article 2. The Causes in the Preces

The reasons, which are found in the *pars motiva* of the *preces,* are commonly called causes. Actually, the one term explains the other, for, from the petitioner's standpoint, the cause (or causes), which he alleges in his petition, is (or are) the reason (or reasons) why he presents his request for a rescript to the superior. As far as the superior is concerned, it is that same reason (or reasons) which causes (or cause) him either to issue his rescript or to grant it more readily than he would have if the reason (or reasons) in question had not been given.[47]

[46] The following example of a petition for a dispensation from a *ratum et non consummatum* marriage exemplifies the three parts of the *preces* for rescripts:

Beatissime Pater:

(Pars narrativa)

Ego infrascriptus, Marcus Smith, filius Leonis et Annae Smith, e Dioecesi Bellunensi, annos natus 26, conditione operarius, domicilium habens in paroecia S. Stephani, via Roma, 16, ad pedes Sanctitatis Vestrae humiliter provolutus, quae sequuntur expono:

Die 3 mart. 1925 nuptias contraxi cum Maria White eiusdem Dioecesis et paroeciae coram parocho et testibus, praemissis denuntiationibus aliisque a iure statutis.

Matrimonio vix inito, mulier gravi morbo correpta atque in amentiam lapsa est. In valetudinario nunc degit, sine spe ex peritorum iudicio ut pristinam sanitatem recuperet. Matrimonium consummatum non fuit.

(Pars postulativa)

Quapropter misericorditer postulo apostolicam dispensationem super matrimonio rato et non cunsummato.

(Pars motiva)

Rationes ad petendam dispensationem sunt: 1) infirmitas gravissima uxoris, 2) periculum incontinentiae, 3) desiderium transeundi ad alias nuptias et familiam efformandi.

Belluni, 12 maii 1936.

/s/ Marcus Smith

[47] Cf. Toso, *Commentaria Minora,* I, 123.

The reasons or causes, then, which are found in petitions for rescripts, can be divided into motivating or final causes,[48] and impelling or impulsive reasons.[49] A motivating or final reason is a cause or an accumulation of causes which efficaciously moves the superior to grant the rescript requested of him. In other words, a final cause motivates the superior to concede the petitioner's request to such an extent that without it the grant would not be made at all, or, at least, not in the same form nor without the imposition of certain conditions.[50] An impulsive cause, on the other hand, is a single or manifold reason which does not actually move the superior to issue his rescript but rather makes it easier for him to accede to the petitioner's request. That is to say, without the impelling cause the superior would still grant the same rescript, but not with the same promptitude and readiness. Hence, an impelling cause merely helps the superior to make up his mind to issue the rescript which is requested of him. It is not, however, sufficient of itself to obtain the request.[51] Cocchi tries to throw more light on the difference be-

[48] That is, *causae motivae, seu finales, seu inductivae, seu principales, seu primariae.*

[49] That is, *causae impellentes, seu impulsivae, seu secundariae.*

[50] Van Hove, *De Rescriptis,* p. 147.

[51] "Causa finalis est, quae ex toto et funditus animum movet disponentis, alias verisimiliter non facturum. Impulsiva vero, quae impellit statuentem, qua cessante statuens adhuc erat statuturus."—Panormitanus, *Commentaria,* Lib. I, tit. IX, ad c. 11, X, *de renuntiatione,* I, 9, n. 18. "Causa finalis . . . ea dicitur, qua non existente, Princeps non concederet id, quod petitur; vel qua vere allegata, illud denegasset, vel saltem non eo pacto ac modo concessisset, quo concessit, sed non nisi adhibito moderamine. Causa vero impulsiva est, qua non existente, Princeps quidem absolute concessisset et eodem pacto ac forma, licet non tam facile, sed multo difficilius concessit."—Pirhing (1606-1679), *Jus Canonicum in Quinque Libros Decretalium* (ed. novissima, 5 vols. in 4, Dilingae, 1722), Lib. I, tit. III, n. LXXXVI (hereafter cited as *Jus Canonicum*). Cf. also Maroto, *Institutiones,* I, n. 284 ad 2°. "Causa *motiva* . . . seu *finalis* . . . est, quae efficaciter movet rescribentem ad concedendam gratiam determinatam, et sine qua gratiam vel non concederet, vel non sub eadem forma vel amplitudine. *Causa impulsiva* est, quae non est sufficiens ad movendum rescribentem ut gratiam concedat, sed conducit ut facilius et citius illam tribuat."—Van Hove, *De Rescriptis,* p. 147.

tween motivating and impelling causes by saying: "*causa motiva potius respicit obiectum: causa impulsiva potius respicit personam. . . .*" [52]

From these descriptions of motivating and impelling causes one can understand why the judgment of the merit and weight of any particular reason which is presented in a petition ultimately depends upon the will and intention of the superior who is asked to grant the rescript involved.[53] Nonetheless, commentators usually offer the following norms as safe and practical guides in determining the precise nature of the different reasons which may have been presented.

Concerning petitions with a single cause—

First of all, if someone advances only one reason in his petition and there is evidence that the rescript requested by him has been granted on account of that reason, the cause is undoubtedly motivating,

> quia princeps, sive Papa non solet absque omni causa rescriptum concedere, et multo minus cum aliquo dispensare: ergo quando allegatur unica causa, recte ipsa censetur motiva. Quinimo tunc locum habebit illud vulgatum axioma: "ratio legis est anima legis, sive dispositionis." [54]

Concerning petitions with several causes—

Secondly, when several causes are presented in one and the same petition and all of them in some way influence the superior

[52] *Commentarium in Codicem iuris canonici ad usum scholarum* (8 vols., Vol. I, 5. ed., Taurinorum Augustae: Marietti, 1938), I, 248 (hereafter cited as *Commentarium*).

[53] "Iudicium de sufficientia causae spectat ad rescribentem qui, attentis expositis, iudicat an sit causa sufficiens et an expediat gratiam concedere. . . . Impetrantis est allegare causas, ob quas spes fundata sit obtinendi concessionem gratiae."—Van Hove, *op. cit.*, p. 148.

[54] Michiels, *Normae Generales,* II, 365. In this connection, however, it must be remembered that at times the Holy See does not specify the reason on account of which it has issued a rescript. This happens, for instance, when Rome grants matrimonial dispensations under the general formula "for certain reasonable causes (*ex certis rationabilibus causis*)." Dispensations which are issued in this manner are often called dispensations *sine causa,* not because there is no sufficient reason for them, but because none is specified in the rescript. Cf. *infra,* p. 90.

in his granting the requested rescript, the first criterion by which to distinguish the weight of the respective reasons given is the *stylus Curiae Romanae.*[55] Through the years, various Instructions emanating from the Holy See have indicated clearly which reasons generally are motivating and which are merely impelling.[56] In fact, because of this approval of certain reasons as final causes in particular instances, commentators often propose lists of reasons, some of which they classify as canonical causes, others as non-canonical. De Smet summed up this matter as follows:

> A cause is canonical when, in accordance with canonical rules and the prudent judgment of the Church, it is sufficient to constitute a final cause, if not for a grave impediment, at least for a lighter one. A canonical cause is, therefore, ordinarily final, but in respect to a determinate impediment, it may be insufficient. On the other hand, non-canonical causes are in themselves merely impulsive, since, taken separately, they are incapable of constituting a final cause for any impediment; if, however, several such causes occur at the same time and are taken collectively, they may produce a final and sufficient cause.[57]

The *stylus Curiae Romanae,* then, is the first criterion one will use in determining the exact nature of the several causes presented by a petitioner.[58]

When the *stylus Curiae* fails to give a basis on which to decide which of the different causes in one and the same petition is motivating and which is impelling, the second criterion one will use in making this decision is the judgment of some

[55] The *stylus Curiae Romanae* will be given more consideration in Section III of this chapter. Cf. pp. 26-32.

[56] Cf., for instance, S. C. de Prop. Fid., instructio, 9 maii 1877—*Collectanea,* II, n. 1470.

[57] *Betrothment and Marriage,* II, 276. While De Smet was concerned in the place just cited with the relationship between canonical and non-canonical causes and matrimonial impediments, the principles which he outlined are general norms that, *mutatis mutandis,* can govern any relationship in which canonical and non-canonical causes are involved.

[58] The *stylus* of a diocesan curia can be the criterion in this matter when the reasons pertain to a grant which is within the proper competence of the diocesan curia involved. Cf. *infra,* pp. 142-144.

prudent person. That is to say, when no positive indication concerning the nature of a particular reason can be found in the practice and custom of the Roman Curia, all the canonical authors who treat this matter teach generally that the decision in question should be left to some prudent person, to the judge, for instance, if a rescript of justice is involved. The judgment of this person is to be based not only on the nature of the cause itself and the gravity of the matter requested, but also on the circumstances connected with the petition.[59] Such a circumstance is, for example, the condition of life of the petitioner. Moreover, it is suggested that, if possible, the person making the decision in question should examine other rescripts similar to the one under consideration to see whether he can thus obtain some indication as to the true nature of the cause in which he is interested. Such an investigation may well give him an insight into the mind of the superior, as it was manifested in his granting of rescripts which are similar to the one under consideration.[60]

Furthermore, two presumptions are offered by the commentators as aids in the making of the judgment under consideration. These presumptions are to be used after the rescript has been granted. The first conjecture is that, when it appears that a superior has granted a rescript on account of a number of causes which, in themselves and individually, are certainly only impelling reasons, the entire aggregate of these causes is to be taken as constituting one single motivating reason. This presumption is based on the Roman Law principle: *"Singula quae non prosunt, simul collecta iuvant."*[61] The second presumption

[59] De Meester, *Juris Canonici et Juris Canonico-Civilis Compendium* (3 vols. in 4, Vol. I, nova ed., Brugis, 1921), I, 199 (hereafter cited as *Compendium*). Cf. can. 84, § 1.

[60] "Quando vero de eo (stylo Curiae) non constat, hoc ipsum [i.e., iudicium de natura causae] arbitrio viri prudentis, seu judicis, relinquitur discernendum, qui dijudicabit attento jure communi, et consuetudine ceteroquin in similibus observari solita, atque pensatis aliis circumstantiis, ex quibus verisimiliter conjecturari potest de voluntate concedentis."—Reiffenstuel, *Jus Canonicum,* Lib. I, tit. III, n. 195; De Smet, *loc. cit.;* Michiels, *ibid.*, pp. 365-366.

[61] C. (4, 19) 5—*Corpus Iuris Civilis,* II, *Codex Iustinianus* (quem Paulus Krueger recognovit et retractavit, ed. stereotypa 10., Berolini, 1929) (here-

which is proposed in this matter is that, when there is doubt about the exact nature of one particular false cause among several true reasons contained in a rescript, the false cause should be presumed to be not a motivating reason but merely an impelling one.[62] The juridic reason which is given to support this presumption is the general principle: *"In dubio standum est pro valore actus, nisi aliud probetur."* [63]

Unfortunately, the authors who rest this second presumption upon the foregoing general principle do not explain how that principle supports the presumption in question. This writer submits, however, that the following considerations explain the connection between the aforesaid principle and the presumption.[64] First of all, in reference to the pre-Tridentine period, it

---

after cited as *Cod. Iust.*). Cf. also S. C. de Sacramentis, instructio, 1 aug. 1931—*AAS,* XXIII (1931), 415; Bouscaren, *The Canon Law Digest,* I, 516.

[62] Th. Sanchez (1550-1610) noted that there were some canonists who held that such a cause should be considered final.—*De Matrimonio,* Lib. VIII, disp. 21, n. 20. The vast majority of pre-Code commentators, however, supported the above-stated position.—Cf. Pirhing, *Jus Canonicum,* Lib. I, tit. III, n. CV; Santi, *Praelectiones,* I, 32.

The writer has not found any author after the Code who disagrees with the above-listed presumption. Cf., e.g., Claeys Boúúaert-Simenon, *Manuale Juris Canonici* (3 vols., Vol. I, 5. ed., Gandae et Leodii: Prostat apud auctores in Seminariis Gandavensi et Leodiensi, 1939), I, 118; Brys, *Juris Canonici Compendium* (2 vols., Vol. I, 10. ed., Brugis: Desclée de Brouwer et Sii., 1947), I, 158.

[63] "Quoties in actionibus aut in exceptionibus ambigua oratio est, commodissimum est id accipi, quo res de qua agitur magis valeat quam pereat." —D. (34, 5) 12—*Corpus Iuris Civilis,* I, *Digesta Iustiniani Augusti* (quem recognovit Theodorus Mommsen et retractavit P. Krueger, ed. stereotypa 15., Berolini, 1928) (hereafter cited as *Digesta*). Cf. Claeys Boúúaert-Simenon, *loc. cit.;* Brys, *loc. cit.*

[64] This connection need be established only for those instances in which the validity of the rescript involved depends solely on whether or not the false reason in question is a final cause. If the validity or nullity of the letter can be determined *for certain* on another basis, the principle involved in this discussion is obviously not applicable. Hence, as far as at least the majority of pre-Code commentators were concerned, the principle in question here had no application to cases in which the cause, if in its nature it was doubtful, proved false because of the petitioner's bad faith. This principle was not applicable to such cases, for during the entire pre-Code period, according to the more commonly accepted doctrine, fraudulent and

was the doctrine of some authors that falsehood found in any *final* cause in a petition laid the consequent rescript open to invalidity, even if the false cause had been presented along with one or more really motivating reasons that were true.[65] Hence, to presume any false cause to be a final and not an impelling reason was to presume the automatic nullity of rescripts of favor and the possible invalidity of rescripts of justice.[66] Secondly, after the Council of Trent, canonists almost unanimously accepted the doctrine which is now in the prescription of canon 42, § 2, of the Code of Canon Law, namely, that, as far as the causes in a petition are concerned, falsehood in them does not invalidate a rescript so long as there is present at least one true *final* cause.[67] In other words, those canonists agree with the present-day authors that untruthfulness in the merely impelling causes which are proposed does not affect the validity of a rescript, except when a petitioner fails to present even one truly motivating reason, and the superior accepts the various impulsive causes which are presented as constituting in the aggregate the single final cause for the grant. In such a case, ordinarily, but not always, each of the individual impelling causes has to be truthful.[68] Consequently, in both the post-Tridentine and the present canonical discipline, the general principle in question seems to have application solely to the case in which the petitioner has presented only a false cause which in its nature is doubtful, and several other causes which are true but at the same time certainly only impelling reasons. It is not certain in this case, therefore, that the false cause involved was

---

deceitful obreption in either the final or the impelling causes in the *preces* laid the subsequent rescript open to invalidity.—Cf. *infra*, pp. 66-68; 72-74.

65 Cf. *infra*, p. 78, note 74. It should be noted here that some pre-Tridentine canonists held that falsehood even in merely impelling causes also had a vitiating effect on rescripts. Cf. *infra*, pp. 74-76. Accordingly, whenever that teaching was accepted, the general principle in question here was useless as the basis on which to presume the validity of a rescript that had been issued in the presence of a false impelling reason.

66 Cf. *infra*, pp. 99-105.

67 Cf., however, *supra*, p. 24, note 64. Cf. *infra*, pp. 69-70; 78.

68 Cf. *infra*, pp. 172-173.

the motivating reason for the issuance of the rescript. Yet, since the letter was granted presumably because of the various causes alleged by the petitioner, there is good reason to believe that the superior took the different impelling reasons that were proposed, together with the false cause in question, to constitute the single final reason for his concession. Under such circumstances, then, to presume, on the one hand, that the doubtful reason is a final cause would be to adjudge the rescript as certainly invalid, for the one and only final cause for the rescript would be false. On the other hand, to presume that the cause is a merely impulsive reason would be to allow for the possibility that the rescript may be valid, provided the false impelling cause is relatively insignificant in relation to the other impulsive reasons taken cumulatively.[69] Hence, *in dubio standum est pro valore actus.*

Section III. Concerning the *Stylus Curiae*

The concept of *"stylus curiae"* deserves special consideration in this study, for besides being a primary criterion in the determination of the exact nature of the various causes in petitions for rescripts the *stylus curiae* has always had a paramount role in deciding what facts and circumstances must be mentioned in the *preces* if they are to be considered truthful.[70]

In Canon Law a curia or court is the body of persons, offices, and tribunals (and Congregations, if the Roman Curia is specifically considered) used by the various ordinaries in their government of the parts of the Church under their respective jurisdictions.[71] The Church has established several curiae. First, there is the Roman Curia. The Roman Curia is the body of Congregations, Tribunals, and Offices through which the Pope

[69] Cf. *infra*, pp. 172-173.

[70] Cf. *infra*, pp. 61-64; 141-147, and can. 42, § 1, which states: "Reticentia veri, seu subreptio, in precibus non obstat quominus rescriptum vim habeat ratumque sit, dummodo expressa fuerint quae de stylo Curiae sunt ad validitatem exprimenda."

[71] Cf. can. 242, which reads: "Curia Romana constat Sacris Congregationibus, Tribunalibus et Officiis, prout inferius enumerantur et describuntur." Cf. also can. 363, § 1, which states: "Curia dioecesana constat illis personis quae Episcopo aliive qui, loco Episcopi, dioecesim regit, opem praestant in regimine totius dioecesis."

regularly governs the universal Church.[72] Hence, it is the highest in power and importance.[73] Each of the branches of the Roman Curia is governed by special norms peculiar to itself, as well as by the general regulations prescribed for the Curia as a whole.[74] Then, there are the other curiae, all subordinate to the Roman Curia, yet independent in some ways of its decisions. These are the curiae which the different ordinaries under the Supreme Pontiff employ in ruling the territories and persons sub-

[72] Monin (1881-1954) presented the following information: the Roman Curia had its beginnings in the very early centuries of the Church's history, for a kind of infant curia was formed out of the synodal meetings that were held in Rome by the Pope with the Italian bishops. Those councils were convoked as early as the third century. Then, too, the Popes depended upon the Roman priests and deacons who formed the *presbyterium* as their helpers and counsellors in administrative matters. In fact, by the middle of the fourth century Pope Damasus had already created the *"Scrinium"* or archive. In the centuries that followed various other administrative curial offices were established by the Pontiffs. From the twelfth century onwards, however, consistories of cardinals were substituted for the *presbyterium* and the councils of Italian bishops. Then in the sixteenth century different Congregations, likewise composed of cardinals, made their appearance.

The Roman Curia in its present form is the work of Pope St. Pius X (1903-1914) who effected a general reform of the Curia with his Constitution, *Sapienti consilio,* of June 29, 1908.—*De Curia Romana* (Lovanii, 1912), pp. 4-9, 152.

Actually, it was not until the eleventh century that the name *"Curia"* was given to the various groups who aided the Popes in their government of the universal Church. Until that time they were designated as the *"Palatium."*—The last two statements are made upon the authority of the Very Rev. Msgr. Thomas O. Martin, former professor of Canon Law Institutes at the Catholic University of America.

[73] All of the dicasteries of the Roman Curia act in the name and with the authority of the Sovereign Pontiff. Accordingly, their power is supreme and universal in their respective spheres of competence, unless the contrary is expressly stated. Nonetheless, the acts of these dicasteries are to be attributed to the Holy Father only when he confirms them *in forma specifica.* Without such confirmation those acts can be revoked or modified on the authority of the dicasteries themselves.—Chelodi, *Ius Canonicum de Personis,* p. 256.

[74] Can. 243, § 1: "In singulis Congregationibus, Tribunalibus, Officiis servanda est disciplina et tractanda sunt negotia secundum normas tum generales tum particulares, quas ipsis Romanus Pontifex praestituerit."

ject to themselves. For instance, there are diocesan curiae, metropolitan curiae, and the curiae of the ordinaries of regulars.[75]

The term "*stylus*," translated style, originally designated either a column, or a tool or instrument used by sculptors. Later, however, the word was used to indicate a form or manner of writing or speaking. It designated also a *modus agendi* that was usually followed in connection with certain acts or dispositions, such as wills, rescripts, and judicial sentences.[76]

Accordingly, in the jurisprudence of the Church the expression "*stylus curiae*" has come to signify the manner or way in which a curia *usually* uses its public power to handle and solve matters within its competence. Furthermore, this expression points to the norms according to which a curia's *modus agendi* is molded.[77] If this *modus agendi* is judicial, that is, if it concerns a *res contentiosa*, it is called *stylus iudicialis;* if it is administrative, that is, if it concerns a *res gratiosa*, it is called *stylus extraiudicialis*.[78]

An important element in this description of the *stylus curiae* is the notion that there is involved in it the constant practice on the part of the curia of using a certain method and specified norms in transacting its business. The style of any curia is not established by the handling of only one determined case. Rather it grows, first of all, out of uniform interpretations and decisions given by the curia in a consistent and constant manner for particular cases, for because of the uniformity among these interpretations and decisions they take on the nature of general norms. Secondly, the *stylus curiae* develops from the uniform

[75] Michiels, *Normae Generales*, I, 625. In this study there is no need to advert to the historical beginnings of these other curiae recognized in the Church's law, for, as has already been noted, prior to the Code of Canon Law the term "rescript" was commonly restricted to signify only the written replies of the Popes. Cf. *supra*, pp. 3-4.

[76] Cf. Cicognani, *Canon Law*, p. 105, and Michiels, *loc. cit.*

[77] Cf. Van Hove, *Commentarium Lovaniense in Codicem Iuris Canonici*, Lib. I, tom. II, *De Legibus Ecclesiasticis* (Editum a Magistris et Doctoribus Universitatis Lovaniensis, Mechliniae—Romae, 1930), p. 332 (hereafter cited as *De Legibus*), and Regatillo, *Institutiones Iuris Canonici* (2 vols., Vol. I, 2. ed., Santander: Sal Terrae, 1946), I, 95.

[78] Michiels, *ibid.*, p. 626.

and concurring sentences which the tribunals of the curia pronounce in the same types of cases.[79] These concepts are applicable to the *stylus* both of the Roman Curia and of other curiae.[80]

The commentators who treat this matter usually distinguish between a formal *stylus curiae* and one which is material. The formal style is concerned with the solemnities or formalities usually employed by a curia in preparing, solving, and executing its transactions, both judicial and non-judicial. The material style has reference to the decisions themselves which a curia gives on some particular matter. That is to say, this kind of *stylus curiae* is constituted by the juridic norms which have been applied in deciding certain specified cases.[81]

Both the formal and the material *stylus curiae* may be considered as a fact (*stylus facti*) or as a law (*stylus iuris*). As a fact, *stylus* means usage or practice; as a law, it denotes the laws and rules which result from that usage or practice.[82]

That the formal *stylus curiae* should have in given circumstances the force of law is easy to understand when one notes the basis upon which this kind of style is often founded. Not infrequently it is based on the prescriptions of the common law,[83] on the norms of special laws and regulations,[84] and on legiti-

[79] "Stylus Curiae est praxis, ex successive datis decisionibus invalescens, similiter iudicandi in eodem genere causarum, cui constanti uniformitate pedetentim accrescit 'auctoritas rerum similiter iudicatarum.'"—Beste, *Introductio in Codicem* (3. ed., Collegeville, Minn.: St. John's Abbey Press, 1946), p. 17. Cf. also Van Hove, *De Legibus*, pp. 332 and 336.

[80] Usually, however, the lawgiver and the canonical commentators pay more attention to the style of the Roman Curia, for the curiae subordinate to the Roman Curia are concerned with only particular matters, and not with affairs affecting the universal Church.

[81] Cf. Van Hove, *loc. cit.*, and Michiels, *loc. cit.*

[82] Cicognani, *loc. cit.*

[83] Cf., for example, the following canons in the Code of Canon Law: can. 39; can. 42, § 1; can. 156, § 3; can. 534, § 2; can. 991; can. 1040 with can. 7, can. 1047; cans. 1051-1057; cans. 1061-1063; can. 1447; can. 1532, § 4, and can. 2249.

[84] Cf. can. 243, § 1. One can find special laws and regulations concerning the various branches of the Roman Curia in the Constitution, *Sapienti*

mately established customary law.[85] Nonetheless, in other instances, even the formal *stylus* is merely a fact, for it is sometimes established in an arbitrary manner and can be changed by the precepts of superiors or major officials of the curia. As a result the requirements for the establishment of customary law are not fulfilled.[86]

As for the material *stylus curiae,* it, too, can have the force of law, even though of itself it is merely a *stylus facti,* for customary law can arise from the repeated decisions coming from a curia upon some particular matter within its competence.[87]

The foregoing assertions that both the formal and material *stylus curiae* can have the force of law suggest two questions, especially in reference to the style of the Roman Curia: [88] first, who are bound to observe the law established by the style of the Roman Curia; second, when is this *stylus iuris* obligatory?

---

consilio, issued on June 29, 1908, by Pope St. Pius X—*AAS,* I (1909), 1 ff. Moreover, by means of Instructions the dicasteries themselves sometimes add their own regulations to these special laws. This is especially true of the various Congregations and their major administrators who can, within the limits of their competence, introduce observances which sometimes affect even the validity of the acts of the Congregations to which they belong. Cf. Van Hove, *De Rescriptis,* p. 146.

[85] It seems helpful to note here that by means of legitimate custom, existing regulations in any curia can be derogated from and new practices *praeter legem communem* can be introduced into the *stylus curiae.* Cf. cans. 27, 28, and 30, and Toso, *Commentaria Minora,* I, 56.

[86] Cf. Felinus Sandeus, *Commentaria,* Lib. I, tit. III, ad c. 2, X, *de rescriptis,* I, 3, nn. 16-18; Van Hove, *op. cit.,* p. 333.

[87] "Ad stylum materialem seu ipsam jurisprudentiam quod attinet . . . notum est decreta formaliter aut aequivalenter generalia a competentibus Curiae Romanae Dicasteriis emanantia habere vim legis, decreta particularia et sententias judiciales vero ex se ligare tantum partes in causa (c. 17, § 3 et 1904, § 2) ideoque Stylum iisdem afformatum ex se esse meri facti seu non praebere objectivi juris normam in similibus casibus pro omnibus obligatoriam."—Michiels, *Normae Generales,* I, 627.

[88] The Roman Curia is considered in particular at this point, because this curia is of primary importance in the matter of rescripts. Moreover, when ordinaries beneath the Pope issue rescripts, very often they act as delegates of the Holy See. Nonetheless, the general principles enunciated hereafter concerning the *stylus Curiae Romanae* apply, *mutatis mutandis,* to the style of other curiae as well.

In answer to the first question, it must be said that certainly the administrators and officials of the Roman Curia are bound by its *stylus iuris.* Moreover, all other persons who become involved in transactions that are within the competence of the Roman Curia must attend to the formalities and comply with the conditions which have been established for the validity or lawfulness of the Curia's acts.[89] This latter statement applies especially to persons who act with power delegated to them by the Holy See, for a delegate must follow the *stylus* of the principal.[90]

As for the second question, that is, when is the *stylus iuris* of the Roman Curia obligatory, one must say that this style is of obligation in the following cases: a) when the Curia has to deal with affairs that belong to its competence; b) when power delegated by the Curia is exercised; c) when acts and documents emanating from the Curia are to be interpreted, and d) when the *stylus Curiae* is accepted as a source of suppletory law, as envisioned in canon 20.[91]

Furthermore, the distinction between *stylus iuris* and *stylus facti* takes on added juridical importance when it is considered in connection with the firmness and stability which the style of the Roman Curia has. The *stylus iuris* of the Roman Curia is based upon and grows out of its laws and statutes. It is, therefore, firm and fixed, and has the same degree of stability as do laws and statutes. Its *stylus facti,* on the contrary, depends both on individual decisions issued by the Curia itself and on precepts laid down by its superiors and major officials. Hence it may vary.[92]

Moreover, it must be noted that very often the *stylus Curiae Romanae* on rescripts is concerned with the granting of favors of one kind or another. By reason of their own nature such

[89] "Cum autem Curiae inferiores, in quantum autonomae sunt, jus habeant ad proprium stylum, obvium est stylum formalem Curiae Romanae ex se non habere vim legis relate ad negotia ab istis Curiis inferioribus propria auctoritate pertractanda."—Michiels, *ibid.,* p. 626.

[90] Cf. Van Hove, *loc. cit.,* and Michiels, *ibid.,* p. 627.

[91] Cicognani, *op. cit.,* p. 107.

[92] Cf. Cicognani, *op. cit.,* pp. 106-107.

concessions are made out of the liberality and generosity of the Holy See, for no one has a right to a favor. Hence, while the Holy See usually concedes its favors according to a general pattern of action which is intended to keep the *stylus Curiae* from becoming too arbitrary, nonetheless this pattern may well be changed. Most often this modification is effected in order to adapt the norms involved to the changing circumstances of time and place, as well as to special cases which are presented.[93] Accordingly, there is a saying that the *stylus facti* of the Roman Curia is sometimes white, sometimes black.[94]

Despite this possibility of variation, which is much more likely in the *stylus facti* than in the *stylus iuris* of the Roman Curia, there are definite ways to ascertain what the *stylus Curiae* is at any given time. There are, first of all, the sources of the different kinds of *stylus.* That is to say, one can learn what the *stylus Curiae* is, concerning a particular matter, by examining pertinent prescriptions in the common law, in special laws and regulations on the subject, and in the customary law on the point in question. One can study also the various interpretations, decisions, and sentences which the Holy See has issued in relation to the matter under consideration. A second indication as to what the *stylus Curiae Romanae* is on a particular point can be found in the many instructions and decrees which the different Congregations, Offices, and Tribunals issue from time to time.[95]

[93] Cf. Van Hove, *De Rescriptis,* p. 146.

[94] Cicognani, *op. cit.,* p. 107.

[95] Cf., for example, S. C. de Prop. Fid., instructio, 9 maii 1877—*Collectanea,* II, n. 1470; S. C. de Sacramentis, *De processibus in causis dispensationis super matrimonio rato et non consummato,* 7 maii 1923—*AAS,* XV (1923), 389-436; Bouscaren, *The Canon Law Digest,* I, 764-792; S. C. de Sacramentis, instructio, 1 augusti 1931—*AAS,* XXIII (1931), 413-415; Bouscaren, *ibid.,* pp. 514-516.

PART II

HISTORICAL SYNOPSIS OF JURIDIC PRINCIPLES AND JURISPRUDENCE ON TRUTH IN *PRECES*

INTRODUCTION

The purpose of this historical synopsis is to present a survey of the basic pre-Code law and jurisprudence in regard to the truth in the *preces* for rescripts. It is hoped that from this presentation of the principles of the traditional canonical discipline in this matter the reader will be able to come to a fuller appreciation of the clarity and conciseness of the norms of the present law in reference to the essential need for truthful petitions, as far as rescripts are concerned. Accordingly, in this survey the writer proposes to place special emphasis on those points of the previously prevailing law and jurisprudence which have a direct connection with the Church's currently binding law in this regard, as it is found in canons 40, 41, 42, 45, and 1054 in the Code of Canon Law.

In reference to the pre-Code law concerning the truth that was demanded in the *preces* for rescripts, it seems to be certain that the Church's own proper legislation in this matter came after the Popes first introduced the pertinent Roman Law Institute of Rescript as a means of the papal government and direction of the individual members of the faithful.[1] At all events, from the time of the introduction of rescripts into the papal administrative mechanism, truthful petitions were always required for the validity of the letters. On this point there can be no doubt, for, until the Church had developed her own law in this regard, the sources indicate that she must have adopted the prevailing civil law of Rome in reference to it. That law was most clear in demanding that the *preces* for rescripts be founded on truth.[2]

The first properly ecclesiastical legislation pertaining to the truth required in the *preces* for rescripts began to appear, as far as the records show, in the year 557.[3] The vast majority of the pre-Code law in this regard was enacted through decretals issued

[1] Cf. *infra*, pp. 38-39.

[2] Cf. *infra*, pp. 38-39.

[3] Cf. *infra*, p. 39, note 5.

by the Popes who reigned before the Council of Trent (1545-1563).[4] In fact, by the time of the Council of Trent the Church's legislation on this subject was almost completely crystallized. Very few new laws on it were enacted between the Council of Trent and the Code of Canon Law. Indeed, while the Council itself and, later on, the Roman Congregations touched upon the law's demand for the presence of truth in petitions for rescripts, for the most part they merely echoed or, perhaps, emphasized what had already been prescribed by the Popes in their decretals.[5] Hence, all the more notable was the legislation of Pope St. Pius X (1903-1914) in his reconstruction of the Roman Curia in 1908. One of the norms established at that time provided that rescripts containing dispensations from minor matrimonial impediments were exempt from the invalidating effect of subreption and obreption in the *preces* for the letters.[6] That norm represented a most significant change in the legal substratum that underlay the pre-Code jurisprudence in reference to the truth and *preces* for rescripts.

The foregoing brief description of the law and the legal norms, which furnished that juridical substratum, may help the reader to appreciate the plan which the writer has adopted in presenting his survey of the doctrine of the pre-Code commentators on the subject matter of this study. His plan is, namely, to set forth the pertinent teaching of those authors in this regard without dividing the time prior to the Code into the different periods that one ordinarily expects to find in a historical survey. Actually, in this study such divisions would be forced and unnatural, and they would cause a great deal of tedious repetition. That repetition would be due to two interrelated factors.

First of all, all the pre-Code authors used the decretal legislation as the basis for most of their commentary on the matter being considered in this work. Secondly, it was the evident practice of those commentators often merely to restate the teachings of their predecessors on a particular point in that early law. If the

[4] Cf. *infra*, pp. 41-50.

[5] Cf. *infra*, pp. 50-54.

[6] Cf. *infra*, p. 54.

point under discussion had been disputed in the past, the later authors indicated the stand which they took on it. Sometimes new reasons were given for their having taken that stand; at other times only the reasons of the earlier canonists were repeated.

This is not to say, however, that there was no noticeable change nor gradual evolution in the pre-Code canonical doctrine concerning the *preces* and the truth required in them. There were definite changes in that doctrine. Far-reaching changes were caused, for instance, by Pope Boniface VIII (1294-1303) when he made *motu proprio* granted rescripts exempt from the invalidating effect of subreption,[7] and by Pope St. Pius X when he excepted rescripts conveying dispensations from minor matrimonial impediments from the nullifying effect of both subreption and obreption.[8] There was also a gradual evolution in the doctrine of the commentators. This is evidenced by the fact that, with the passing of time, it frequently happened that one or the other of the different opinions on a particular disputed point became recognized as the common or at least the more common teaching in the matter concerned, precisely because of the support given it by the later canonists.

In fact, while the change and the evolution which took place do not warrant a division of this historical survey into different periods of time, they do make it worth one's while, and even necessary, to consider the doctrine of the pre-Code commentators on the subject matter of this dissertation. The value of such a consideration lies in the fact that it was the teaching of those authors which had much to do with the development of the jurisprudence that surrounded the practical application of the lawgiver's demand for truthful *preces.* Moreover, it is their teaching which now gives one an insight into the manner in which the canonical experts of the period prior to the Code understood the sometimes complex and not-too-clear decretal legislation that implemented the essential condition *"si preces veritate nitantur."*

[7] Cf. *infra,* p. 48.

[8] Cf. *infra,* p. 54.

CHAPTER II

PRE-CODE LEGISLATION AND LEGAL NORMS

SECTION I. FORMAL INTRODUCTION OF THE CONDITION *"si preces veritate nitantur"* INTO THE LAW ON RESCRIPTS

The first express mention of the essential condition *"si preces veritate nitantur,"* as a formal element of the law on rescripts, is found in a decree of the Emperor Zeno in the year 477:

> Universa rescripta . . . quae vel annotatio, vel quaevis pragmatica sanctio nominetur, sub ea condicione proferri praecepimus, si preces veritate nitantur, nec aliquem fructum precator oraculi percipiat impetrati, licet in iudicio adserat veritatem, nisi quaestio fidei precum imperiali beneficio monstretur inserta.[1]

Pope Alexander III (1159-1181) canonized this Roman Law expression seven centuries later when he wrote: "*. . . et in huiusmodi literis* [*i.e., literis apostolicis*] *intelligenda est haec conditio, etiamsi non apponatur: 'si preces veritate nitantur'. . . .*"[2]

It must not be thought, however, that by officially incorporating the aforesaid condition into their respective laws Zeno and Alexander were thereby enunciating new principles. The fact of the matter is that the Roman legal machinery, on the one hand, was practicing the principle underlying that expression long before 477. Indeed, the force of that principle was felt at least as early as the year 294 in virtue of a law enacted by the Emperors Diocletian and Maximian in reference to rescripts of justice.[3] On the other hand, the Popes had seen fit to adopt the

[1] C. (1. 23) 7—*Cod. Iust.*

[2] C. 2, X, *de rescriptis*, I, 3—Jaffé, *Regesta Pontificum Romanorum ab condita Ecclesia ad annum post Christum natum MCXCVIII* (ed. 2. correctam et auctam auspiciis Gulielmi Wattenbach, curaverunt F. Kaltenbrunner, P. Ewald, S. Loewenfeld, 2 vols., Lipsiae, 1885-1888), n. 14317 (hereafter cited as JK, JE, JL).

[3] Cf. C. (1. 22) 2—*Cod. Iust.*

Roman Law Institute of Rescript for their own use certainly by the year 385.[4] They undoubtedly accepted the norms which governed this institute in Roman Law until the time when they could officially formulate the Church's own law on rescripts.[5]

Section II. The Meaning of the Word "Truth"

In trying to ascertain the meaning of the word "truth," as it was used in the clause *"si preces veritate nitantur,"* one looks in vain for a philosophical definition of this term in the various laws which the Emperors and the Popes enacted in this regard. In this matter, those lawmakers were acting primarily as legislators and not as philosophers. Accordingly, as far as the validity of rescripts was concerned, they were interested mainly in showing the legal or juridical meaning of the word "truth." Their approach, then, was not a positive one, that is, by way of an express definition of what they meant by that term in connection with the *preces* for rescripts. Rather, they showed its meaning in a negative manner by setting down cases in which they declared by law that in this or that instance the petitioner's *preces* had not been founded on truth.

Thus, in the Roman Law the Emperors Diocletian and Maximian stated that an exception on the grounds of falsehood in the petition for a particular rescript might be filed either whenever a lie or duplicity had been detected *in a statement of law or of fact in the* preces *involved,* or whenever fraud had been committed by the petitioner, insofar as he had intentionally

[4] The first papal rescript which has been preserved in full was issued by Pope Siricius (384-399) in 385. It is the opinion of some authors, however, that rescripts had been granted by Popes who reigned before the time of Pope Siricius.—Cf. O'Neill, *Papal Rescripts of Favor,* p. 14.

[5] The first law concerning the truth that was required in the *preces* for rescripts, which Gratian recorded in his *Decretum,* was that of Pope Pelagius I (556-561), issued in 557. It is worthy of note that, in commenting on this law of Pope Pelagius, Gratian quoted, besides others, the two texts of Roman Law, referred to above, to support his opinions. Since Gratian pointed to no previous properly ecclesiastical laws in this matter, his use of the aforesaid texts from the Roman Law seems to indicate that prior to the time of Pope Pelagius I the Church had adopted the Roman Law principles in this regard as her own law.—Cf. c. 16, C. XXV, q. 2, and the *Dictum Gratiani* after this text.

remained silent concerning some point which should have been expressed.[6] Likewise, the Emperors Theodosius and Valentinian decreed that only where necessity required it should words whose meaning was doubtful to the petitioner be inserted in his *preces*. Obviously, the purpose of that precaution was to guard against ambiguity which would have possibly prevented the Emperor from rendering his decision on the matter at hand in accordance with right reason.[7]

Similar statements were made by the Popes for the Church's law. In the year 557 Pope Pelagius I wrote, for example, that it had been established by general law that those sacred things which had been granted at the instance of any petitioner prevailed and were effective only when they were in accordance with right reason and the law; those which were obtained by subreption or by a false petition, however, were of no benefit to the petitioner.[8] An even more important law in this regard was that which Pope Innocent III (1198-1216) issued in 1208. In that law Pope Innocent set down four distinct points which had a direct bearing on the proper understanding of what it meant to have the *preces* founded on truth. He noted, first of all, that a petition could be lacking in truth either *because some item of truth had been suppressed* or *because some falsehood had been expressed*. His second point was that one had to consider the intention of the grantor in judging whether or not the *preces* for a particular rescript were *de facto* truthful. His third point was that not any and every lack of truth in a petition laid the subsequent rescript open to invalidity. Finally, Pope Innocent indicated that, even when a petition was falsified in good faith, the concession that was obtained because of the untruthfulness involved was nullified for the intended beneficiary of the rescript.[9]

Hence it may be said that under the law the word "truth," when it was used in connection with the *preces* for rescripts,

[6] C. (1. 22) 2—*Cod. Iust.*

[7] Cf. C. (1. 19) 8—*Cod. Iust.*

[8] C. 16, C. XXV, q. 2.

[9] C. 20, X, *de rescriptis*, I, 3; Potthast, *Regesta Pontificum Romanorum inde ab anno post Christum natum MCXCVIII ad annum MCCCIV* (2 vols., Berolini, 1874-1875), n. 3519 (hereafter cited as Potthast).

signified a legally sufficient objective conformity between what was stated in the petitions for rescripts and the facts and circumstances that actually existed in the cases of the prospective beneficiaries of the letters.[10]

SECTION III. DECRETAL LEGISLATION ON TRUTH IN THE *Preces*

The essential need of having truthful *preces* for rescripts was amply evidenced by the great amount of legislation which appeared in reference to this matter in the decretals of the Popes before the Council of Trent (1545-1563). All of that legislation was, indeed, important. There were some laws, however, which had an especially significant bearing upon the relationship between petitions and the truth that was required in them. Those were the decretals to which the pre-Code commentators appealed most frequently in propounding their doctrine concerning the truth and the *preces* for rescripts.

In order to avail the reader of a ready opportunity to study the more important of these laws, both in their text and in their context, the writer proposes here to quote in full certain particular decretals which are especially pertinent to the subject matter of this dissertation.[11] He has been prompted to present the following quotations by the fact that the decretals in question were always given to decide particular cases that had been brought to the attention of the Sovereign Pontiffs. Yet, in developing their doctrine concerning the essential necessity of truthful *preces*, the commentators drew from these decretals

[10] Cf. *infra*, pp. 56-58.

[11] All of the quotations which follow in this section are taken from the *Corpus Iuris Canonici* (editio Lipsiensis II, post Aemilii Ludovici Richteri curas instruxit Aemilius Friedberg, 2 vols., Lipsiae: Ex officina Bernhardi Tauchnitz, 1879-1881; ed. anastatice repetita, 1928). Any italics which appear in them correspond to italized words or passages in the foregoing edition of the *Corpus Iuris Canonici*. Italics are used in that edition to indicate words and passages which were in the original text of the law at its initial promulgation, but which were absent therefrom in its later promulgation. The "†" is used to mark the place where St. Raymond of Pennafort interrupted the text of the particular law being quoted and simply inserted, "etc. Et *infra*," in reference to another law wherein there could be found the passage which belonged originally in that place in the decretal in question. The laws quoted in the subsequent pages follow a topical rather than a chronological order.

most of the general principles or norms that were basic to a proper understanding of the legislator's demand for truth in the petitions for rescripts. Unfortunately, however, the authors did not always agree among themselves as to the correctness of the principles that were taken from this or that decretal. Accordingly, the writer hopes that by quoting at least some of the more fundamental decretal legislation concerning the matter at hand, the reader will thereby have an occasion to understand the circumstances that surrounded the laws to which the commentators very often referred. He is not including in this place any of the authors' commentaries upon these laws, except the rubric to, that is, the summary of, the individual texts and a brief notation of the specific bearing which each law had upon the pre-Code jurisprudence concerning the relationship between the *preces* and the truth required in them.[12]

To begin with, there was the law of Pope Alexander III (1159-1181) which made the condition *"si preces veritate nitantur"* a formal part of the Church's legislation on rescripts. The rubric to this law reads as follows: *"In rescripto apostolico subintelligitur clausula: 'si preces veritate nitantur.' Et si rescriptum prohibet causae cognitionem, est de falsitate suspectum."* The text of the law states:

> Ex parte *venerabilis fratris nostri* Conventrensis episcopi nostris est auribus intimatum, quod, quum de causa, quae inter G. et F. clericos vertitur super praebenda de Novalis, cognoscens legitime eidem F. secundum tenorem literarum nostrarum, continentium, quod, si constaret, ipsum F. de periurio esse convictum, et perpetuo illi renunciasse praebendae, *appellatione cessante* amoveretur ab ea; eo cognito et probato, praebendam adiudicasset eandem, ipse in vocem appellationis prorupit, et ad te, quod ei praebendam praecise at absque causae cognitione restitueres, literas nostras reportavit, † *et episcopum, qui post appellationem eum praebenda spoliavit, auctoritate alicui beneficium conferendi appellatione cessante privares, donec per se, vel per nuncium, aut per literas suas de tanto excessu satisfacturus ad sedem apostolicam accederet, et praenominatum G., si eundem F. in iam dicta praebenda praesumeret molestare, vinculo excommunicationis usque ad dignam satisfactionem adstringeres.* Verum quoniam non

[12] An extensive commentary on these laws is presented in Chapter III. Cf. *infra*, pp. 55-106.

credimus, *nos* ita praecise scripsisse, *et si taliter scripsimus, hoc ex nimia occupatione contigit,* et in huiusmodi literis intelligenda est haec conditio, etiamsi non apponatur: "si preces veritate nitantur": *fraternitati tuae per apostolica scripta praecipiendo* mandamus, quatenus inspectis literis, quas episcopo praedicto direximus, si inveneris, quod secundum praedictum modum ei scripserimus, *et in literis nostris appellatio fuerit inhibita,* et in literis, quas *tibi* praefatus F. reportavit, non fuerit habita mentio priorum literarum, sententiam praefati episcopi *omni occasione et appellatione cessante* confirmes, et saepedictum F. cum literis nostris, quas tibi detulit, ad praesentiam nostram venire compellas.[13]

A most basic law in the matter of the need for truthful petitions was that of Pope Innocent III (1198-1216), issued in 1208. This law was most fundamental to the pre-Code jurisprudence concerning the truth required in the *preces* for rescripts of justice, in regard to which it was primarily enacted. It was applied, however, also to rescripts of favor. The authors used the norms of this decretal in commenting upon the truth in relation to the causes or reasons alleged for rescripts,[14] upon the extent of the effect which false petitions had upon rescripts,[15] and upon the manner in which the aforesaid effect was produced in connection with rescripts of justice.[16] The rubric to this law states:

> Difficile et famosum c. et est clavis totius tituli [tit. III, *de rescriptis*]. Et h. d. in summa: Exprimens falsum, vel tacens verum in rescripto, si malitiose, caret prorsus impetratis. Sed si per simplicitatem vel ignorantiam aut obtinuisset vero expresso, et suppresso falso saltem literas in forma communi, et delegatus procedit servato iuris ordine, et non speciali forma rescripti; secus, si nullo modo literas habuisset.

The text reads:

> Super literis, quae ab aliquibus ex malitia, et a nonnullis ex ignorantia, tacita veritate vel suggesta falsitate impetrantur a nobis, diversos intelleximus diversa sentire, aliis asserentibus, eos debere prorsus carere omni commodo literarum, quum

[13] C. 2, X, *de rescriptis,* I, 3; JL, n. 14317.

[14] Cf. *infra,* pp. 65-73.

[15] Cf. *infra,* pp. 91-99.

[16] Cf. *infra,* pp. 99-102.

mendax precator carere debeat penitus impetratis; aliis vero dicentibus, quod, etsi forma carere debeant in literis nostris expressa, nihilominus *tamen* iuxta rigorem iuris sit a delegato iudice in negotio procedendum. Nos igitur inter eos, qui per fraudem vel malitiam, et illos, qui per simplicitatem vel ignorantiam literas a nobis impetrant, huiusmodi credimus discretionem adhibendam, ut hi, qui priori modo falsitatem exprimunt vel supprimunt veritatem, in suae perversitatis poenam nullum ex illis literis commodum consequantur, ita videlicet, quod delegatus, postquam sibi super hoc facta fuerit fides, nullatenus de causa cognoscat. Inter alios autem, qui posteriori modo literas impetrant, duximus distinguendum, quae falsitas suggesta fuerit, vel quae veritas sit suppressa. Nam si talis expressa sit falsitas vel veritas occultata, quae, quamvis fuisset tacita vel expressa, nos nihilominus saltem in forma communi literas dedissemus: delegatus, non sequens formam in literis ipsis appositam, secundum ordinem iuris in causa procedat. Si vero per huiusmodi falsitatis expressionem vel suppressionem etiam veritatis literae fuerint impetratae, qua tacita vel expressa nos nullas prorsus literas dedissemus, a delegato non est aliquatenus procedendum, nisi forsitan eatenus, ut partibus ad suam praesentiam convocatis de precum qualitate cognoscat, ut sic in utroque casu eadem ratio, quae delegantem moveret, moveat etiam delegatum, et ubi delegans suas literas denegaret, delegatus etiam suae cognitionis officium nullatenus interponat. [*Dat. Ferentini XV. Kal. Nov. Pont. nostri Ao. XI. 1208.*] [17]

Pope Innocent III issued another law which was used by some authors to argue that even the impelling causes for rescripts of favor had to be truthful.[18] The rubric to this law is as follows:

Per literas iustitiae non tenetur episcopus providere habenti perpetuam vicariam vel sufficiens patrimonium, nec valent literae gratiae ad beneficium obtinendum, in quibus impetrans tacuit perpetuam vicariam. Hoc dicit comprehendendo utrumque intellectum.

Its text states:

Postulasti per sedem apostolicam edoceri, utrum alicuius ecclesiae perpetuo vicario, de proventibus vicariae bonisque paternis habenti unde valeat commode sustentari, tenearis per illam formam communem: "Quum secundum Apostolum," in

[17] C. 20, X, *de rescriptis*, I, 3; Potthast, n. 3519.

[18] Cf. *infra*, pp. 74-75.

ecclesiastico beneficio providere. Ad quod sic duximus respondendum, quod, quum per formam praedictam necessitatibus pauperum clericorum, qui nullum sunt ecclesiasticum beneficium assecuti, *sicut ibidem exprimi consuevit,* sedes apostolica duxerit succurrendum, perpetuus vicarius, nisi de vicaria fecerit mentionem, commodum reportare non debet de huiusmodi literis, utpote veritate tacita impetratis. Non enim beneficio *ecclesiastico* carere debet dici, cui competenter de perpetuae vicariae proventibus est provisum. Et pro habente beneficii sufficientis subsidium ex certa scientia super obtinendo alio beneficio de levi non scribimus, quin faciamus de primo in nostris literis mentionem. [*Tu denique etc. Dat. Lat. VI. Id. Ian. Pont. nostri Ao. XVI. 1214.*] [19].

Other commentators appealed to a law of Pope Boniface VIII (1294-1303) to substantiate by deduction their teaching that falsehood in the impelling causes given for rescripts of favor did not invalidate the letters, unless the untruthfulness involved had arisen from bad faith.[20] The summary of the content of this decretal is set forth thus:

Si Papa det licentiam legato suo recipiendi auctoritate apostolica resignationes beneficiorum legationis suae, libere in manibus suis factas, et illa beneficia conferendi; secundo Papa, de praedicta postestate non habita mentione, canonicatum et praebendam, si vacat, vel quam primo vacaverit in aliqua ecclesia legationis, mihi conferat; tertio canonicus ipsius ecclesiae renunciet, et legatus etiam, ignorans collationem mihi factam, confert tibi praebendam praedictam; non tenet collatio legati, sed mihi illa praebenda debetur. Hoc dicit Ioann. Andr.

The text of the law reads:

Dudum venerabili fratri nostro S. episcopo Praenestino, quem ad patres destinavimus Gallicanas, recipiendi auctoritate nostra resignationem ab obtinentibus beneficia ecclesiastica in eisdem partibus, qui ea vellent libere in eius manibus resignare, ac beneficia ipsa personis idoneis conferendi per nostras literas potestate concessa, nos postmodum, de concessione huiusmodi non habita mentione, Nicolao de Bonefac., camerario dilecti filii nostri N. tituli sancti Laurentii in Damasco presbyteri cardinalis, canonicatum Lexoniensis ecclesiae, quae in partibus

[19] C. 27, X, *de rescriptis,* I, 3; not listed in Potthast.

[20] Cf. *infra,* pp. 76-77.

illis exsistit, et praebendam nulli alii de iure debitam, si qua tunc vacabat in dicta ecclesia, contulimus, et sibi providimus de eisdem. Si vero nulla talis praebenda vacabat ibidem: nos praebendam, proximo inibi vacaturam, conferendam dicto camerario, quum vacaret, donationi apostolicae duximus reservandam, decernentes extunc [sic] irritum et inane, si secus super hoc a quoquam contingeret attentari, certis sibi ad hoc exsecutoribus deputatis. Quumque postmodum Nicolaus Vasalli clericus canonicatum et praebendam, quos in dicta Lexoniensi ecclesia obtinebat, in dicti episcopi manibus resignasset, et dictae potestatis praetextu eos idem episcopus, collationis, provisionis, reservationis et decreti praedictorum forsan ignarus, Guilielmo Vasalli presbytero contulisset, dicti exsecutores, collatione non obstante praedicta literarum nostrarum auctoritate praebendam eandem dicto camerario, velut sibi debitam, contulerunt, quem dictus presbyter, praetextu collationis per dictum episcopum sibi factae, quod praebendam ipsam pacifice possidere valeat, non permittit; propter quod idem camerarius nobis supplicavit humiliter, ut providere sibi super hoc de opportuno remedio dignaremur. Nos igitur, attendentes, quod, etsi memorato episcopo praedictam concessimus potestatem, penes nos tamen nihilominus remansit maior, licet eadem potestas etiam in praedictis, propter quod nostra, qui eandem praeoccupavimus potestatem, potior debet esse conditio, praesertim quod secundum canonicas et legitimas sanctiones per speciem generi derogatur, quanquam de genere in derogante specie mentio nulla fiat; considerantes quoque, quod nos, exposito nobis de potestate praedicta, nihilominus literas gratiosas daremus in dictis partibus, non habita mentione de ipsa, quia foret absurdum, si tam lata nostra impediretur potestas, et si in omnibus provisionum nostrarum literis, quas concederemus in partibus supra dictis, oporteret nos de saepe dicta potestate specialem facere mentionem. . . .[21]

Moreover, in connection with the causes alleged for rescripts, the authors held that in the case of a petition which contained several really final reasons, unless bad faith was present, it was sufficient for the validity of the subsequent rescript that only one of those causes was truthful.[22] They pointed to a law which

[21] C. 14, *de praebendis et dignitatibus*, III, 4, in VI°. The foregoing quotation contains the pertinent part of this decretal from which was deduced the canonical doctrine that in the presence of good faith it was sufficient, as far as the causes presented for rescripts of favor were concerned, that only the final reason given for such letters was true.

[22] Cf. *infra*, p. 69.

Pope Alexander III enacted between 1159 and 1181 as bearing out this doctrine. The rubric to this law reads: "*Si Papa mandat in rescripto de duobus inquiri alternative, ad certum effectum consequendum sufficit alterum probari.*" The law itself provides as follows:

> Inter ceteras consultationes tuas [*id nobis*] fuit propositum coram nobis, quid tenere debeas, quum aliqua sub disiunctione mandantur, quorum unum verum est, alterum falsum, utputa si proponatur, quod si talis sit sacerdotis filius, et in sacerdotio genitus, qui proximo in tali ecclesia ministravit, vel quod illicite ecclesiam occupavit eandem. Huic ergo quaestioni taliter respondemus, *quod convenit,* iudici quodcumque istorum constiterit, illi praelibatam ecclesiam adiudicari debere. Et idem in similibus observandum est. *Sane si etc.* (*cf. c. 8. de off. iud. del. I. 29*).[23]

In reference to the time at which the *preces* had to be founded on truth, it was an almost unanimous doctrine among the pre-Code authors that the petitions for rescripts *in forma gratiosa* had to be truthful only at the time of their *tempus datae.*[24] To support this doctrine, the commentators appealed to Pope Innocent III's law of 1213, the rubric to which reads:

> Non valet dispensatio, obtenta a Papa super matrimonio inter consanguineos contracto, si ibi causa falsa sit expressa, nisi postea eam Papa confirmaret. H. d. secundum verum et communem intellectum.

Its text states:

> Quia circa (*Et infra:* [*cf. c. 6. de bigam. I. 21*]). Porro de nobili viro N., pro cuius dispensatione, indulgentia scilicet remanendi cum ea, quae ipsum quinto consanguinitatis gradu contingit, a sede apostolica obtinenda falsa nobis causa fuerat allegata, proles videlicet, quum tamen ante dispensationem obtentam unica filia, quam habeat, viam fuerit universae carnis ingressa, prout tua consultatio continebat, dissimulare poteris, ut remaneat in copula sic contracta, quum ex separatione, sicut asseris, grave videas scandalum imminere. [*Tu denique etc. Dat. Signiae V. Non. Oct. Pont. nostr. Ao XVI. 1213.*] [25]

[23] C. 4, X, *de rescriptis,* I, 3; JL, n. 13878.

[24] Cf. *infra,* pp. 79-82.

[25] C. 6, X, *de consanguinitate et affinitate,* IV, 14; Potthast, no. 4820.

The commentators referred in this regard also to a law of Pope Boniface VIII, which was summarized in this manner: "*In literis ad beneficia impetratis inspicitur tempus datae. Unde per illas beneficium curatum obtinere non poterit, qui, licet nunc sit maior, illo tempore minor erat. Ioann. Andr.*" The law itself reads:

> Si eo tempore, quo tibi de beneficio cum cura vel sine cura mandavimus provideri, ad obtinendum curatum beneficium idoneam non habebas aetatem: tibi, licet nunc legitimae effectus sis aetatis, auctoritate literarum huiusmodi, quum tempore datae ipsarum adhuc non esses idoneus, de beneficio curam animarum habente nequaquam poterit provideri. Beneficium autem sine cura, quum ad ipsum sufficientem tunc aetatem haberes, per eas licite poteris obtinere.[26]

Until the year 1908, when Pope St. Pius X made rescripts containing dispensations from minor matrimonial impediments exempt from the invalidating effects of subreption and obreption, only rescripts issued *motu proprio* were partially immune from the otherwise universal scope of the lawgiver's requirement of truthful *preces* for the validity of rescripts.[27] It was Pope Boniface VIII who effected this exemption in favor of *motu proprio* issued rescripts. The rubric to the law involved states: "*Obstat taciturnitas obtenti beneficii, licet modici, nisi constet, provisionem factam proprio motu Papae; qui demum intelligitur, si hoc in litera exprimatur. H. d. Zenz.*" Its text is as follows:

> Si motu proprio alicui, aliquod beneficium obtinenti, conferamus aliud, de illo non habita mentione: non ob hoc gratiam huiusmodi, quae de nostra mera liberalitate processit, invalidam volumus reputari. Secus, si ad petitionem illius, vel alterius pro eodem oblatam gratiam huiusmodi faciamus. Tunc enim, quantumcunque modicum beneficium taceatur in ea, ipsam veluti subreptitiam vires nolumus obtinere. Motu quoque proprio tunc solum gratia fieri censeatur, quum hoc expresse cautum fuerit in eadem.[28]

In regard to the manner in which the invalidating effect of false *preces* was produced upon rescripts, it was the more com-

[26] C. 9, *de rescriptis*, I, 3, in VI°.

[27] Cf. *infra*, pp. 87-89.

[28] C. 23, *de praebendis et dignitatibus*, III, 4, in VI°.

mon opinion of the pre-Code commentators that this effect did not result *ipso iure,* as far as rescripts of justice were concerned.[29] The authors deduced this doctrine from such laws as the following one of Pope Lucius III (1181-1185). The summary of this decretal reads: *"Valet secundum rescriptum impetratum ab adversario, licet non faciat mentionem de primo, si primus impetrans dolo vel negligentia non fuit usus illo."* The text states:

> Si autem aliquis, auctoritate posteriorum literarum per adversarium in iudicium tractus, obiecerit, literas se priores habere, de quibus in posterioribus mentio non habetur, si eis dolo vel negligentia uti postposuerit, excusari non debet. Si autem, quia delegati iudicis copiam nequiverit habere, per posteriores literas non poterit conveniri.[30]

There were a few commentators, however, who held that the aforesaid effect was produced *ipso iure* upon rescripts of justice whenever the falsehood involved was due to bad faith.[31] To substantiate their claim, these authors appealed to another law issued by Pope Lucius III and also to other decretals of similar tenor. The rubric to this law of Pope Lucius is worded thus: *"Non valet rescriptum impetratum ad beneficia, si in eo tacetur dignitas impetrantis."* The text of his law reads:

> Ad aures nostras *te significante* pervenit, quod plerumque decani, archdiaconi, praecentores vel alii ecclesiasticis praediti dignitatibus, super minoribus beneficiis *per interpositas personas* literas impetrantes, nomen supprimunt dignitatis suae, et simplici nomine se appellant, tanquam non habeant aliquem personatum, † *ideoque rescripto nostro postulas edoceri, si fraus ista tacendi praeiudicium eis debeat generare?* Consultationi *igitur* tuae taliter respondemus, quod, quum non sit intentionis nostrae, ut personae pluribus reditibus abundantes per literas nostras pauperes clericos super minoribus beneficiis inquietent, literas, in quibus actor* suae nomen dignitatis supprimit, vires nolumus *aliquas* obtinere. *Postremo etc.* (*cf. c. 36. de app. II. 28*).[32]

[29] Cf. *infra,* pp. 99-102.

[30] C. 9, X, *de rescriptis,* I, 3; JL, n. 15185. Cf. also c. 23, X, *de rescriptis,* I, 3; Potthast, n. 3671 (Innocent III: 1209).

[31] Cf. *infra,* pp. 101-102.

[32] C. 8, X, *de rescriptis,* I, 3; JL, n. 14965. The editor of the *Corpus Iuris Canonici* indicated that in some manuscripts the term *"auctor"* was

When rescripts of favor were involved, the nullifying effect of false petitions was produced *ipso iure* according to the almost unanimous teaching of the pre-Code commentators.[33] The basis of this doctrine was found in such laws as the one of Pope Honorius III (1216-1227), which is quoted here. The rubric to this decretal states: "*Si habens literas Papae ad beneficium eis propter annuam pensionem renunciat, non valent literae beneficiales per eum hoc tacito impetratae.*" Its text is as follows:

> Ad audientiam nostram *te significante* pervenit, quod quidam clerici, obtentis a sede apostolica literis super provisione sua in aliquibus ecclesiis tibi *lege dioecesana* subiectis, recipientes ab eis annuas pensiones, seu alia beneficia, ab eorum impetitione desistunt, renunciantes *nostrarum* beneficio literarum, † *deinde ad sedem apostolicam accedentes super provisione sua obtinent alias literas ab eadem, de literis antea impetratis non habita mentione, et sic gratia benignitatis apostolicae abutentes, ecclesias multipliciter inquietant. Ne igitur tales de suae circumventionis astutia glorientur,* Fraternitati tuae mandamus, quatenus eos, qui, post literas *nostras* taliter venditas, alias, de illis mentione non habita, impetrabunt de cetero, vel hactenus impetrarunt, carere decernas commodo earundem, et ecclesias, *contra quas fuerint impetratae,* non permittas earum occasione vexari, revocando in irritum, si quid earum praetextu inveneris esse factum.[34]

SECTION IV. LEGISLATION OF THE COUNCIL OF TRENT ON TRUTH IN THE *Preces*

The Fathers of the Council of Trent made three specific references to the necessity of having truth in the petitions for rescripts. The first came in regard to a bishop's right to take summary cognizance of favors relative either to the absolution from crime or to the remission of punishment which had been imposed

---

used for "*actor**" in the foregoing text. Cf. also c. 26, X, *de rescriptis,* I, 3; Potthast, n. 5026 (Innocent III: 1198-1215).

[33] Cf. *infra,* pp. 102-105.

[34] C. 31, X, *de rescriptis,* I, 3; Potthast, n. 7789. Cf. also c. 19, X, *de rescriptis,* I, 3; Potthast, n. 353 (Innocent III: 1198); c. 23, *de praebendis et dignitatibus,* III, 4, in VI° (quoted above on p. 48); c. 2, *de filiis presbyterorum et aliis illegitime natis,* I, 11, in VI° (Boniface VIII: 1294-1303).

by the same ordinary. Since their words expressed so well the spirit behind the letter of Pope Innocent III's laws on this point, they are here reproduced in full:

> And since it sometimes happens that under false pleas, which, however, appear probable enough, certain persons fraudulently obtain favors of the kind, whereby the punishments imposed on them by the just severity of their bishops are either wholly remitted or mitigated; and since it is a thing not to be tolerated that a lie, which is so exceedingly displeasing to God, should not only go unpunished, but should even obtain for him who tells it the pardon of another crime; it is therefore ordained and decreed as follows: a bishop residing in his own church may *per se ipsum*, as the delegate of the Apostolic See, and without judicial process, take cognizance of the cheating and stealing of a favor obtained under false pretenses for the absolution of any public crime or delinquency, concerning which he himself had instituted an inquiry, or for the remission of a punishment to which he himself had condemned the criminal; and he shall not admit that favor after it shall have been lawfully established that it was obtained by the statement of what is false or by the suppression of what is true.[35]

The Council's second reference had much the same tone and dealt precisely with rescripts containing dispensations. In this regard it was decreed, first, that all dispensations which were to be sent outside the Roman Curia were to be committed to the ordinaries of those who had obtained them, and, secondly, that those dispensations which were granted as a favor would have no effect until the ordinaries, as delegates of the Apostolic See, had established summarily and extra-judicially that the terms of the petition were free from fraud and deception.[36]

Trent's third mention of truthful petitions for rescripts had to do with permissions which Rome had given to alter a last will and testament. There again the Fathers of the Council made it clear that no change whatsoever was to be executed until the bishops, acting as the Apostolic See's delegates, had ascertained

[35] Conc. Trident., sess. XIII, *de ref.*, c. 5—Schroeder, *Canons and Decrees of the Council of Trent:* Original Text with English Translation (St. Louis: B. Herder Book Co., 1941), p. 84 (hereafter cited as Schroeder).

[36] Conc. Trident., sess. XXII, *de ref.*, c. 5—Schroeder, pp. 155-156.

summarily and extra-judicially that nothing had been stated in the petition which suppressed what was true or suggested what was false.[37]

Section V. Legal Norms Issued After the Council of Trent on Truth in the *Preces*

After the Council of Trent it was the Roman Curia which did most in the way of laying down norms which touched, in one way or another, upon the fundamental principles concerning the truth that was required in the *preces* for rescripts. The following regulations are of importance in this study.

In 1846 the Sacred Congregation of Bishops and Regulars issued a decree by which it indicated, first, that a favor granted in a rescript *in forma commissoria* was to be considered as being suspended until the executor had been able to verify the conditions contained in the rescript (the most general of which was *si preces veritate nitantur*), and, secondly, that even if the granting of the favor would have benefited the Church at the time when the rescript had been issued in Rome, the petition involved had to be true also at the time when the rescript was to be executed, or else the execution was not to take place.[38]

Concerning the investigation to be made by the executor into the truth of the *preces*, it should be noted that prior to 1885 the Apostolic Datary and the Apostolic Chancery had been accustomed to attach to their rescripts when granted *in forma commissoria* the clause *"si preces veritate niti repereris,"* which seemed to demand more than the clause *"si preces veritate nitantur,"* which was at least understood in every rescript. In fact, the former clause led canonists in general to teach that the investigation of the *preces* of those rescripts to which it was attached was necessary for the validity of the execution of the letters, unless the executor himself otherwise knew that the peti-

[37] Conc. Trident., sess. XXII, *de ref.*, c. 6—Schroeder, p. 428.

[38] S. C. Ep. et Reg., *Nolana*, 13 iun. 1846—*Codicis Iuris Canonici Fontes*, cura Emi Petri Card. Gasparri editi (9 vols., Romae [postea Civitate Vaticana]: Typis Polyglottis Vaticanis, 1923-1939, Vols. VII-IX ed. cura et studio Emi Iustiniani Card. Serédi), n. 1946 (hereafter cited as *Fontes*).

tions were true.[39] The reason for that conclusion was that the clause *"si preces veritate niti repereris"* was looked upon as constituting a part of the form of the execution, and the least of the requirements which made up such a form had to be observed if the execution was to be valid. The other clause, on the contrary, did not introduce any new form, but was merely an expression of the law itself.[40] In virtue of a decree of the Holy Office, issued on August 28, 1885, however, the original clause *"si preces veritate nitantur"* was ordered to be substituted for *"si preces veritate niti repereris."*[41] Moreover, on April 27, 1886, the Sacred Penitentiary declared that the executor's investigation of the truthfulness of the *preces* was thenceforth to be demanded only for the lawfulness, not for the validity, of the execution of its rescripts.[42] This practice was adopted by the whole Curia when it was reformed in 1908.[43]

The above-mentioned decree of the Holy Office had been preceded in 1852 by an answer from the Sacred Congregation of Bishops and Regulars, which indicated clearly that clauses in rescripts which demanded truthful petitions as a condition for the validity of the letters were not meaningless and mere formalities that could be considered as not having been inserted or

[39] Th. Sanchez, *De Matrimonio,* Lib. VIII, disp. XXIV, n. 26; De Justis, *De Dispensationibus Matrimonialibus,* Lib. I, cap. VI, n. 249; Benedictus XIV (1740-1758), *Institutiones Ecclesiasticae* (3. ed., 2 vols., Venetiis, 1788), I, 87, n. 34; Zitelli (d. 1887), *De Dispensationibus Matrimonialibus* (Romae, 1884), p. 86 (hereafter cited as *De Dispensationibus*); cf. also De Smet, *Betrothment and Marriage,* II, 310, note 1; O'Neill, *Papal Rescripts of Favor,* p. 175.

[40] Cf. Zitelli, *op. cit.,* p. 87.

[41] *Acta Sanctae Sedis* (41 vols., Romae, 1865-1908), XXVII (1895-1896), 512 (hereafter cited as *ASS*).

[42] "Utrum ad validitatem executionis requiratur nova et canonica verificatio causarum vi Litterarum Apostolicarum instituenda, casu quo Ordinarius de causis dispensationis exactam, et per iuratos testes habitam, informationem ceperit, antequam preces, pro obtinenda dispensatione, Sanctae Sedi porrexisset.

"Negative."—*Collectanea,* II, n. 1655, no. 3.

[43] Cf. De Smet, *loc. cit.*

understood at all. In fact, the unfavorable answer which the Congregation gave against a person whose petition for a prior rescript had not been truthful was practical proof of how essentially necessary it was, as a rule, to express the truth in the *preces.*[44]

Indeed, until 1908 the general rule concerning truthful petitions applied to all rescripts except those issued *motu proprio.*[45] Under the regulations of the reformed Curia, enacted on September 29, 1908, a change was made in this regard, since according to these new norms

> dispensations from minor [matrimonial] impediments shall all be granted for reasonable causes approved by the Holy See; under this form they will have the same force as if given in virtue of a *motu proprio* and with certain knowledge (*certa scientia*), and so will not be open to question on the ground either of obreption or of subreption.[46]

[44] S. C. Ep. et Reg., *Conchen.*, 3 sept. 1852—*Fontes*, n. 1965.

[45] Cf. *supra*, p. 38.

[46] Ordo Servandus in S. Congregationibus, Tribunalibus, Officiis Romanae Curiae, 29 sept. 1908, Pars II, *Normae peculiares*, cap. VII, art. III, n. 21—*AAS*, I (1909), 91-92. This regulation will be given further consideration below.—Cf. pp. 89-90.

CHAPTER III

DOCTRINE OF THE PRE-CODE COMMENTATORS

Section I. The Significance of the Condition *"si preces veritate nitantur"*

It was Pope Alexander III (1159-1181) who canonized the Roman Law expression *"si preces veritate nitantur"* and made it a formal part of the Church's law on rescripts.[1] From the time of its official introduction into the ecclesiastical legal system all canonists recognized it, whether it was expressed or merely understood, as being the most important essential condition that had to be fulfilled if the rescripts of the Sovereign Pontiffs were to be valid.[2] Indeed, Baldus de Ubaldis (1327-1400) noted that, over and above the will of the legislator, this condition had to be understood in rescripts because of the very nature of these letters.[3]

The reason why so much importance was attached to the fulfillment of this condition was that, unless it had been complied with, the Pope ordinarily could not be said to have granted his rescripts reasonably and voluntarily, as he certainly intended to do.[4] His action would have been unreasonable, on the one hand, because in the case of many rescripts of favor his rescripts

[1] C. 2, X, *de rescriptis,* I, 3; JL, n. 14317. Cf. *supra,* pp. 42-43.

[2] Cf. Tuschus (1534-1620), *Practicae Conclusiones Iuris in omni foro frequentiores* (8 toms., Lugduni, 1634; *Additiones,* Tom. IX, Lugduni, 1670), Tom. VI, concl. 217, n. 29 (hereafter cited as *Practicae Conclusiones*); Reiffenstuel (1642-1703), *Jus Canonicum,* Lib. I, tit. III, n. 141; O'Neill (1900-1943), *Papal Rescripts of Favor,* p. 117.

The clauses *"si ita est"; "si vera sunt, quae precibus complexa sunt,"* and others conveying the same meaning were sometimes substituted for *"si preces veritate nitantur."*

[3] *Super Decretales* (Lugduni, 1547), ad c. 2, X, *de rescriptis,* I, 3, folio XXII.

[4] There were special norms to govern this matter when rescripts issued *motu proprio* and such as contained dispensations from minor matrimonial impediments were concerned.—Cf. *infra,* pp. 87-90.

were actually *contra* or *ultra ius*. Accordingly, for the Pontiff to act reasonably in granting something that was contrary to or over and above what the common law permitted, there should have been present some true cause for so doing. Moreover, although his rescripts of justice were *secundum ius*, the Pope usually issued them to decide some controversy, and hence it was essential that he should have known the actual facts of the case in question. It was through the *preces* for rescripts that the Holy Father obtained this necessary information. Therefore, a truthful petition was a *conditio sine qua non* for a valid rescript. On the other hand, the Pope's action would have been involuntary precisely because the lack of truth in the *preces* would have caused him to be in error about and to be ignorant of the true circumstances of the case. Yet, an action that proceeded from error and ignorance could not be called truly voluntary. This consideration was of the utmost importance here, because if a rescript had been granted involuntarily it was almost as if no rescript had been issued at all, since *"substantia rescripti dependet a voluntate concedentis,"*[5] and *"deficiente ea* [*voluntate concedentis*], *vires non obtinent* [*rescripta*]."[6]

It is little wonder, then, that the commentators who dealt with this essential requirement wrote a great deal in their attempts to explain what it meant to have a petition that was based on truth.

Article 1. The Meaning of the Word "Truth"

One looks in vain to find an express definition of truth in the writings of the pre-Code canonists. Like the lawgiver himself, they seemed more interested in describing the truth by indicating when and how it would or would not be present in the *preces*.[7] For instance, Fagnanus (1598-1678), repeating the teaching of

[5] Fagnanus (1598-1678), *Commentaria in Quinque Libros Decretalium* (5 vols. in 4, Venetiis, 1709), Lib. I, tit. III, ad c. 20, X, *de rescriptis*, I, 3, n. 62 (hereafter cited as *Commentaria*).

[6] Gonzalez-Tellez (d. after 1673), *Commentaria*, Lib. I, tit. III, ad c. 20, X, *de rescriptis*, I, 3, n. 10, and ad c. 2, X, *de rescriptis*, I, 3, n. 17. Cf. also Hostiensis (d. 1271), *Commentaria in Quinque Decretalium Libros* (6 vols. in 4, Venetiis, 1581), Lib. I, tit. III, ad c. 20, X, *de rescriptis*, I, 3, n. 18 (hereafter cited as *Commentaria*).

[7] Cf. *supra*, pp. 39-41.

Panormitanus (1386-1453), maintained that, if a petitioner failed to mention anything and everything that would have made it less easy for the Pope to grant the rescript requested, his petition was not based on truth.[8] Gonzalez-Tellez taught that a petitioner was bound to propose to the Pope everything which had a bearing on the justice of the cause, and which could move the Sovereign Pontiff either to grant or to refuse the rescript desired.[9] Otherwise his petition would be lacking in the truth which the law required. Tuschus noted the further requirement that these causes and facts had to be set down expressly and specifically, and not merely in a general fashion.[10] Santi (1830-1885) spoke of a petition's being falsified in one of two ways, namely through a *"falsitatis insinuatio"* or a *"veritatis silentium."*[11]

These statements represent a cross-section of the teaching of the canonists of the period under consideration here concerning the meaning of truth as it was required in the *preces* for rescripts. Hence, for these authors, the word "truth" really conveyed two notions: first, an absence of falsehood in such petitions, and second, an honest statement of the facts and circumstances of the cases involved. Accordingly, when it was said that truthful petitions were necessary, they saw a twofold requirement being set forth, namely, a negative demand that there should be no falsehood expressed in the *preces*, and a positive one that there should be the clear expression of any and every fact or circumstance which would obtain or prevent the obtaining of the requested rescript. In fact, in some cases the com-

8 "Omne tacitum, quo expresso Princeps non tam facile dedisset litteras, reddit rescriptum subreptitium."—*Ibid.*, ad c. 1, X, *de rescriptis*, I, 3, n. 15. Cf. Panormitanus, *Commentaria*, Lib. I, tit. III, ad c. 20, X, *de rescriptis*, I, 3, n. 7.

9 "Qui rescriptum impetrat, tenetur Pontifici proponere omnia ea, quae ad causae iustitiam spectant, quaeque ipsum ad rescribendum, vel non, movere possunt."—*Ibid.*, ad c. 3, X, *de rescriptis*, I, 3, n. 6.

10 "Subreptio nihil aliud est, quam taciturnitas eius, quod exprimi debet, ex quo expresso, vel non facta fuisset concessio vel difficilius, quod habet locum, etiamsi expressio fieret generice et non clare."—*Ibid.*, n. 1; cf. also *ibid.*, n. 17.

11 *Praelectiones*, I, 32; cf. also De Smet (1868-1927), *Betrothment and Marriage*, II, 339.

mentators extended these two demands even to the impelling causes which might appear in a petition.[12]

In this regard it must be kept in mind that a petition was normally composed of three parts. Therefore the demands for the above-described truth had to be fulfilled in all three sections of the *preces*.[13]

Article 2. The Lack of Truth: Subreption and Obreption

In describing the lack of truth in the petitions, as well as in the rescripts themselves, the pre-Code canonists used the terms "subreption" and "obreption." Before the Council of Trent (1545-1563) no differentiation was generally made in the precise meaning of these two words; nor was either one of them restricted to apply to either of the two ways in which a petition could be falsified.[14] In fact, some of the post-Tridentine authors continued to use the terms interchangeably to designate both the expression of falsehood in the *preces* and the omission of a particular point of the truth that should have been stated therein. Fagnanus, for example, wrote:

> Subreptio igitur, vel obreptio est expressio falsi, vel taciturnitas veri, quo non expresso, vel tacito, Papa nullo modo litteras concessisset, sed potius denegasset vel concessisset quidem sed non ita facile, aut verisimile est concessurum non fuisse.[15]

[12] Cf. *infra*, pp. 66-68, 72-73, 74-76.

[13] Cf. *supra*, pp. 15-19.

[14] Panormitanus, *loc. cit.* Hostiensis made the following distinction between subreption and obreption: "Dicuntur quandoque literae subreptitiae, i. furtivae, per quas nulla datur iurisdictio, nec tenet processus ut hic. Vel dicitur quod hoc fuit exceptum ex eo quod aliis fuerat causa commissa et appellatum et ideo irritus est processus secundus. Quandoque verso dicuntur obreptitiae quia aliquid ibi suggestum est, vel suppressum sed per tales datur iurisdictio et nisi excipiatur tenet processus."—*Ibid.*, ad c. 22, *de rescriptis*, I, 3, n. 1. Pope Innocent IV (d. 1254) also found a special distinction between subreption and obreption, which Panormitanus summarized in this manner: "Appellat subreptitias, quando falso expresso vel veritate suppressa, literae fuerunt impetratae. . . . Obreptitias vero appellat, quando per involutionem verborum puta ironice vel calide'loquendo literae effugiunt deliberatam conscientiam Principis."—*Ibid.*, ad c. 22, X, *de rescriptis*, I, 3, n. 7. Cf. Innocentius IV, *In Quinque Libros Decretalium Commentaria* (Venetiis, 1570), ad c. 22, X, *de rescriptis*, I, 3, n. 3.

[15] *Ibid.*, ad c. 20, X, *de rescriptis*, I, 3, n. 8.

In treating the two terms as synonyms, these authors were merely imitating the Popes themselves.[16] Their reason for so doing, according to many of the authors, was that, as far as the effect which either of these defects had on the validity of the subsequent rescript was concerned, there was no appreciable difference.[17] In this regard, however, Tuschus was careful to point out that the statement of falsehood in the rescript itself always had a vitiating effect upon it, whereas the omission of some point of truth did not invalidate the letter except insofar as it was expressly said to do so.[18] Then, too, it was commonly held that the expression of falsehood concerning some matter which should have been mentioned in the petition was equivalent to the suppression of the truth.[19]

Nonetheless, by the seventeenth century there was a definite trend among canonists to reserve the term *"obreption"* to signify the expression of falsehood, and the word *"subreption"* to indicate either the actual suppression of some truth that should have been expressed, or the concealment of such truth by means of a confusing and indistinct statement of it.[20] This was in line with the literal meanings of these two words.[21] It is noteworthy that Ludovicus Engel, who died in 1674, said that in his time this restrictive use of the two terms was the more commonly accepted practice.[22] As a matter of fact, this latter usage

[16] Gonzalez-Tellez, *ibid.*, ad c. 20, X, *de rescriptis,* I, 3, n. 4.

[17] Cf. Gonzalez-Tellez, *loc. cit.;* Wernz (1842-1914), *Ius Decretalium,* I, n. 184.

[18] *Ibid.*, n. 2.

[19] Cf. Th. Sanchez (1550-1610), *De Matrimonio,* Lib. VIII, disp. 21, nn. 31-32.

[20] Pirhing (1606-1679), *Jus Canonicum,* Lib. I, tit. III, n. LXXXVI. The writer himself is using these terms in this restricted sense throughout this dissertation.

[21] Cf. Schmalzgrueber (1663-1735), who, after noting that the two words were often used interchangeably, wrote: "Proprie tamen diversum quid sonant, nam obreptio proprie committitur per narrationem vel expressionem falsi: subreptio per reticentiam, sive suppressionem veri."—*Ius Ecclesiasticum,* Lib. I, tit. III, par. 3, n. 14. Cf. also *infra,* p. 28, for the literal meanings of the two terms.

[22] "Magis tamen communiter obreptitie impetratum dicitur, quod est impetratum per falsa narrata, subreptitie vero, quod est impetratum super

seemed to become more exclusive the closer the authors came to the promulgation of the Code.[23]

In reference to subreption and obreption, the question was raised whether the presence of these defects should be judged absolutely, that is, according to the petition that was sent to Rome, or according to the summary of the *preces,* which was contained in the rescript itself. The authors were divided in solving this difficulty. Some maintained that it was to the petition itself that one should look to judge whether either subreption or obreption was present so as to vitiate the rescript obtained.[24] Others held that this judgment had ultimately to be based on the summary of the petition in the rescript that came back from Rome.[25] Actually, this matter presented no practical problem when the summary of the *preces* in the rescript adhered faithfully to the petition that had been presented, for then, no matter which basis had been used for the judgment, the end result would have been the same.

Article 3. The Practical Criterion of a Truthful Petition

The pre-Code canonists found that, in order to have a practical understanding of the principle *"si preces veritate nitantur,"* they had to go beyond their general statement that a petition was founded on truth when no falsehood was expressed therein and

tacitam sive occultam veritatem, circumstantiam, aut qualitatem, quae rescribenti exprimi debuisset."—*Collegium,* Lib. I, tit. III, n. 11. "Expressio falsitatis dicitur proprie obreptio. Taciturnitas veritatis dicitur subreptio." —Tuschus, *ibid.,* n. 24.

It may be noted here that Gonzalez-Tellez reversed these definitions for the two words.—Cf. *ibid.,* ad c. 20, X, *de rescriptis,* I, 3, n. 4, where he wrote: "Subreptio dicitur, cum videlicet precatores falsitatem exprimunt, falsique et mendacibus supplicationibus rescripta impetrant. Obreptio dicitur cum veritas in precibus reticetur, aut cum aliud celatur, quod expressum Principis animum in diversam traheret sententiam."

[23] Cf. Vecchiotti (d. 1870), *Institutiones,* p. 106; Zitelli, *De Dispensationibus,* p. 22; Santi, *Praelectiones,* I, 32; De Smet, *Betrothment and Marriage,* II, 339.

[24] Reiffenstuel, *Jus Canonicum,* Lib. I, tit. III, n. 152; Zitelli, *op. cit.,* p. 28.

[25] Th. Sanchez, *De Matrimonio,* Lib. VIII, disp. 21, n. 57; D'Annibale (1815-1892), *Summula,* I, 236, nota 2.

when the petitioner had not suppressed any points of truth which he was required to mention in his *preces*. This problem still faced them: *in practice*, when was a petition truthful in the eyes of the law? The majority of the authors solved the problem with an answer consisting of two parts.

First of all, they said that the truth which the law demanded was that which had an intrinsic connection with the substance of the matter requested in the petition. Hence, if the false statement or the point of truth that was suppressed was merely something accidental to the substantial matter, or if it bore only an extrinsic relationship to the petitioner's request, such a defect would not have essentially falsified the *preces* as far as the law was concerned.[26]

The juridic reason which underlay the first part of this solution was, on the one hand, that any vitiating defect concerning what was looked upon as the substantial part of the petition would destroy or undermine the Pope's intention to grant the request. Yet, it was a universally accepted principle that the substance of a rescript depended on the will of the grantor, so much so that if the Pontiff's will or intention to grant the rescript was lacking the rescript had no value whatsoever.[27] On the other hand, when the defect of subreption or obreption was found in something that was merely accidental to the request and had no intrinsic bearing on the matter asked for, such a lack of truth would not have affected the Pope's intention to grant the rescript (unless, perhaps, the subreption or obreption was caused by malice or

[26] "Illud adhuc observandum est, quod si falsa narratio, sive ex proposito, sive ex ignorantia facta nec directe nec indirecte concernat materiam in rescripto contentam aut ejus causam . . . non vitietur rescriptum."—Engel, *ibid.*, n. 14; "Si veritas tacita, vel falsitas expressa mere extrinsice et per accidens, et impertinenter se habeat ad rem postulatam, non vitiatur rescriptum."—Pirhing, *Jus Canonicum,* Lib. I, tit. III, n. CVI. "Debet res, quae subticetur, aut falso allegatur esse talis, quae secundum jura et praxim curiarum pertineat ad substantiam causae. Utrumque debet esse de re tali, quae ad negotium, de quo datur rescriptum, per se, seu intrinsice pertineat, adeoque necessario sit exprimenda."—Schmalzgrueber, *ibid.*, n. 15. Cf. De Smet, *loc. cit.*

[27] Cf. Pirhing, *loc. cit.;* Fagnanus, *Commentaria,* Lib. I, tit. III, ad. c. 20, X, *de rescriptis,* I, 3, n. 62; Gonzalez-Tellez, *Commentaria,* Lib. I, tit. III, ad c. 20, X, *de rescriptis,* I, 3, n. 10.

fraud, in which case, as will be seen below, it was generally held that, as a penalty, the rescript was vitiated).[28]

The second part of the solution which the canonists presented to indicate when a petition could be said to be legally truthful consisted in proposing a standard which men were to use in determining what constituted the substantial matter of petitions for the different types of rescripts. That is to say, they indicated the practical norm which one was to look to in deciding what had to be mentioned if the *preces* were to be based on truth. This standard or norm was almost universally admitted to be the demands both of the common law and of the style and practice of the Roman Curia, which, indeed, indicated the mind of the Holy Father himself in this regard. For example, Tuschus maintained that the whole matter of subreption depended on whether the law or the custom of the Popes, in granting their rescripts, required the expression of the particular facts in question.[29] In fact, he quoted Felinus Sandeus (1444-1503) as saying: *"quod non potest dari certa regula, quod taciturnitas inducat subreptionem, nisi ex eis, quae de stylo Principis consuevere exprimi et repetit."* [30] Moreover, it is not surprising to find Tuschus take this stand because he looked upon subreption as resulting in a penalty or a punishment, and so he concluded that subreption could be present only when the law so indicated.[31]

Some years later Pirhing, speaking about the mention of certain qualities in the *preces*, taught that, if a petitioner failed to set down qualities the expression of which was not required by the common law or the style or custom of the Roman Curia, he was not to be concerned about his petition's having been surreptitious. He went on to say, however, that the petition was

[28] Cf. Pirhing, *loc. cit.*, and *infra*, pp. 91-92.

[29] "Declara . . . totam materiam [subreptionis] complectitur hoc modo, ut ea, quae reperiuntur scripta in iure et exprimenda sunt, si non exprimantur, subreptio intrat sine difficultate, et idem in iis, quae de stylo concedentis sunt inducta. . . . "—*Practicae Conclusiones,* Tom. VI, concl. 217, n. 15.

[30] *Loc. cit.*

[31] "Subreptio est quaedam poena, seu punitio; ideo non habet locum, nisi in casibus a iure expressis."—*Ibid.*, n. 2.

definitely lacking in the expression of the required truth if these two sources did demand mention of the facts that had been omitted. This was true even though the Pope would have granted the very same rescript, in exactly the same form, and with precisely the same facility, had the suppressed truth been mentioned.[32] His reasons for the foregoing doctrine, which reasons were agreed to by all the other pre-Code canonists who expressed themselves on this point, were, in regard to the law:

> quia jura exigunt harum qualitatum expressionem ad formam substantialem impetrationis; sine forma autem actus non potest subsistere; forma enim rei mutata, proxime interimitur sive mutatur etiam rei substantia,

and, in reference to the style of the Curia: *"quia stylus Curiae jus facit et consuetudo pro lege habetur."* [33]

Schmalzgrueber summed up the general teaching of the authors before the Code of Canon Law on this point when he wrote: *"Debet res, quae subticetur, aut falso allegatur esse talis, quae secundum jura et praxim curiarum pertineat ad substantiam causae."* [34]

Accordingly, then, it was the common law of the Church and the *stylus Curiae* that were to serve as the practical criterion of a truthful petition. When this criterion failed to indicate whether a particular petition was based on the necessary truth,

[32] Pirhing, *ibid.*, n. C.

[33] *Loc. cit.*

[34] *Loc. cit.;* cf. also De Angelis (1824-1881), *Praelectiones Juris Canonici* (4 toms., Romae-Parisiis, 1877-1878), Tom. I, pars I, p. 67; Soglia (1779-1855), *Institutiones Juris Publici Ecclesiastici* (5. ed., Parisiis, 1853), pp. 64-65 (hereafter cited as *Institutiones*). Vecchiotti, *Institutiones*, p. 106; De Smet, *Betrothment and Marriage*, II, 339.

For a list of the points which were required to be mentioned in the *preces* for various kinds of rescripts, cf. Panormitanus, *Commentaria*, Lib. I, tit. III, ad c. 8, nn. 1-3; ad c. 17, n. 2; ad c. 20, n. 8; ad c. 27, n. 3; ad c. 31, n. 1; ad c. 32, nn. 2, 10; ad c. 34, n. 6; ad c. 42, nn. 1, 3, X, *de rescriptis*, I, 3; Schmalzgrueber, *ibid.*, nn. 9-10; Zitelli, *De Dispensationibus*, pp. 25-26. For a listing of the points which were to be expressed in petitions for rescripts containing dispensations from matrimonial impediments, cf. S. C. de Prop. Fid., instructio, 9 maii 1877—*Collectanea*, II, n. 1470 (where the principal canonical causes for matrimonial dispensations were also enumerated and briefly explained), and De Smet, *ibid.*, p. 292 sqq.

the same directions were to be followed as were given in the question of deciding the exact nature of some cause that had been set down in the *preces*.[35]

Article 4. The Truth in Relation to the Causes Alleged in Petitions [36]

There was no doubt among the pre-Code commentators that the *final* or *motivating* reason or reasons which a petitioner alleged in his *preces* for the rescript which he hoped to obtain constituted a part of the substantial matter of the petition. The authors did not always agree among themselves, however, as to the precise bearing which the principle *"si preces veritate nitantur"* had on the impelling causes that might appear in petitions.

There was not as much controversy on this point in regard to rescripts of justice as there was when rescripts of favor were concerned. The reason for this difference was that Pope Innocent III had done much to clarify the law in this matter in regard to rescripts of justice, whereas the decretal law evidently gave a basis for varying opinions on this point in reference to rescripts of favor. Hence, the commentators were able to find solid reasons for the divergent opinions which they propounded. Moreover, this question of the nature of a petitioner's reasons depended almost entirely upon the proper interpretation of the will of the Sovereign Pontiff. Consequently, it is not surprising that at times one finds the canonists offering directly contrary views on whether or not it was necessary to have not only truthful final causes but also truthful impelling reasons in the petitions for rescripts.

For the sake of clarity in presenting the doctrine of the commentators on this point, the writer proposes to consider the matter, first, in connection with rescripts of justice, and then, in relation to rescripts of favor. Both types of rescripts will be treated in the light of the twofold source of falsehood in the

[35] Cf. *supra*, pp. 22-26.

[36] The subject matter of this article necessarily involves a consideration of the extent of the invalidating effect which false causes have on rescripts. The extent of the vitiating effect of untruthful *preces* in general is treated below.—Cf. pp. 91-99.

petitions, namely, the petitioner's malice or fraud, and his simplicity or ignorance. It must be noted here that rescripts containing dispensations from minor matrimonial impediments are not included within the scope of this discussion.[37]

A. Rescripts of Justice

In formulating their doctrine concerning the truthfulness of the reasons which petitioners alleged in order to obtain rescripts of justice, the commentators used as the main basis of their teaching a law which Pope Innocent III had issued in 1208. This law was considered the key to the solution of many of the difficulties which arose in relation to petitions for rescripts.[38] The law in question referred primarily to rescripts of justice. In it Pope Innocent noted the important distinction between untruthfulness caused by the petitioner's malice or fraud, and that which arose from his simplicity or ignorance.[39] He also confirmed another distinction which was recognized by the canonists of his day in reference to rescripts of justice, namely, that between the substance and the form of such rescripts. The substance of a rescript of justice was the jurisdiction which was granted through it; the form was the *modus procedendi* which the Pope wanted his judge-delegate to follow in the case for which the letter was granted.[40]

Furthermore, the Pontiff laid down the following principles, which constituted the core of the canonical doctrine thereafter concerning the truth which the law required in the causes proposed in the *preces* for rescripts of justice: first—

[37] Cf. *infra*, pp. 89-90.

[38] Cf. Rubric to c. 20, X, *de rescriptis*, I, 3; Potthast, n. 3519. Cf. also Fagnanus, *Commentaria*, Lib. I, tit. III, ad c. X, *de rescriptis*, I, 3, n. 1.

[39] "Nos igitur inter eos, qui per fraudem vel malitiam, et illos, qui per simplicitatem vel ignorantiam literas a nobis impetrant, huiusmodi credidamus discretionem adhibendam. . . ."—C. 20, X, *de rescriptis*, I, 3. Cf. *supra*, pp. 43-44.

[40] "Nam si talis expressa sit falsitas vel veritas occultata, quae, quamvis fuisset tacita vel expressa, nos nihilominus saltem in forma communi literas dedissemus: delegatus, non sequens formam in literis ipsis appositam, secundum ordinem iuris in causa procedat."—*Loc. cit.* Cf. Panormitanus, *Commentaria*, Lib. I, tit. III, ad c. 20, X, *de rescriptis*, I, 3, n. 5.

> . . . huiusmodi credidamus discretionem adhibendam, ut hi qui priori modo [per fraudem vel malitiam] falsitatem exprimunt vel supprimunt veritatem, in suae perversitatis poenam nullum ex illis literis commodum consequantur, ita videlicet, quod delegatus postquam sibi super hoc facta fuerit fides, nullatenus de causa cognoscat;

second—

> Inter alios autem, qui posteriori modo [per simplicitatem vel ignorantiam] literas impetrant, duximus distinguendum, quae falsitas suggesta fuerit, vel quae veritas sit suppressa. Nam si talis expressa sit falsitas vel veritas occultata, quae, quamvis fuisset tacita vel expressa, nos nihilominus saltem in forma communi literas dedissemus: delegatus, non sequens formam in literis ipsis appositam, secundum ordinem iuris in causa procedat.

and third—

> Si vero per huiusmodi falsitatis expressionem vel suppressionem etiam veritatis literae fuerint impetratae, qua tacita vel expressa nos nullas prorsus literas dedissemus, a delegato non est aliquatenus procedendum, nisi forsitan eatenus, ut partibus ad suam praesentiam convocatis de precum qualitate cognoscat, ut sic in utroque casu eadem ratio, quae delegantem moveret, moveat etiam delegatum, et ubi delegans suas literas denegaret, delegatus etiam suae cognitionis officium nullatenus interponat.[41]

a) Untruthfulness from bad faith

From the first of these principles, the vast majority of the commentators concluded that when truth was lacking in a petition because of malice, fraud, or deceit, it mattered little whether the falsehood was in the final or only in the impelling cause in the *preces*. They reasoned that, since the legislator had made no distinction between the two kinds of causes, he must have meant his penalty to apply to either kind of reason whenever a malicious lack of the truth was involved. Moreover, they maintained that it made little difference whether only one or several of the causes proposed were lacking in truth. They applied this doctrine both to rescripts containing a single grant and to those having several concessions, all of which were directly attribut-

[41] *Loc. cit.*

able to the false causes in the *preces* for the letters. They believed that the Pope had intended that, as a penalty for the fraud, malice, or deceit involved, whatever was granted in the rescript and was intimately connected with the defective cause or causes should bring no benefit to the intended recipient, "*cum mendax precator carere debet penitus impetratis.*" [42]

Furthermore, there were some authors who taught that this rule applied even to cases in which a petition contained two or more distinct reasons or sets of reasons for a corresponding number of separate and unrelated grants, and malicious obreption was found in only one of the causes. These canonists believed that the penalty, which Pope Innocent had decreed for the petitioner's evil-mindedness, was so far-reaching that it vitiated the entire rescript, in spite of the other truthful causes offered for the other distinct requests.[43]

There were other authors, however, who maintained that an opinion contrary to the above-stated doctrine in this matter was equally probable. In other words, these commentators considered it safe to hold that if the malicious obreption in the cases described above affected only the cause or causes, final or impelling, which were presented for one of the matters requested in the petition, while the other distinct grants were given for reasons which were truthful, these latter parts of the rescript would not be vitiated in virtue of Pope Innocent's first principle. Two reasons were given for this opinion. First, when two differ-

[42] Panormitanus, *ibid.*, n. 2; Fagnanus, *ibid.*, nn. 10, 24; Gonzalez-Tellez, *Commentaria*, Lib. I, tit. III, ad c. 20, X, *de rescriptis*, I, 3, n. 6; Sanguineti (1829-1893), *Iuris Ecclesiastici Institutiones* (3 ed., Romae, 1896), p. 96 (hereafter cited as *Institutiones*); Aichner (1816-1910), *Compendium Juris Eclesiastici* (6 ed., Brixinae, 1887), p. 25, nota 8 (hereafter cited as *Compendium*).

[43] Thus, Gonzalez-Tellez wrote: "Rescripta ergo per subreptionem, aut obreptionem impetrata, nullius sunt momenti, nullumque precatori commodum afferre possunt . . . : quae doctrina procedit, licet in eodem rescripto diversa proponantur; nam quoad omnia tale rescriptum vitiatur."—*Loc. cit.* Among others the following authors supported this opinion: Panormitanus, *loc. cit.;* Fagnanus, *loc. cit.;* Vecchiotti, *Institutiones*, pp. 106-107; Santi, *Praelectiones*, I, 32; Sanguineti, *loc. cit.;* Aichner, *loc. cit.;* Bargilliat (1853-1926), *Praelectiones Juris Canonici* (30. ed., 2 vols., Parisiis, 1915), I, n. 414, ad e.

ent grants were placed in one rescript, there were virtually two rescripts, and the rescript actually issued was merely *per accidens* or, as it were, only materially one. Secondly, the vitiation of the rescript involved in this case had been established by the law as a penalty for the petitioner's fraud or malice. Penalties, however, were to be interpreted strictly. Consequently, this vitiating effect was not to be extended to that part of the rescript which was not maliciously or fraudulently defective because of obreption in the causes presented only for one or the other of the grants contained in the letter. Rather, the penalty was to affect only those matters which had a definite and direct connection with the defective reasons.[44]

Hence, these two opinions actually arose because of a difference in the interpretation of Pope Innocent's first principle. On the basis of their intrinsic merits each theory could be said to have been probable. If one judges them on the basis of extrinsic authority, however, the former opinion seems to have been preferred to the latter.

b) *Untruthfulness from good faith*

When it was a question of obreption that was caused by the petitioner's simplicity or ignorance, only the final cause had to be truthful. This was the general teaching of the commentators before the Code of Canon Law. It was based on the second and third principles enunciated by Pope Innocent in his law of 1208, for in them the Pontiff was definitely concerned only with those reasons which actually motivated the grantor to accede to the petitioner's request.[45] Therefore, while the authors recognized the desirability of having a completely truthful petition, they all admitted that it was not required by the lawgiver that the impelling reasons in the *preces* for rescripts of justice had also to

[44] Pirhing, *Jus Canonicum,* Lib. I, tit. III, n. CIX; Schmalzgrueber, *Jus Ecclesiasticum,* Lib. I, tit. III, nn. 15, 17; De Angelis, *Praelectiones Juris Canonici,* Tom. I, pars I, p. 69.

[45] Cf. *supra,* pp. 65-66. Cf. Panormitanus, *loc. cit.;* Fagnanus, *ibid.,* nn. 52, 62; Gonzalez-Tellez, *ibid.,* nn. 9, 11; Pirhing, *ibid.,* n. CI; Santi, *loc. cit.;* Zitelli, *De Dispensationibus,* p. 23; Bargilliat, *loc. cit.*

be based on truth, as long as the obreption appearing in them arose from the petitioner's ignorance or simplicity.[46]

Once this fundamental norm had been considered, the commentators turned their attention to cases involving the multiple rescript, that is, a rescript that contained more than one grant. Of course, when a single final cause was presented for a rescript, it had to be true, or everything which was contained in the letter was vitiated.[47] This conclusion was admitted by all the commentators. Furthermore, in the case of a petition which contained several final causes all of which had been presented together for the rescript requested, the authors held that it was sufficient if only one of these reasons was founded on the required truth. This was especially true when the motivating reasons had been presented in an alternative or disjunctive manner. Tuschus seemed to be speaking the mind of the other canonists of his own time and those who came after him when he wrote: *"Libellus plures continens causas sufficientes, non debet in omnibus justificari."* [48] The reason which was most often proposed to support this teaching was a principle of Roman Law, which had been incorporated into Pope Boniface's *Regulae Juris,* namely, *"In alternativis debitoris est electio et sufficit alterum adimpleri."* [49]

It must be emphasized that the commentators had in mind here only the case where more than one really final cause had been given. Where only impelling reasons had mistakenly been presented as so many final causes, all of them had to be true according to the more common, though not universal, teaching of the pre-Code authors. The argument for this majority opinion

[46] Cf. Pirhing, *ibid.*, n. CIII. Usually, the terms "ignorance" and "simplicity" were looked upon as being synonymous and represented any kind of ignorance, even crass ignorance, provided that it did not amount to rashness on the part of the petitioner.—Cf. Th. Sanchez, *De Matrimonio,* Lib. VIII, disp. 21, nn. 62, 66.

[47] Cf. Pope Innocent's third principle, *supra,* pp. 65-66.

[48] *Practicae Conclusiones,* Tom. VI, concl. 217, n. 3.

[49] Reg. 70, R. J., in VI°. Cf. c. 4, X, *de rescriptis,* I, 3; JL, n. 13878; cf. *supra,* pp. 46-47; cf. Th. Sanchez, *ibid.*, n. 42.

took the following form. Since all of the causes had been merely impelling reasons, the Pope had evidently considered that when they were taken together, they were sufficient to constitute a single final cause. In fact, it was precisely the conjunctive or cumulative value of these reasons that had moved the Pontiff to grant the rescript. Consequently, each of these causes had a definite bearing on the substantial matter of the rescript, even though individually they were merely impelling in their nature. Each of them had to be true, therefore, or else the one final cause for the rescript would have been false.[50]

Furthermore, there seems to have been unanimous agreement among the commentators when they considered multiple rescripts and the truth that had to inhere in the different reasons proposed, respectively, for the various concessions contained in such letters. In this regard the following situations were contemplated by the pre-Code authors.

First of all, where two different reasons were given for two altogether separate and distinct grants, only that part of the rescript was vitiated the final cause of which had been infected with obreption. The reasons which the commentators gave for this position were, first, that even though the two grants were actually made through a single rescript, virtually there were two rescripts, and, second, that *"Utile per inutile vitiari non debet."*[51]

Secondly, where different causes were proposed for the various matters that were requested, but the grants were closely connected, for instance, insofar as the one was something accessory to the principal grant, or insofar as they were all intended for the same purpose, in such a case the final cause of each grant had to be truthful, or else the whole rescript would have been defective. This was precisely because of the close connection between the different matters granted in the one rescript. As another reason many of the authors pointed to the legal axiom: *"Accessorium naturam sequi congruit principalis."*[52] If, however, the truth

[50] Schmalzgrueber, *ibid.*, n. 18; Vecchiotti, *ibid.*, p. 107.

[51] Reg. 37, R. J., in VI°. Cf. Panormitanus, *loc. cit.;* Gonzalez-Tellez, *ibid.*, n. 6; Schmalzgrueber, *ibid.*, n. 17; Bargilliat, *loc. cit.*

[52] Reg. 42, R. J., in VI°. Cf. Gonzalez-Tellez, *loc. cit.;* Schmalzgrueber, *loc. cit.;* Th. Sanchez, *ibid.*, n. 77; Bargilliat, *loc. cit.* This axiom was ap-

was lacking only in the final cause of something granted as an accessory to the principal concession in the rescript, the principal grant was not vitiated with that which was merely accessory.[53]

B. Rescripts of Favor

Turning from rescripts of justice to rescripts of favor, one finds the doctrine of the commentators full of controversy and of directly contrary opinions concerning the correct application of the principle *"si preces veritate nitantur"* to the causes in petitions for the latter type of rescripts. This divergence of opinion was due to a number of factors. There was, for instance, no clear-cut decretal legislation on this point concerning rescripts of favor, as there was in Pope Innocent's law of 1208 in reference to rescripts of justice. Then, too, the commentators themselves were at odds with one another on whether that law of Pope Innocent should have been applied to rescripts of favor with the same force as it was to rescripts of justice. Moreover, the difference of opinion in this matter was caused by another difference, which was actually admitted by all the authors, namely, the fundamental difference between these two types of rescripts. Schmalzgrueber summed up this difference by saying that the two were dissimilar: *"cum [rescripta gratiae] fere juris relaxationes sint, magis sint odiosa quam ea, quae lites concernuntur et propterea facilius vitientur."* [54] In view of this fundamental difference some of the commentators [55] were convinced that whatever requirements were made for rescripts of justice should also be applicable with equal rigor to rescripts of favor. Hence, Pope Innocent's norms for rescripts of justice should have governed

---

plicable, however, only when the principal and accessory grants had the same nature.—Bartoccetti, *De Regulis Juris Canonici* (Romae: A. Belardetti, 1955), p. 164.

[53] Cf. the second principle of Pope Innocent, *supra*, p. 66. Cf. also Felinus Sandeus, *Commentaria*, Lib. I, tit. III, ad c. 20, X, *de rescriptis*, I, 3, n. 2.

[54] *Ibid.*, n. 15. It was noted above that rescripts of justice were *secundum ius*.—Cf. *supra*, p. 10.

[55] Cf., e.g., Fagnanus, *Commentaria*, Lib. I, tit. III, ad c. 20, X, *de rescriptis*, I, 3, nn. 13-14.

rescripts of favor also. Other authors believed that certain completely different rules, derived from various other decretals, should be used.[56]

a) Untruthfulness from bad faith

The authors disagreed even in regard to a case involving maliciously or fraudulently false causes or reasons. Some of them applied Pope Innocent's first principle to petitions for rescripts of favor in the same way as it affected the *preces* for rescripts of justice. That meant that whenever malice or fraud was involved, any lack of the required truth, even in only the impelling reasons, constituted a violation of the essential condition *"si preces veritate nitantur."* This theory was undoubtedly the more common opinion among the commentators before the Code of Canon Law.[57] De Smet summed up the teaching of the proponents of this opinion thus:

> If the error is due to bad faith, i.e., if in the *supplica* a false statement is knowingly made or the truth is out of malice suppressed, the dispensation is always vitiated, even when the error affects only matters of minor importance, provided, of course, that it bears on a point affecting the dispensation. Thus, if a nonexisting cause is fraudulently alleged, the dispensation is null, even though the cause in question be merely impulsive.

[56] Cf. Engel, *Collegium,* Lib. I, tit. III, n. 12.

[57] Among those who adhered to this opinion were Panormitanus, *ibid.,* n. 5; Fagnanus, *loc. cit.;* Tuschus, *Practicae Conclusiones,* Tom. VI, concl. 217, n. 18; Gonzalez-Tellez, *ibid.,* n. 7; Pirhing, *ibid.,* n. VC; Schmalzgrueber, *loc. cit.;* Corradus Pyrrhus, *Praxis,* Lib. I, c. 1, n. 10; Soglia, *Institutiones,* I, 64; Giovine (19th cent.), *De Dispensationibus Matrimonialibus Consultationes Canonicae* (2 vols., Neapoli, 1863), I, par. CXX (hereafter cited as *De Dispensationibus*); J. Planchard (19th cent.), *Dispenses Matrimoniales Règles a Suivre pour les Demander, les Interpréter, les Mettre a Exécution* (Angoulême, 1882), n. 293; Zitelli, *De Dispensationibus,* pp. 23, 50; H. Feije (1820-1894), *De Impedimentis et Dispensationibus Matrimonialibus* (3. ed., Lovanii, 1885), n. 722 (hereafter cited as *De Impedimentis*); Santi, *Praelectiones,* I, 32; I. De Becker (1857-1936), *De Sponsalibus et Matrimonio Praelectiones Canonicae* (2. ed., Lovanii, 1913), pp. 356, 368; De Smet, *Betrothment and Marriage,* II, 339; Wernz, *Ius Decretalium,* I, n. 153, II.

The proof of our statement is easy. In c. 20, X, I, 3, Pope Innocent X [sic] ordains that those who, by fraud or malice, "allege what is false or suppress what is true, shall, in punishment of their perverse conduct, derive no advantage from the dispensation"; the maxims of the law are to the same effect: *"fraus et dolus alicui patrocinari non debent"* (fraud and trickery should profit no one), *"mendax precator carere debet penitus impetratis"* (a lying petitioner must be deprived of what he has obtained).[58]

Nonetheless, there were a very few authors who denied that the scope of Pope Innocent's first principle was so extensive. They maintained that fraud or malice had no bearing upon a case in which only the impelling reasons were lacking in truth. Their argument was based on this line of reasoning. The vitiation of a rescript, when the petition for it had been maliciously or fraudulently false, was established as a penalty for the petitioner's *dolus*. *Dolus,* however, here presupposed the violation of some requirement that had been laid down either by the common law or by the *stylus Curiae*. Yet, when the final cause had been truthful, and when all of the points of the truth which should have been set down were expressed, the requirements from either of these sources would have been fulfilled. Therefore, there was no room for *dolus,* and, as a reasonable consequence, no room for the penalty established for *dolus*. Hence, it was not necessary, even in such a case, that the impelling causes in the *preces* be based on the truth.[59]

Looking now to the case where a petition contained two or more distinct reasons for a corresponding number of separate and unrelated favors, and where malicious obreption was found in only one of the causes which pertained to only one of the favors requested, one finds the same difference of opinion among the authors here as in reference to rescripts of justice.[60] That is to say, some of the canonists maintained that even in such a

[58] *Ibid.,* pp. 339-340.

[59] P. Laymann (1574-1635), *Theologia Moralis* (5 vols. in 1, Duaci, 1635), Lib. I, tract. IV, c. 22, n. 22; D'Annibale, *Summula,* I, n. 238. Cf. Th. Sanchez, *De Matrimonio,* Lib. VIII, disp. 21, nn. 73-74, 79.

[60] Cf. *supra,* pp. 66-68.

case the entire rescript with all its contents would have been vitiated, unless each and every cause had been truthful. Others admitted that it was at least probable that only that favor in the rescript would have been invalidated which had had a direct connection with the defective cause or causes.[61]

b) Untruthfulness from good faith

Pre-Code authors also disagreed among themselves when they dealt with rescripts of favor and reasons that were false because of a petitioner's good faith, that is, his ignorance or simplicity. In fact, one can discern three conflicting opinions in this regard. The proponents of each theory felt that they had a solid basis in the decretal law on which to rest their teaching.

There were, first of all, those authors who maintained that the principle *"si preces veritate nitantur,"* if understood correctly in reference to petitions for rescripts of favor, required that not only the final causes but also the merely impelling reasons proposed in the *preces* had to be founded on truth. They felt that if the truth had been expressed or the falsehood not stated, that expression or omission, as the case might have been, either would have kept the Pope from granting the favor at all, or else would have made it much more difficult for him to accede to the petitioner's request.[62] This opinion was not widely accepted, however, after the Council of Trent. In fact, the present writer could find only two authors thereafter who definitely supported it, namely, Cardinal Tuschus and Corradus Pyrrhus.[63]

The proponents of this theory offered three reasons to defend

[61] For the various authors who supported these different theories, and their reasons for doing so, cf. *supra,* pp. 67-68.

[62] Felinus Sandeus, *Commentaria,* Lib. I, tit. III, ad c. 27, X, *de rescriptis,* I, 3, n. 1; Panormitanus, *Commentaria,* Lib. I, tit. III, ad c. 27, X, *de rescriptis,* I, 3, n. I. Cf. Th. Sanchez, *De Matrimonio,* Lib. VIII, disp. 21, n. 10. Th. Sanchez himself did not hold this opinion.

[63] "Et subreptio gratiae vitiat gratiam, sive subreptio fuerit causa finalis ipsius gratiae, sive etiam impulsiva, ut quia concessisset, sed difficilius, et sic causa non sit finalis, multo magis, si finalis."—Tuschus, *Practicae Conclusiones,* Tom. VII, concl. 720, n. 3; Corradus Pyrrhus, *Praxis,* Lib. I, c. 1, n. 10.

their position. First, they pointed to a decretal of Pope Innocent III in which the Sovereign Pontiff decided that a rescript, specifically one conferring a benefice, had been invalid because the petitioner had failed to mention that he already held a permanent vicarage. The Holy Father had expressed the reason for his decision in the words: *"Et pro habente beneficii sufficientis subsidium ex certa scientia super obtinendo alio beneficio de levi non scribimus."* [64] These canonists concluded that because the Pope said, *"de levi non scribimus,"* he was indicating that in petitions for rescripts which were intended to confer benefices, even the impelling reasons proposed had to be truthful, or else the subsequent rescript would have been invalid. They extended this rigorous doctrine so as to include not only rescripts conferring benefices but also those containing privileges and all other favors.[65] Secondly, on the basis of the axiom: *"Qui cito dat, bis dat,"* by an *argumentum a contrario,* they maintained that one who would have granted a request only with a greater amount of difficulty and delay, if he had known the complete truth, could not be said to have granted the entire favor asked for, but only a part of it, and that, as it were, reluctantly. Therefore, the concession actually made in the case where a part of the truth was lacking because of false impelling reasons in the *preces* was partially involuntary. Consequently, the entire grant based on those reasons was vitiated, for the rescript obtained its force only from the will of the grantor. Thirdly, the defenders of this theory noted that the suppression of some point of the truth in the *preces,* the expression of which was required by the law, or by custom, or by other circumstances of the case, was equivalent to the statement of a falsehood in the petition. They asserted that it was generally held that such an expression of falsehood vitiated the favor conceded as often as the falsehood notably induced the Pontiff to grant the request more easily.

[64] C. 27, X, *de rescriptis,* I, 3; not listed in Potthast (1214). Cf. *supra,* pp. 44-45.

[65] Cf. Felinus Sandeus, *ibid.,* ad c. 20, X, *de rescriptis,* I, 3, n. 3, and *Glossa* ad c. 1, *de constitutionibus,* I, 2, in VI°, s.v. *noscatur.* This gloss is attributed to Joannes Andreae (1272-1348).

Accordingly, they concluded that the same was true about the suppression of truth in the petition when it had a similar effect upon the grantor.[66]

These were the reasons why a very small number of authors held that the pre-Code law on rescripts required that not only the *final* causes but also the *impelling* reasons in a petition for a rescript of favor had to be founded on truth. The value of these reasons, however, and consequently of the theory itself, was seriously questioned by the overwhelming majority of the canonists after the Council of Trent. They could not be convinced that there was any basis at all in the decretal law for the doctrine that a favor was vitiated in the presence of good faith because one or the other of the impelling causes that had been advanced for it was defective with regard to the truth.[67]

This fact undoubtedly explains why the majority of the pre-Code commentators who wrote after the Council of Trent subscribed to the opinion that, when good faith was involved, only the lack of truth in the *final* cause for a rescript of favor made the favor granted therein null and void. They held this conclusion as true even though it would have been more difficult for the Pope to grant a certain favor if the impelling reason or reasons given for it had not been obreptitious.[68] Pirhing summed up the teaching of those authors when he wrote:

> Probabilius tamen est, rescriptum quodcumque, sive justitiae, sive gratiae, non esse subreptitium, nisi suppressio veritatis, vel expressio falsitatis ad rem postulatam per se, et intrinsice pertinentis, contingat circa causam finalem seu principalem concessionis, quia scilicet Princeps, falsitate non allegata, vel veritate expressa et cognita, probabiliter rem petitam non

66 Cf. Th. Sanchez, *loc. cit.*

67 Cf. Pirhing, *Jus Canonicum,* Lib. I, tit. III, n. CIII.

68 Among the authors who supported this teaching were Fagnanus, *Commentaria,* Lib. I, tit. III, ad c. 20, X, *de rescriptis,* I, 3, n. 69; Gonzalez-Tellez, *Commentaria,* Lib. I, tit. III, ad c. 20, X, *de rescriptis,* I, 3, n. 9; Engel, *Collegium,* Lib. I, tit. III, n. 12; Pirhing, *loc. cit.;* Th. Sanchez, *ibid.,* n. 74; Schmalzgrueber, *Jus Ecclesiasticum,* Lib. I, tit. III, n. 16; Giovine, *De Dispensationibus,* I, par. CXXI; Santi, *Praelectiones,* I, 32; H. Feije, *De Impedimentis,* n. 726; Wernz, *Ius Decretalium,* I, n. 153, II; De Smet, *Betrothment and Marriage,* II, 340.

concessisset, vel non tali modo ac forma concessisset, sed cum certa restrictione, aut conditione. Quod si vero subreptio sive per expressionem falsi, sive suppressionem veri, tantum fiat circa causam impulsivam concessionis, quia nimirum, ea etiam remota, et veritate cognita, quamvis concessisset difficilius, non debet censeri rescriptum obreptitium, nisi jus vel stylus Curiae veri expressionem specialiter requirat. . . .[69]

The authors who proposed this opinion found a basis for it in the decretal legislation of Pope Boniface VIII (1294-1303). This Pontiff had made it clear that, in spite of the lack of truth in an impelling reason proposed by the petitioner to obtain a benefice, the rescript which had been granted stood to benefit the petitioner.[70]

Another argument which was offered in support of this opinion was that the reason obreption in a final cause vitiated a favor granted on account of it implied that actually the relevant concession emanated from the ignorance of the Pope. Since ignorance took away the Pontiff's intention to make the grant at all, the favor was necessarily worthless. The absence of a false impelling cause, however, would merely have kept the Pope from granting the favor so easily. It would not have in any way destroyed the Pontiff's intention to accede to the petitioner's request. Hence, the issued rescript retained its force precisely because that force was based on the Holy Father's intention in giving the rescript, and nothing had been done to undermine his intention.[71]

Thomas Sanchez mentioned still a third opinion in regard to the necessity of having truthful impelling reasons in the *preces* for rescripts of favor.[72] According to this theory rescripts were not vitiated by every suppression of the truth in the petitions.

[69] *Loc. cit.*

[70] "Considerantes quoque, quod nos, exposito nobis de potestate praedicta, nihilominus literas gratiosas daremus in dictis partibus, non habita mentione de ipsa. . . ."—C. 14, *de praebendis et dignitatibus,* III, 4, in VI°. Cf. *supra,* pp. 45-46.

[71] Cf. Th. Sanchez, *ibid.,* n. 11.

[72] *Ibid.,* nn. 12 and 17. Among the supporters of this opinion were P. Laymann, *Theologia Moralis,* Lib. I, tract. IV, c. 22, n. 22, and D'Annibale, *Summula,* I, n. 238.

Rather, subreption was present only when there was omitted some point of the truth which the law required to be expressed. This doctrine was based on the principle that the will of the Pope was presumed to be the same as the intention of the law. It was founded also on the generally recognized fact that a rescript conferring a benefice upon someone who was guilty of some wrongdoing was valid as long as the wrongdoing had not brought on some impediment established in the law. Furthermore, the proponents of this theory argued that the invalidation of a rescript was actually a penalty, and *"In poenis benignior est interpretatio facienda."* [73]

Actually, no explicit mention was made in this doctrine of either final or impelling causes. Sanchez, however, regarded it as another way of expressing the teaching of the second and more common opinion mentioned above. Hence, in practice those who held to it required that only the final causes had to be considered when the principle *"si preces veritate nitantur"* was applied to rescripts of favor in cases involving obreption caused by the petitioner's simplicity or ignorance.

In reference to cases involving obreption from ignorance or simplicity and the *preces* with several final causes presented together for one or more favors in a single rescript of favor, the more common opinion among the commentators was that the same norms which were set forth in this regard for rescripts of justice were equally valid in reference to rescripts of favor.[74]

[73] Reg. 49, R. J., in VI°.

[74] Cf. *supra*, pp. 69-71. Th. Sanchez noted, however, that there were some canonists, for instance, Felinus Sandeus (*Commentaria*, Lib. I, tit. III, ad c. 20, X, *de rescriptis*, I, 3, n. 3), who maintained that if several equally principal causes were set down in the *preces* for rescripts of favor, each of them had to be truthful, or else the favor or favors granted in the rescript would be invalid. Their reasons for this position were the following: first, since the value of causes in relation to the requested rescripts depended entirely on the judgment and the will of the Pope, and since the matter asked for was purely a favor in its nature, the Pontiff did not wish to grant the petition, unless all the causes alleged were true, although at another time he might have granted the favor for anyone of the causes then proposed together; second, since the law demanded the truth of the *preces*, which term was set down in its plural form and, consequently, comprehended everything in the petition, if one or the other of the causes

The same can be said of cases involving obreption from good faith and multiple rescripts of favor.[75]

Article 5. The Time at Which the Preces Had to Be Founded on Truth

Another question which the pre-Code commentators tried to answer in their explanation of the significance of the condition *"si preces veritate nitantur"* was this: at what precise time was it necessary that the *preces* be truthful? In answering this question, the authors had to take into consideration not only the four distinct points of time, at any or all of which the law could have required petitions to be founded on the prescribed truth, but also the different ways in which rescripts were sometimes granted. That is to say, the answer to this question depended very much on whether a rescript was granted *in forma gratiosa* or *in forma commissoria,* and, if the grant was made *in forma commissoria,* on whether the commissioned executor was a mere executor, or a necessary, or a voluntary one.[76]

The four points of time, which could have been involved in the obtaining of some request from Rome by means of a rescript, were, first, the time when the petition was sent to the Holy Father; second, that at which the Pope personally granted the petitioner's request and applied it directly to him without using the services of any intermediary; third, the time at which an

---

presented was false, the *preces* could not be said to be truthful; third, since in the case of a dispensation there was usually attached to the rescript the clause, "super his te diligenter informes, et si repereris, quod preces veritate nitantur, super quo tuam conscientiam oneramus, dispensa," it must have been the intention of the Pope that all the causes be truthful, for the relative pronoun in the phrase *"super quo"* evidently referred to all the reasons alleged; and, fourth, since the clause *"si preces veritate nitantur"* was conditional, it constituted at least a part of the form of the rescript, and every individual part of the form would have to be observed if the rescript was to be valid. Hence, all the reasons mentioned in the petition were required to be founded on truth.—Cf. Th. Sanchez, *ibid.,* n. 43. The writer was able to find no author who supported this opinion during the period between the Council of Trent and the present Code.

[75] Cf. *supra,* pp. 70-71. Cf. also Th. Sanchez, *ibid.,* n. 44, and Vecchiotti, *Institutiones,* p. 107.

[76] Cf. *supra,* pp. 13-14.

executor was appointed and his mandate was sent to him from Rome; and fourth, the moment when the executor carried out his mandate either by applying to the petitioner the grant which had been made by the Pope himself, or by using the power delegated to him by Rome to grant the petitioner's request in consequence of the original *preces*. Hence, the problem was to decide at which of these times the *preces* had to be truthful.

In solving this question, almost all of the commentators who considered the matter taught that it was not necessary for the *preces* to be founded on the truth at the time when they left the petitioner's hand to be sent to Rome.[77] This general rule applied to all rescripts in whatever form they were issued. The authors supported their teaching on this point in an indirect fashion, namely, by proving that, in reference to rescripts issued *in forma gratiosa*, it was required and sufficient that the *preces* be true at the time when the Pope actually granted the rescript, that is, at the *tempus datae*. This proof was based primarily on decretal legislation.

The authors pointed, first of all, to a law of Pope Innocent III, enacted in 1213, in which the Pontiff indicated that, if a rescript was to be valid, the reasons presented for it had to be true when the Pope granted the petitioner's request. Hence, it was neither required nor sufficient that the petition had been truthful before the papal action upon the *preces*. The specific case which the Pontiff was treating in this decretal was that of a petitioner who had asked for a matrimonial dispensation on the grounds that a child had been born to him and the woman whom he then wished to marry. Although there had been a child, she had died before the time at which the dispensation had actually been granted. Because of that fact the Pope decided that the peti-

[77] "Neque obstat textus c. 20 ubi Inn. III statuit, eos qui falsitatem per malitiam exprimunt, in suae perversitatis poenam nullum ex apostolicis litteris commodum consequi, hoc enim verum duntaxat est, quando causa etiam tempore concessionis falsa est. Ex quo sequitur, falsitatem causae eo usque esse extrinsecam, et ideo per illam rescriptum dispensationis non vitiari."—Schmalzgrueber, *Jus Ecclesiasticum,* Lib. IV, pars III, tit. XVI, n. 159; H. Feije, *De Impedimentis,* n. 727; Bargilliat, *Praelectiones,* I, n. 414, ad g. De Justis, however, held that the *preces* had to be truthful at this time.—Th. Sanchez, *De Matrimonio,* Lib. VIII, disp. 30, n. 2.

tion involved had not been truthful in the manner required by the law.[78] The commentators' second reference was to a decretal of Pope Boniface VIII. In this document it was decreed in regard to a person who had received a rescript entitling him to a particular benefice that, since the petitioner did not have the age required for the holding of such a benefice at the time when the rescript was issued, he could not obtain it. This decree was to be enforced even though the petitioner in question had perhaps become old enough to hold the benefice by the time that it was to be conferred on him.[79]

The commentators also found a strong argument in the very clause that expressed the principle concerning truthful petitions. That is to say, they maintained that in regard to a rescript granted *in forma gratiosa,* the condition *"si preces veritate nitantur"* could mean only one thing, namely, that the petition presented to the Pope was true at the time at which he granted the request. That condition could not possibly be fulfilled, however, if the *preces* were true only at some time in the past or were to become verified only at some point in the future. They argued that it was the Pope's intention to grant the request then and there. His intention was conditioned on the truthfulness of the petition then and there. Hence, if the petition was not verified at that moment, the rescript was actually granted involuntarily by the Pontiff. Consequently, they concluded that the rescript had been vitiated from the very beginning *ex defectu consensus.* This conclusion left room for the operation of another legal principle: *"Non firmatur tractu temporis quod de jure ab initio non subsistit."* [80]

On the basis of these arguments, the commentators almost unanimously taught that petitions for rescripts issued *in forma*

[78] "Cum tamen ante dispensationem, viam fuerat universa carnis ingressa unica filia, quam habebat."—C. 6, X, *de consanguinitate et affinitate,* IV, 14; Potthast, n. 4820. Cf. *supra,* p. 47. Cf. also Schmalzgrueber, *loc. cit.;* Th. Sanchez, *ibid.,* n. 4.

[79] "Cum tempore datae non esset idoneus."—C. 9, *de rescriptis,* I, 3, in VI°. Cf. *supra,* p. 48. Cf. also Gonzalez-Tellez, *Commentaria,* Lib. I, tit. III, ad c. 30, X, *de rescriptis,* I, 3, n. 19; Engel, *Collegium,* Lib. I, tit. III, n. 18.

[80] Reg. 18, R. J., in VI°. Cf. Engel, *loc. cit.*

gratiosa had to be founded on truth at the time when the request was granted by the Pope.[81]

This same doctrine was applied also to rescripts granted *in forma commissoria* when the executor had merely the ministry of execution and nothing more. It must be remembered that in such cases the grant was *de iure* complete when the rescript left Rome. The executor only applied it *de facto* to the intended recipient.

It seems, however, that by the seventeenth century, if not before, this form of executory commission was relatively rare, as compared with those cases wherein either a necessary or a voluntary executor was employed.[82] More rare were rescripts granted *in forma gratiosa.* In fact, the practice of granting rescripts which were to be executed by either a voluntary or a necessary executor became ever increasingly prevalent. Such had regularly been the case when rescripts of justice were involved. From the seventeenth century onwards rescripts of favor were also ordinarily issued in one of these two forms, so much so that by the nineteenth century Santi could quote the Apostolic Datary as saying: *"Dispensatio regulariter nonnisi in forma commissoria conceditur. In forma gratiosa aut nunquam aut nonnisi rarissime concedi consuevit."* [83] Hence, in reference to the three centuries immediately preceding the Code, from a practical viewpoint, it was most important to know precisely the time at which the *preces* had to be truthful when a petitioner received his request through either a necessary or a voluntary executor.

Unfortunately, the commenators differed in settling the time element in regard to the *preces* for such rescripts. Some taught that the petition had to be based on truth at the time when the Pope commissioned the executor to grant what was requested, as well as at the moment of the execution of the rescript in question. Their demand for the presence of the truth at that prior time made their doctrine different from that of many other

[81] Cf. Panormitanus, *Commentaria,* Lib. I, tit. III, ad c. 7, X, *de rescriptis,* I, 3, n. 5.

[82] Cf. Schmalzgrueber, *ibid.,* n. 160.

[83] *Praelectiones,* I, 35. Cf. Wernz, *Ius Decretalium,* I, n. 155, II.

canonists. Nonetheless, their argument for this more comprehensive position was a plausible one. It was based on the very nature of the manner in which such rescripts were issued. They maintained that when the Pope granted a rescript *in forma commissoria* with either a necessary or a voluntary executor, the apostolic letters carried with them the petitioner's favor or other grant as having been conferred not completely by the Pontiff himself. Rather, they contained either a mandate or faculties, respectively ordering or empowering the executor to give the petitioner in its fullest measure what he had asked for from the Holy Father.[84] The use of that mandate or those faculties, however, was always based upon the condition *"si preces veritate nitantur."* Indeed, what was even more important to these authors in their argumentation on this point was the fact that the very rescript which contained the mandate or delegation for the executor likewise depended for its validity upon the verification of that same condition. Consequently, if the petition had been lacking in the required truth at the time when the Pontiff issued that rescript, the Pope would not have commissioned an executor to accede to the petitioner's request. Since that was the case, the mandate or delegation given to the executor was invalid from the beginning precisely *ex defectu intentionis* on the part of the Holy Father. That meant that even though the petition had become founded on truth by the time of the execution of the rescript and the mandate or faculties which it brought, the execution itself would have been invalid, since: *"Non firmatur tractu temporis quod de jure ab initio non subsistit."*[85] Consequently, the rescript itself could bring no benefit to its intended beneficiary.[86]

[84] A rescript with a necessary executor contained a mandate for the execution of the letter; a rescript with a voluntary executor conveyed to that person the faculties to grant or deny the petitioner's request, according to his own conscience and prudent judgment.—Cf. *supra*, p. 14.

[85] Reg. 18, R. J., in VI°.

[86] Among the proponents of this opinion were Th. Sanchez, *De Matrimonio,* Lib. VIII, disp. 30; Suarez (1584-1617), *Opera Omnia,* Vol. VI, *Tractatus de Legibus et Legislatore Deo,* lib. VI, cap. 20, p. 101, §§ 13-14; De Justis, *De Dispensationibus Matrimonialibus,* Lib. VIII, c. 6, nn. 296-299; H. Feije, *De Impedimentis,* n. 727.

Despite the fact that these authors were convinced that a petition had to be truthful even at the moment when the Pope, acting on a petitioner's *preces,* had commissioned an executor to handle the matter, some of them were willing to admit that the truthful condition of the *preces* did not have to subsist throughout the whole period between the commission of the executor and the execution of the rescript. Nevertheless, even these commentators held firmly to the doctrine that a petition had to have the required truth at the time of the commission of the executor and at the time of the execution of the rescript.[87]

At all events, the majority of the authors, certainly of those who wrote after the Council of Trent, were of the opinion that only at the time of the execution of the relevant rescript was it required that the *preces* for the letter be founded on truth.[88] As these canonists saw it, whether or not a petition had been false before the time of the rescript's execution was ordinarily immaterial. Their reason was that the rescript itself did not contain the favor or other matter requested by the petitioner, at least, not in the most perfect form in which the Pope contemplated acceding to the request. Rather, only the mandate or the faculties which respectively ordered or authorized the rescript's execution came from Rome, and that execution was conditioned precisely on whether the *preces* were truthful. Accordingly, if the petition was not truthful at the moment of the execution of the rescript, the execution could not be validly and lawfully performed.[89]

In sum, therefore, authors were of the common, though not unanimous, opinion that the presence of the truth in petitions at the time of the rescript's execution alone was sufficient to satisfy the requirements of the law for the validity of the grant to the beneficiary. They argued that when a petition was truthful

[87] Suarez, *loc. cit.;* H. Feije, *loc. cit.*

[88] Cf. Schmalzgrueber, *ibid.,* n. 161. *Contra,* Jacobus de Zochis de Ferraria (d. 1457) in *Repetitionum in Universas fere Iuris Canonici Partes, Materiasque sane Frequentiores, Volumina Sex* (cura L. A. Giunta, Venetiis, 1587), ad c. 20, X, *de rescriptis,* I, 3, n. 54 (hereafter cited as *Repetitiones*).

[89] Cf. Schmalzgrueber, *loc. cit.*

at the time of the execution of a rescript, the condition *"si preces veritate nitantur,"* upon which the executor's mandate and faculties depended for their proper and valid fulfillment, was verified precisely because that condition affected the actual granting of the matter requested. That grant took place in the case of a rescript in commissorial form when it was applied by the executor to the prospective beneficiary, rather than when the order or power to grant it was given. Consequently, the execution of the rescript was valid, and the petitioner obtained what he had requested in the petition that had originally been sent to Rome.[90]

It must be noted here that the authors who supported this last opinion excepted from it the case in which a cause given in the *preces* had been false when the petition was sent to Rome, but was maliciously and willfully made true by the time of the execution of the rescript. Such would have been the case, for instance, where sexual relations had been falsely alleged as the reason for obtaining a matrimonial dispensation, and then by the time that the dispensation was actually applied to the involved parties, that cause was actually established. In cases like this it was held that the fact that the petition was true when the rescript was executed did not satisfy the condition *"si preces veritate nitantur"* as far as the law was concerned.[91]

A particular problem which was considered in this regard, especially by authors between the Council of Trent and the Code, concerned the situation in which a rescript containing a matrimonial dispensation had been validly and lawfully executed, but then, between that time and the day of the marriage, all of the final causes had ceased to exist. So the question was asked: did the law on rescripts demand that the petition be true also when

[90] "Nam tunc jam censetur impleta conditio, sub qua pontifex potestatem dispensandi delegat; mandat enim delegato, ut dispenset, si invenerit, rem de facto se ita habere, prout proponitur in precibus: quod in hac specie facti verum est."—Schmalzgrueber, *ibid.*, n. 162. Among the other commentators who supported this opinion were De Smet, *Betrothment and Marriage,* II, 341; Reiffenstuel, *Jus Canonicum,* Lib. IV, *Appendix de dispensationibus matrimonialibus,* n. 223; C. Pyrrhus, *Praxis,* Lib. VIII, c. 6, nn. 24-28; Wernz, *Ius Decretalium,* I, n. 155, II; Bargilliat, *Praelectiones,* I, n. 414, ad g.

[91] Cf. De Smet, *ibid.*, nn. 341-342; H. Feije, *loc. cit.*

the dispensation was actually put into use? In answering it, some commentators thought that the law did extend its requirement for truthful petitions that far; others held that it did not.

Thomas Sanchez supported the more rigorous view in this controversy.[92] The principal reasons advanced for this position were the following: first, according to the legal axiom: *"Cessante causa, cessat effectus,"* if there was a cessation of the final cause on account of which the dispensation had been granted, the dispensation itself had to be looked upon as being revoked; second, another principle of law ruled that *"Actus agentium non operantur ultra intentionem illorum"*; the Pope, however, could not be thought to grant any dispensation except with at least the implied condition *"dummodo causa permaneat."* Since in this case the cause of the dispensation had ceased, therefore the dispensation, and consequently also the rescript, was no longer valid.[93]

On the other hand, there were many commentators who held that the dispensation, together with the rescript by which it was conveyed, retained its validity in spite of the cessation of its final cause before the time of the celebration of the marriage. In fact, this latter opinion was considered the more probable one and certainly one that it was safe to follow in practice.[94] In support of their doctrine, these authors argued that, when the dispensation had been granted, as it had been at the moment when the rescript was executed, the impediment in question was removed absolutely, that is, once and for all. Since that was the effect of the dispensation upon the impediment, the action of the dispensation was perfectly complete, so that even if there was a cessation of the final cause on account of which the Pope had granted the dispensation, the impediment did not again arise, for: *"Factum legitime retractari non debet, licet casus postea eveniat, a quo non potuit inchoari."* [95]

Furthermore, Schmalzgrueber took issue with the cogency of the reasons presented by the proponents of the conflicting opinion

[92] *Ibid.*, n. 14.

[93] Cf. Th. Sanchez, *loc. cit.*

[94] Schmalzgrueber, *ibid.*, n. 164; H. Feije, *op. cit.*, n. 728.

[95] Reg. 73, R. J., in VI°. Cf. Schmalzgrueber, *loc. cit.*

on this question. In reference to their first argument based on the axiom: *"Cessante causa, cessat effectus,"* he noted that that principle applied only to cases in which the effect of the relevant dispensation was not fully perfected and accomplished, and not to those in which that effect was absolute and final, as was the situation here. As for their second reason, he insisted that any condition upon which the Pope granted the dispensation had reference to the time at which the favor was actually granted and became effective. Hence, if the condition had been fulfilled at that time, the grant was valid and the impediment was removed once and for all.[96]

Section II. The Effect of False Petitions on Rescripts

When Pope Alexander III (1159-1181) formally introduced the condition *"si preces veritate nitantur"* into the Church's law on rescripts, he indicated that that essential condition was to apply to all papal rescripts.[97] Indeed, from that time onwards there were no canonists who denied the importance of the fulfillment of that condition in relation to the validity of the many rescripts that came from Rome. In time, however, two important exceptions were made in regard to the effect which the violation of that principle was to have. The first exception concerned rescripts granted *motu proprio.* The second involved rescripts which contained dispensations from the minor matrimonial impediments.

Article 1. Motu Proprio Granted Rescripts

It was Pope Boniface VIII (1294-1303) who excepted *motu proprio* granted rescripts from the general rule concerning the vitiating effect which a lack of truth in the *preces* ordinarily brought.[98] It seems that the doctrine which the canonists drew from that Pontiff's legislation was universally accepted.

96 *Ibid.,* n. 165.

97 "Et in huiusmodi literis intelligenda est haec conditio, etiamsi non apponatur: 'si preces veritate nitantur'. . . ."—C. 2, X, *de rescriptis,* I, 3; JL, n. 14317. Cf. Panormitanus, *Commentaria,* Lib. I, tit. III, to the foregoing chapter, n. 3.

98 Cf. c. 23, *de praebendis et dignitatibus,* III, 4, in VI°, and *supra,* p. 48.

That doctrine adverted to two general rules. The first rule was that the *motu proprio* of the Pope regularly abstracted from invalidity as following upon any and all subreption, even though it was intentional, and from any and every vitiating consequence which that defect might have had on a rescript.[99] The second was that the Pontiff's *motu proprio* still adverted to the element of obreption; therefore its usual invalidating effect remained to deprive the petitioner of the benefit granted in the Pope's rescript.[100] Obreption was here understood by the majority of the authors as the false statement of the sole remaining final cause for the *motu proprio* issued rescript.

The reason for this distinction between subreption and obreption in this regard was summarized by Schmalzgrueber in this way:

> Ratio disparitatis est, quia quando tacetur veritas, pontifex ab illa ad concessionem non movetur; neque sciri potest, an bene informatus de rei veritate gratiam denegasset; imo cum ea gratia procedat ex mera liberalitate principis, potius praesumi potest, quod etiam veritate cognita, adhuc illam concessurus fuisset. E contrario, quando causa falsa exprimitur, satis apparet, quod concessio ex errore processerit, igitur cum errantis nullus sit consensus.[101]

As far as obreption was concerned, there were no exceptions to the general rule stated above.

Furthermore, there were three instances in which the *motu proprio* of the Pope did not exclude the usual effect even of subreption. They obtained, first, when because of the suppression of the truth the rights of a third person were injured; secondly, when the incapacity of the recipient to receive the particular re-

[99] "Subreptio dolosa vitiat rescriptum. Limita nisi litterae fuerint obtentae motu proprio Papae, quia tunc subreptio etiam scienter facta non vitiat et hoc propter virtutem motus proprii Principis, quae omnem subreptionem excludit."—Fagnanus, *Commentaria,* Lib. I, tit. III, ad c. 20, X, *de rescriptis,* I, 3, n. 37.

[100] "Non tamen aequaliter clausula motu proprio supplet subreptionem ex falsitatis expressione provenientem."—Gonzalez-Tellez, *Commentaria,* Lib. I, tit. III, ad c. 2, X, *de rescriptis,* I, 3, n. 19.

[101] *Jus Ecclesiasticum,* Lib. I, tit. III, n. 11.

script in question was concealed; and thirdly, when the intrinsic qualities of the benefice that was to be conferred were hidden by the suppression of the truth.[102]

Article 2. Rescripts Containing Dispensations from Minor Matrimonial Impediments

Until 1908, *motu proprio* issued rescripts were the only ones which were excepted from the otherwise universal application of the principle that the validity of rescripts always depended upon the truthfulness of the *preces* presented for them. In that year, however, under the regulations of the reformed Curia, another type of rescript was exempted from the vitiating effect of both subreption and obreption. That was the rescript which carried dispensations from the minor matrimonial impediments. The new regulations stated:

> Dispensations from minor impediments shall all be granted for reasonable causes approved by the Holy See (*ex certis rationabilibus causis a Sancta Sede probatis*); under this form they will have the same force as if given in virtue of a *motu proprio* and with certain knowledge (*motu proprio et ex certa scientia*), and so will not be open to question on the ground either of obreption or of subreption.[103]

It will be helpful for one, in trying to understand the import of this norm, to keep in mind that at the time it was the practice of the Holy See sometimes to grant dispensations under the general formula "for certain reasonable causes (*ex certis rationabili-*

[102] Schmalzgrueber, *loc. cit.*

[103] Ordo Servandus in S. Congregationibus, Tribunalibus, Officiis Romanae Curiae, 29 sept. 1908, Pars II, *Normae peculiares*, cap. VII, art. III, n. 21—*AAS*, I (1909), 91-92.

The minor matrimonial impediments at that time were consanguinity and licit affinity in the third and fourth degrees, illicit affinity in the first and second degrees, spiritual relationship, and public decency.

This rule applied expressly only to rescripts with dispensations granted by the Sacred Congregation of the Sacraments, but there was some probability that it could be extended also to rescripts issued by the Sacred Penitentiary, and even by bishops.—Cf. De Smet, *Betrothment and Marriage*, II, 282, note 3.

bus causis)" or the like. Dispensations which were issued in that manner were often called dispensations *sine causa,* not because there was no sufficient cause for them, but because none was specified in the rescript. That lack of specification of a determinate reason was sometimes due to the fact that no strictly canonical causes had been alleged in the petitioner's *preces.* At other times it was an indication that Rome did not require the verification of the cause or causes for the validity of the rescript and the dispensation which it brought. The latter was the case under the new discipline of the Roman Curia for dispensations from impediments of minor degree.[104]

As for the regulation itself, it evidently made a wider exception to the general necessity of having truthful petitions than had been accorded to *motu proprio* granted rescripts, for it indicated that neither subreption nor obreption, even from bad faith, would have any effect upon the rescripts within its scope. The exemption which was established by it seems not to have been intended to embrace the *pars postulativa* of the *preces,* but only the *pars narrativa* and *pars motiva.*[105] Thus De Smet noted in this regard:

> This rule, determining that dispensations from minor impediments are not subject to any hazard on the ground of obreption, or subreption, must, in our opinion, be restricted to the causes, and does not apply to the declaration of the impediments themselves; consequently, a substantial error on this point would annul the rescript, as seems implied by the context.[106]

Nonetheless, this new discipline of the Roman Curia did establish an important exception in reference to the application of the principle *"si preces veritate nitantur."* Its significance is evidenced by the fact that the non-fulfillment of that condition in cases involving all other rescripts granted *ad instantiam* always brought with it a vitiating effect upon the letters.

[104] Cf. De Smet, *ibid.,* p. 283.

[105] For a description of these different parts of the *preces,* cf. *infra,* p. 91, note 107.

[106] *Ibid.,* p. 309, note 1.

Article 3. Rescripts Other Than Such as Were Issued Motu proprio and Such as Contained Dispensations from Minor Matrimonial Impediments

A. The Extent of the Effect of False *Preces* on Rescripts

As far as all other rescripts were concerned, the principle *"si preces veritate nitantur"* applied to each of the three parts in the petitions presented for them.[107] Consequently, even though defective reasons seem to have been the more usual cause of the falsification of the *preces,* subreption or obreption in any other section of a petition could have vitiated the subsequent rescript. For that reason it is important for the reader to keep in mind what has already been said concerning the doctrine of the commentators in reference to when the various parts of a petition could be regarded as lacking in the required truth.[108]

In dealing with the effect which false petitions had on both rescripts of justice and rescripts of favor, the authors, in imitation of Pope Innocent III in his law of 1208, distinguished between that subreption and obreption which arose from the petitioner's fraud or malice and that which was caused by his ignorance or simplicity.[109] In fact, the source of these defects had an important bearing on the doctrine of the commentators on the matter now under discussion.

Concerning the effect of a malicious or fraudulent lack of truth in the *preces,* there were two schools of thought among the pre-Code canonists. Both schools included both rescripts of justice and rescripts of favor in their respective doctrines on this point.

The first school was represented by those authors who maintained that this type of subreption and obreption always vitiated the entire rescript for which the false petition had been presented.

[107] Those parts were the *pars narrativa,* in which the facts and circumstances of the petitioner's case were set forth, the *pars postulativa,* in which the request was expressed, and the *pars persuasiva,* in which the causes were given.—Cf. *supra,* pp. 16-19.

[108] Cf. *supra,* pp. 60-79.

[109] Cf. Jacobus de Zochis de Ferraria in *Repetitiones,* ad c. 20, X, *de rescriptis,* I, 3, nn. 1, 12.

They argued that such a total vitiation of the rescript with all its contents was the clear intention of Pope Innocent III when he wrote:

> Ut hi qui priori modo [i.e., per fraudem vel malitiam] falsitatem exprimunt vel supprimunt veritatem in suae perversitatis poenam nullum ex illis literis commodum consequantur.[110]

Accordingly, they concluded that it was immaterial whether or not the defect in the petition had a direct connection with all the favors or other concessions given in the rescript. The very fact that the subreption or obreption was due to the petitioner's evil-mindedness was sufficient to bring on, as a penalty, the vitiation of the entire rescript.[111] This was the more common doctrine among the commentators before the Code of Canon Law.

Nonetheless, the authors who constituted the other school of thought in this matter taught that even in these circumstances it was probable that there was vitiated only that part of the rescript which had a direct dependence upon the malicious subreption or obreption in the *preces*.[112] That is to say, these commentators maintained that if the entire rescript with all its contents had been granted by reason of the defect, or was immediately connected with it, then the whole letter was vitiated. The same was true when the several parts of the one rescript were interrelated. Such was the case, for instance, when all the concessions were given for the same purpose. It happened also when the other concessions were dependent upon the principal grant, as when one part was given as an accessory to the principal concession. When the various concessions in the one re-

[110] C. 20, X, *de rescriptis*, I, 3; Potthast, n. 3519. Cf. *supra*, pp. 43-44.

[111] Among the authors who supported this opinion were Panormitanus, *Commentaria*, Lib. I, tit. III, ad c. 20, X, *de rescriptis*, I, 3, n. 2; Fagnanus, *Commentaria*, Lib. I, tit. III, ad c. 20, X, *de rescriptis*, I, 3, nn. 10-24; Gonzalez-Tellez, *Commentaria*, Lib. I, tit. III, ad c. 20, X, *de rescriptis*, I, 3, nn. 6-7; Vecchiotti, *Institutiones*, pp. 106-107; Santi, *Praelectiones*, I, 32; Sanguineti, *Institutiones*, p. 96; Aichner, *Compendium*, p. 25, nota 8; Bargilliat, *Praelectiones*, I, n. 414, ad 3.

[112] Among the authors who supported this opinion were Pirhing, *Jus Canonicum*, Lib. I, tit. III, n. CIX; Schmalzgrueber, *Jus Canonicum*, Lib. I, tit. III, nn. 15-17; De Angelis, *Praelectiones Juris Canonici*, Tom. I, pars I, p. 69.

script were altogether distinct and independent of each other, however, then only that grant was vitiated which was essentially connected with the subreption or obreption in the *preces*.[113]

The proponents of this opinion attempted to justify their position by arguing that when two completely independent concessions were given together in one and the same rescript, there were virtually two rescripts. The rescript which had actually been granted was one only materially. Moreover, they insisted that the vitiation of the rescript in this case was the result of the penalty established by the law which punished the petitioner's evil-mindedness; penalties, however, were to be given a strict interpretation; therefore, this vitiating effect of subreption and obreption in the *preces* was to be extended no further than to that concession in the rescript which had a direct connection with the defect in the petition.[114]

The proponents of both of these opinions adverted to and contemplated rescripts of justice as well as rescripts of favor in their respective doctrines on this point. Almost all of them, however, recognized an important difference between the two types of rescripts in regard to their relationship to malice and fraud. That difference was this: whenever there was doubt about the presence or absence of maliciousness in the false *preces* for rescripts of favor, *dolus* was to be presumed. In false petitions for rescripts of justice, *dolus* was not to be presumed except in two instances, both of which involved obreption alone. Those two cases obtained, first, when obreption was discovered in a matter of great importance, and secondly, when a falsehood was stated about the petitioner's personal condition.

The reason for this distinction between the two types of rescripts was that it was more difficult to obtain a rescript of favor than a rescript of justice. Consequently, the possibility of a petitioner's lying or maliciously suppressing the truth was greater

[113] "Sed etsi subreptio, non per simplicitatem vel ignorantiam, sed per dolum seu malitiam contingat circa unam tantum partem rescripti, probabile est, illam tantum partem vitiari, non alteram, si partes rescripti sint omnino separatae, videlicet super diversis negotiis, aut causas, et per accidens solum, sine ulla connexione, vel subordinatione, in eodem rescripto ponantur."—Pirhing, *loc. cit.*

[114] Pirhing, *loc. cit.;* Schmalzgrueber, *loc. cit.;* De Angelis, *loc. cit.*

in requests for the former type of rescript than in petitions for the latter kind.[115]

The distinction between rescripts of justice and rescripts of favor had a great deal of practical importance. Its importance was due especially to the fact that the majority of the pre-Code commentators held to a much more lenient doctrine concerning the vitiating effect of the false *preces* when the defects in them arose from the ignorance or simplicity of a petitioner requesting a rescript of justice. This more lenient teaching was summed up by Fagnanus in three general principles or norms, and practically all of the other authors subscribed to them.

The first norm was this:

> Expressio falsitatis, vel taciturnitas veritatis ex simplicitate, vel ignorantia proveniens, si non sit causa concessionis, eo quod expressa veritate, vel tacita falsitate, Princeps nihilominus litteras concessisset, rescriptum non vitiat.[116]

There can be no doubt that the juridical substratum of this norm was the second of the three principles which Pope Innocent III had laid down on this point in regard to rescripts of justice.[117] In this matter the Pontiff had indicated that, despite non-malicious untruthfulness in the *preces* for a rescript of justice, its recipient stood to benefit from it as long only as the form and not the substance of the rescript had been infected with the subreption or the obreption.[118] Still, it must be kept in mind that, even in such circumstances, the false petition had been somewhat prejudicial to the petitioner, for it deprived him of the benefit of having his case tried according to the special mode of procedure which the Pope had granted. As a result, he had to be satisfied with a trial conducted according to the norms of the common law.

[115] Cf. Fagnanus, *ibid.*, nn. 41-44; Th. Sanchez, *De Matrimonio,* Lib. VIII, disp. 21, n. 68.

[116] Fagnanus, *ibid.*, n. 52. Cf. also Panormitanus, *loc. cit.;* Engel, *Collegium,* Lib. I, tit. III, n. 12; Pirhing, *ibid.*, n. CI; Schmalzgrueber, *ibid.*, n. 16; Santi, *loc. cit.;* Zitelli, *De Dispensationibus,* p. 23; De Smet, *Betrothment and Marriage,* II, 340; Wernz, *Ius Decretalium,* I, n. 153, II.

[117] Cf. *supra,* p. 66.

[118] Cf. *supra,* p. 66.

Of course, the commentators had to make some adjustments when they attempted to apply Pope Innocent's principle to rescripts of favor, since such rescripts were not considered to be constituted of substance and form as rescripts of justice were. Fagnanus gave an excellent example of how this principle applied to rescripts of favor in these circumstances. It involved the case in which a person had asked for a benefice *cum cura vel residentia* at a time when he was unknowingly impeded from holding that specific type of benefice. He was eligible, however, for a *beneficium simplex.* The Pope had answered this petitioner's request by sending a mandate to his bishop to confer on him the former kind of benefice. So the question arose on whether or not the rescript was completely useless because of the impediment in the way of its being executed as it stood. The commentators decided that the rescript could still benefit the petitioner. They felt that the bishop could confer on him the less demanding kind of benefice, namely the *beneficium simplex,* for which the petitioner was actually eligible. The reason for this decision was precisely *"quia multo potius Papa hoc concessisset."* [119]

This first norm is sufficient to indicate the different lines of thought the writers followed in treating respectively of subreption or obreption as caused by the petitioner's *dolus* and as caused by his ignorance or simplicity. In regard to the former, on the one hand, they reasoned that, since *dolus* was a serious crime, it had to be punished with an appropriate penalty. The most fitting penalty that could be inflicted was to deprive the petitioner of any benefit that the rescript might have brought him. That, according to the authors, was the *finis legis* of Pope Innocent's decretal of 1208, as far as his first principle was concerned. On the other hand, when a petition was falsified in good faith, the authors believed that the lawgiver wanted to pardon, whenever he could, any fault on the part of the petitioner in presenting the false *preces.* That explained why the legislator was more lenient when this type of defect was involved.[120]

119 Fagnanus, *ibid.,* n. 55.

120 Cf. Gonzalez-Tellez, *Commentaria,* Lib. I, tit. III, ad c. 20, *de rescriptis,* I, 3, n. 10.

Nevertheless, the commentators still maintained that one of the most fundamental principles involved in the matter of rescripts was *"cum rescripta pendeant a voluntate concedentis, deficiente ea, vires non continent."* [121] That principle led to the formulation of their second general norm concerning the effect which non-maliciously false *preces* had on both rescripts of justice and rescripts of favor.

Fagnanus expressed that general norm in this manner:

> Expressio falsitatis, vel suppressio veritatis per simplicitatem, vel ignorantiam, vitiat rescriptum in totum, si sit substantiae rescripti inductiva, seu fundamentum, vel causa totius concessionis, id est, si Princeps tacita falsitate, vel expressa veritate, nullo modo dedisset litteras.[122]

In this matter, the authors were merely restating the third principle that had been set down in Pope Innocent III's law of 1208.[123] In restating it, they applied it not only to rescripts of justice but also to rescripts of favor.

The juridic reasoning which underlay this general rule was that the value of a rescript depended not on the negligence, ignorance, or error of the petitioner, but rather on the intention of the grantor to issue the rescript, for it was from that intention that the letter had its force. In this case, however, there was no such intention. Therefore, the rescript was vitiated.[124] Hence, according to this second norm the vitiation of the relevant rescript arose not from the fault of the petitioner, but from the absence of the intention of the Pope to issue it at all.

In spite of the convincing argument which was used to support this second general rule, some of the commentators, especially those of the sixteenth and seventeenth centuries, tried to establish an exception to it because of a decretal issued by Pope Boniface VIII. That decretal concerned the case in which some-

[121] Gonzalez-Tellez, *loc. cit.*

[122] *Ibid.*, n. 62. Cf. also Panormitanus, *loc. cit.;* Gonzalez-Tellez, *ibid.*, n. 9; Tuschus, *Practicae Conclusiones*, Tom. VII, concl. 720, n. 26; Schmalzgrueber, *loc. cit.;* Pirhing, *loc. cit.;* Th. Sanchez, *De Matrimonio*, Lib. VIII, disp. 21, nn. 62-66.

[123] Cf. *supra*, p. 66.

[124] Cf. Tuschus, *loc. cit.;* Gonzalez-Tellez, *loc. cit.;* Pirhing, *loc. cit.;* Schmalzgrueber, *loc. cit.*

one had asked for and received a benefice from the Holy Father after the petitioner's bishop had conferred another benefice upon him. The bishop's action had been unknown to the petitioner, and so he did not mention in his *preces* to the Pope that he already had a benefice. Ordinarily such an omission would have rendered null and void the rescript conferring the second benefice. Yet in this case the Pope decided that the person could keep both benefices if they were compatible; but if they were such as could not be held by one and the same beneficiary, then he was to choose the one that he preferred. The reason which Pope Boniface gave for this decision was "*cum tempore impetrationis nescires. . . .*"[125] That reason led some commentators to believe that, when subreption was caused by ignorance which was in no way due to any negligence on the part of the petitioner, it never vitiated the subsequent rescript.[126]

The third and last norm in regard to the effect of non-malicious subreption or obreption was formulated by Fagnanus thus:

> Subreptio per simplicitatem, vel ignorantiam quae non fuit causa totius concessionis, sed partis illius dumtaxat, scriptum non vitiat in totum, sed eatenus tantum, quatenus fuit causa concessionis.[127]

At the outset, it must be noted that this rule did not apply to those cases in which the different parts or concessions in a single rescript were interrelated. Nor did it operate when a rescript contained a concession which was actually an accessory to the principal grant. These exceptions were made because in such cases the subreption or obreption had an intimate connection with everything that was contained in the rescript.[128]

Another exception sometimes invoked against this third rule

[125] "Gratia, quam super beneficio a sede apostolica te impetrasse proponis, vitiosa reputari non debet, quamvis de alio beneficio, ab episcopo tuo antea tibi absenti et ignoranti collato, nullam, cum tempore impetrationis nescires, feceris mentionem."—C. 7, *de rescriptis,* I, 3, in VI°.

[126] Gonzalez-Tellez (*ibid.,* ad c. 8, X, *de rescriptis,* I, 3, n. 14) and Th. Sanchez (*ibid.,* n. 60) supported this opinion. This writer did not find any authors who took up this question after the time of these two commentators.

[127] *Ibid.,* n. 72.

[128] Cf. Fagnanus, *loc. cit.*

concerned rescripts containing privileges. That is to say, a few authors held that even non-malicious subreption and obreption effected a complete vitiation of such letters.[129] The reason given for this teaching was based upon the nature of a privilege. A privilege was considered to be a private law. Consequently, whenever the Pope granted a privilege in a rescript, his intention was to concede a particular privilege, that is, one so defined and so specified that, if for any reason the petitioner could not receive it, his rescript was totally useless to him. In other words, the concession was held to be so absolutely exclusive that it applied solely to the precise privilege mentioned in the apostolic letter.[130]

Fagnanus, however, was most outspoken against this exception. His argument, which bespoke the mind of the vast majority of the pre-Code canonists, was that the intention of the Pope in granting rescripts containing privileges was no more absolutely precise and exclusive than it was when he issued rescripts conferring benefices. Now, it was generally admitted that his third norm applied to these latter rescripts. Fagnanus argued, therefore, that it should be equally applicable to the former letters. Accordingly, he concluded that in this matter of subreption and obreption the rescripts conveying privileges were to be treated exactly like rescripts granting benefices.[131]

As for the rule itself, the reasoning behind it was based on the fact that, when two altogether distinct concessions were made in the same rescript, there were virtually two rescripts. The letter actually issued was one only materially and incidentally (*per accidens*). This factor opened the way for the authors to apply the legal principle: *"Utile per inutile non debet vitiari."* [132] Ac-

129 Among these authors was Felinus Sandeus, *Commentaria,* Lib. I, tit. III, ad c. 20, X, *de rescriptis,* I, 3, n. 3.

130 Cf. Felinus Sandeus, *loc. cit.* The writer believes that the here-stated exception applied to the first general norm given in this matter rather than to this third rule. Cf. *supra,* p. 94. It was treated, however, in connection with this latter rule by the pre-Code authors. For that reason it has been given the same place in this study.

131 *Ibid.,* nn. 79-80; cf. also Engel, *Collegium,* Lib. I, tit. III, n. 12.

132 Reg. 37, R. J., in VI°.

cordingly, the vitiating effect of the non-malicious subreption or obreption in the *preces* was confined to that part of the rescript with which these defects had a direct and intimate connection.[133]

B. The Manner in Which False *Preces* Produced Their Effect Upon Rescripts

In this analysis of the manner in which false *preces* produced their effect upon rescripts, it is necessary to treat rescripts of justice and rescripts of favor separately, for the majority of the commentators saw each of them affected in its own specific way.

a) Rescripts of justice

As for rescripts of justice, it was by far the more common opinion among the pre-Code authors that these rescripts were never automatically invalid because of the presence of malicious or non-malicious subreption or obreption in petitions for them. More precisely, it was held by most of the canonists that rescripts of justice were invalidated by these defects only after the following procedure had been completed: first, a legitimate exception on the grounds of subreption or obreption in the petitioner's *preces* had been raised by the recipient's adversary;[134] secondly, the opposing party had proved that these defects were present;[135] thirdly, the judge had declared, on the basis of that proof, that the rescript in question had been vitiated because of a surreptitious or obreptitious petition. Until those three things had taken place, the recipient of the defective rescript stood to

[133] Cf. Schmalzgrueber, *ibid.*, n. 16.

[134] In this regard, Panormitanus held that, if a judge-delegate unlawfully refused to admit the above-listed exception, the fact that the petitioner's adversary had rightfully raised the exception was sufficient to nullify the process involved, "quia iudex procedendo ad ulteriora venit contra ordinem iuris. . . ." He noted, however, that Pope Innocent IV and Bernardus Compostellanus (d. ca. 1261) maintained that "iustius et securius esse ut appelletur si iudex non vult admittere exceptionem."—*Commentaria,* Lib. I, tit. III, ad c. 3, X, *de rescriptis,* I, 3, n. 9.

[135] In this connection Panormitanus noted: "Pars si omisit opponere exceptionem apertam, potest iudex ex officio actum irritare saltem ante quam sententia transeat in rem iudicatam."—*Ibid.,* ad c. 22, X, *de rescriptis,* I, 3, n. 9.

benefit from the letter and whatever was contained in it.[136] Consequently, when the pre-Code authors said that subreption and obreption vitiated a rescript of justice, most of them meant that such a rescript was liable to be rendered null solely by means of the process just indicated. It was not their intention to indicate that invalidity followed automatically from a lack of the required truth in the *preces*.[137]

In support of this doctrine the commentators appealed principally to previous decretal legislation on this point. They referred, first of all, to Pope Innocent III's law of 1208, in which the Pontiff had ruled that a malicious lack of the truth in the *preces* vitiated the rescripts in question. At the same time, however, the Pope had indicated that the judge who was to handle the principal action was to render a decision on the exception raised against the plaintiff's rescript by his opponent. He then concluded by saying that only after that exception had been upheld was the judge to refrain from entertaining the principal cause for which he had been delegated through the rescript.[138] If the rescript had been automatically null and void, there would, indeed, still have been reason for the judge to take up the exception against it. Yet, the whole proceeding depending upon the rescript and anterior to the discovery of the nullity would have been null and void before that incidental question had been decided.

Secondly, the authors cited two other decretals, both of which

[136] In this regard, however, Panormitanus taught that if a process had been constructed upon a rescript which was said to be false but was declared by the judge to be true, and later the letter was actually found to be false, the process in question was invalid. He cited Pope Innocent IV, Joannes Andreae, and others as agreeing with him in this doctrine. The reason underlying this position was "quia fabricator falsi rescripti non potuit dare iurisdictionem nec in principali nec in incidenti . . . quia ex quo rescriptum non emanavit a Principe, iste potest dici intrusus et sic non debent valere gesta etiam dato communi errore. . . ."—*Ibid.*, ad c. 20, X, *de rescriptis,* I, 3, n. 11.

[137] Cf. Panormitanus, *ibid.*, ad c. 23, X, *de rescriptis,* I, 3, n. 3; Fagnanus, *ibid.*, ad c. 1, X, *de rescriptis,* I, 3, nn. 5-7; Pirhing, *ibid.*, nn. LII, LXXXV; Schmalzgrueber, *ibid.*, n. 14; Vecchiotti, *Institutiones,* I, 107; Sanguineti, *Institutiones,* p. 96; Santi, *Praelectiones,* I, 37; Wernz, *Ius Decretalium,* I, n. 153, II; Bargilliat, *Praelectiones,* I, n. 414, ad d.

[138] Cf. Pope Innocent III's first principle, *supra*, pp. 65-66.

had given the same decision. Those decretals dealt with a situation in which a rescript had been obtained by a petitioner who had failed to mention that his opponent himself had previously obtained a rescript for the same case. Ordinarily that second rescript would have been vitiated by the very fact that the petition for it had not contained mention of the first rescript. In the case in question, however, the decision of the lawgiver was that the second rescript was to stand as valid. He gave two reasons for that decision. His first reason was that the petitioner's opponent had failed to use his rescript within a year's time. The second was that this opponent could not prove that his failure to do so had been due to the impossibility of his finding a judge to whom to present the apostolic letter. Consequently it was argued that that second rescript must never have been invalid, for otherwise it would have been revalidated through the negligence of the first party and through the passage of time. Such a revalidation was not admitted by the law, however, for a rescript received its force from the will of its grantor. Besides, *"Non firmatur tractu temporis quod de jure ab initio non subsistit."* [139]

It was on the basis of these laws that the majority of the canonists taught that rescripts of justice were not *ipso iure* invalid because of subreption or obreption. Rather, they maintained that such rescripts were rendered null and void only through the successful raising of an objection on those grounds by the petitioner's adversary.

Despite the solid foundation which this majority opinion had, there were a few commentators who offered a contrary doctrine on this point.[140] Led by Gonzalez-Tellez, they maintained that, when there was question of the vitiation of a rescript of justice by malicious subreption or obreption, the effect was produced *ipso iure.*

[139] Reg. 18, R. J., in VI°. Cf. c. 9, X, *de rescriptis,* I, 3; JL, n. 15185 (Lucius III: 1181-1185); c. 23, X, *de rescriptis,* I, 3; Potthast, n. 3671 (Innocent III: 1209); cf. *supra,* pp. 48-49. Cf. also Santi, *loc. cit.*

[140] Gonzalez-Tellez, *ibid.,* n. 8; R. Maschat (1692-1747), *Cursus Iuris Canonici* (2 vols., Romae, 1757), Lib. I, tit. III, n. 10; and Sebastianelli (1855-1920), *Praelectiones Iuris Canonici* (2. ed., 3 vols., Romae, 1905-1906), I, 62.

They founded their teaching on expressions which the lawgiver used in reference to the effect which such defects had upon rescripts, for example, *"ibi nullum ex litteris," "nullatenus de causa cognoscat," "careat penitus impetratis,"* [141] *"vires nolumus obtinere,"* [142] and *"viribus carere decernas."* [143] From those expressions they concluded that the lawgiver was unmistakably indicating that the effect in question was automatic. Consequently the rescripts so affected had to be regarded as *ipso iure* null and void.[144]

At first sight this argument seems to carry a certain amount of weight. In fact, the present writer could find no author among those whom he was able to consult who refuted it point by point, as far as the individual texts were concerned. Nevertheless it appears to the writer that those texts lose a great deal of their probative value in relation to the above-stated opinion when they are interpreted in the light of the context in which they were placed in the decretal legislation. Moreover, he was not able to find among the proponents of this theory any satisfactory contradiction of the convincing arguments presented by the opposite school in this controversy. Consequently, it is the writer's opinion that the former of the two foregoing doctrines had not only more extrinsic authority on its side but also a more solid intrinsic juridic foundation.

b) Rescripts of favor

Turning now to rescripts of favor and the effect which subreption and obreption in their *preces* had upon them, one finds that it was the almost unanimous teaching of the commentators that these rescripts were invalid *ipso iure* whenever the petitions for them were lacking in the required truth.[145]

[141] C. 20, X, *de rescriptis,* I, 3. Cf. *supra,* pp. 43-44.

[142] C. 8, X, *de rescriptis,* I, 3; JL, n. 14965 (Lucius III: 1183-1184). Cf. *supra,* p. 49.

[143] C. 26, X, *de rescriptis,* I, 3; Potthast, n. 5026 (Innocent III: 1198-1215).

[144] Cf. Gonzalez-Tellez, *loc. cit.*

[145] Cf. Panormitanus, *ibid.,* ad c. 19, X, *de rescriptis,* I, 3, nn. 1, 5, 6; Fagnanus, *Commentaria,* Lib. I, tit. III, ad c. 1, X, *de rescriptis,* I, 3, nn.

Once again the authors found the basis for their teaching on this point in the decretal law. They cited, for instance, a law of Pope Innocent III, issued in 1198, in which the Pontiff had written concerning a favor that had been obtained surreptitiously: ". . . *mandamus . . . quicquid factus est occasione literarum ipsarum irritum decernatis. . . .*" [146] They referred also to a decretal of Pope Honorius III (1216-1227). In it the Pontiff dealt with a case in which someone had obtained a benefice in virtue of a rescript, then sold it, and subsequently requested another benefice, without mentioning what had happened previously. In deciding this case, the Pope wrote:

> . . . mandamus, quatenus eos, qui post literas taliter venditas, alias, de illis mentione non habita, impetrabunt de cetero, vel hactenus impetrarunt, carere decernas commodo earundem. . . .[147]

A decision of Pope Boniface VIII was also mentioned, because in it there was this clear statement: "*Tunc enim, quantumcumque modicum beneficium taceatur in ea* [*petitione*], *ipsam veluti subreptitiam vires nolumus obtinere.*" [148] The authors quoted Pope Boniface VIII again in reference to a dispensation that had been obtained in virtue of a false petition: "*Veluti per subreptionem obtenta* [*dispensatione*], *nullius penitus est momenti.*" [149]

Using these laws as a starting point, the commentators proceeded to argue in this fashion: the value of any rescript depended entirely on the intention of the grantor, the Pope; but when rescripts of favor were concerned, the Popes had indicated that they intended the letters to have no value whatsoever whenever they had been obtained by means of false petitions; there-

5-7; Pirhing, *Jus Canonicum,* Lib. I, tit. III, nn. LII, LXXXV; Schmalzgrueber, *Jus Ecclesiasticum,* Lib. I, tit. III, par. 3, n. 16; Giovine, *De Dispensationibus,* par. XCVII; Santi, *loc. cit.;* Bargilliat, *Praelectiones,* I, n. 414, ad d.

146 C. 19, X, *de rescriptis,* I, 3; Potthast, n. 353. Cf. Santi, *loc. cit.*

147 C. 31, *de rescriptis,* I, 3; Potthast, n. 7789. Cf. *supra,* p. 50.

148 C. 23, *de praebendis et dignitatibus,* III, 4, in VI°. Cf. Giovine, *De Dispensationibus,* § CXVII.

149 C. 2, *de filiis presbyterorum et aliis illegitime natis,* I, 11, in VI°. Cf. Giovine, *loc. cit.*

fore, rescripts of favor that were thus obtained were automatically null and void. In other words, such rescripts could be considered as never having been granted at all, precisely because the Pontiff would not have intended to grant them had he known the truth.[150]

As for the reason why rescripts of favor should have differed from rescripts of justice in this regard, Panormitanus noted that the law itself gave no express reason.[151] Nonetheless, the authors advanced several reasons for this difference. They noted, first of all, that rescripts of justice were granted more easily than were rescripts of favor. Inversely, therefore, the latter should be expected to be more quickly and more easily vitiated. This was so, especially, because a petitioner who had obtained a rescript of favor through subreption or obreption showed himself to be more ungrateful than a person who had thus been granted a rescript of justice.[152]

The authors also pointed to the fact that recipients of rescripts of favor, on the one hand, received through them a right either *in re* or *ad rem* insofar as the object of the particular rescript was concerned. Hence, such letters were looked upon as defining and determining the matter in question. Rescripts of justice, on the other hand, were granted as a preparatory step to the settling of some issue. This purpose was evidenced by the fact that it was through them that a judge was delegated to determine the rights of the petitioner and his opponent in a given case, or, as often happened, a *modus procedendi* was outlined to be used to ensure a just and equitable handling of some disputed point. Consequently, rescripts of favor were more likely to be prejudicial to a third person than were rescripts of justice.[153]

[150] Cf. Santi, *loc. cit.*

[151] *Ibid.*, ad c. 31, X, *de rescriptis*, I, 3, n. 14.

[152] Cf. Fagnanus, *ibid.*, ad c. 31, X, *de rescriptis*, I, 3, n. 37; Schmalzgrueber, *ibid.*, n. 14. Their reasoning on this point was no doubt based on the fact that normally the recipient of a favor had no right whatsoever to the concession. The recipient of a rescript of justice, however, was often trying to protect some right which he had from the common law. So, in granting this latter type of rescript, the Pope was merely affording him a means of vindicating that right.

[153] Cf. Schmalzgrueber, *loc. cit.*

Then, too, rescripts of favor had no connection with any kind of litigation. There was no opportunity, therefore, for them to be challenged on the grounds of their having been obtained through false *preces*. Hence, there was more danger of an improper use in connection with them than there was with rescripts of justice. Consequently the necessity of invalidating them by means of direct action of the law was greater than it was for rescripts of justice.[154]

Finally, the commentators saw this reason for the difference in question: the clause *"si preces veritate nitantur"* served a different purpose respectively in rescripts of favor and in rescripts of justice. That is to say, this condition had been inserted in the former letters to demonstrate the intention of the Pope to concede the requested favor if the petition for it was truthful, and not to grant it if the *preces* were false. It had been attached to the latter rescripts, however, *"tantum ad institutionem judicis, quomodo secundum justitiam procedere debeat."* Hence, the force of the clause *"si preces veritate nitantur"* was to be considered as different respectively in the two types of rescripts. From that consideration it was concluded, in regard to rescripts of favor, that the non-fulfillment of the aforesaid condition brought automatic nullity upon the letters. In reference to rescripts of justice, such a non-compliance simply rendered the letters liable to annulment in virtue of an exception successfully raised by the petitioner's adversary.[155]

c) *Mixed rescripts*

In view of the practical import of the distinction between rescripts of justice and rescripts of favor, the question naturally arose on how mixed rescripts were to be treated when subreption or obreption had been found in the petitions for them in such wise as to vitiate these letters completely. In other words, were

[154] ". . . quia in litteris gratiosis cum non sit pars, quae possit excipere de subreptione, impetrans verisimiliter diu pergeret in detentione beneficii injuste occupati. Unde cessante provisione hominis, necesse fuit ut lex provideret inficiendo gratiam, ut sic falsus precator consuleret conscientiae suae, aut per gratiam perinde valere aut per cessionem beneficii. . . . At vero in litteris justitiae adest pars cujus interest, quae potest opponere exceptionem subreptionis et appellare."—Fagnanus, *loc. cit.*

[155] Schmalzgrueber, *ibid.*, n. 12.

such rescripts automatically invalid or not? The commentators answered this question by appealing, whenever possible, to the rule of law which stated: *"Accessorium naturam sequi congruit principalis."* [156] Accordingly, in regard to cases to which this legal principle was applicable, and, indeed, in reference to all cases involving completely vitiated mixed rescripts, they concluded, on the one hand, that, if the principal concession in the rescript had to do with matters of justice or the execution of the law, then the letter should be handled as a simple rescript of justice. On the other hand, when a favor of some kind was the principal grant, the rescript in question was to be governed by the norms that applied to rescripts of favor.[157]

[156] Reg. 42, R. J., in VI°. "Fallitur vero regula quando accessoria non sunt mera accidentia principalis sed aliqua individualitate et independentia gaudent, vel sunt diversae naturae ac principale."—Bartoccetti, *De Regulis Juris Canonici,* p. 164.

[157] Cf. Pirhing, *Jus Canonicum,* Lib. I, tit. III, nn. LII, LXXXV. If the entire mixed rescript was not vitiated by the falsehood in its *preces,* the different parts of the letter could be taken separately, so that the rescript itself could be considered as virtually at least two rescripts. On this basis the part of the letter which was directly affected by the nullifying untruthfulness in the *preces* could be judged separately from the other unaffected part or parts, which still remained to benefit the prospective beneficiary of the letter. Cf. *supra,* pp. 67-68, 70-71, 73-74, 78-79.

PART III

CANONICAL COMMENTARY ON THE PRESENT LAW IN THE CODE OF CANON LAW

INTRODUCTION

In the present legislation of the Church the basic norms implementing the principle *"si preces veritate nitantur"* are found in canons 39 to 42 of the Code of Canon Law. Canon 39 ascribes to this principle the nature of being an essential condition in rescripts. Canon 40 prescribes that it is to apply to all rescripts. The lawgiver, however, immediately excepts two kinds of rescripts from the otherwise all-inclusive application of this essential principle. The first exception is expressed in canon 45, which concerns rescripts issued *motu proprio;* the other is treated in canon 1054, which deals with dispensations from minor matrimonial impediments. Canon 40 is further modified by canon 42 insofar as the latter canon specifies the subject matter of the truth that is regarded as essential in the *preces.* Finally, the important consideration as to when it is necessary for the *preces* to be founded on truth is dealt with in canon 41.

Some of the norms which are contained in these canons are clearly repetitions of pre-Code legal principles, most of which have long been in force in regard to the necessity of having truthful *preces.* Canons 39 and 40, for example, echo the law-making pronouncements of the Emperor Zeno in 477 A.D. and of Pope Alexander III between 1174 and 1181.[1] Canon 45 repeats a principle enunciated by Pope Boniface VIII between 1294 and 1303.[2] Canon 1054 restates a norm laid down by Pope St. Pius X in his reform of the Roman Curia in the year 1908.[3]

As for the other norms of the aforesaid canons, they are to a certain extent identical with the tenets of the more common canonical opinions that prevailed throughout the period before the Code of Canon Law.[4] Hence, in many instances norms which once had only the authority that came from the pre-Code

[1] Cf. *supra,* pp. 42-43.

[2] Cf. *supra,* p. 48.

[3] Cf. *supra,* p. 54.

[4] Cf. *supra,* pp. 60-64, 69-71, 76-79, 80-82, 84-85.

commentators and their juridic arguments now have the force of law. As a result many of the doubts which were encountered in times past in this part of the Church's law on rescripts have been eliminated by the law itself. Moreover, the law which these norms express is today often explained and clarified by much of the canonical reasoning of authors who lived long before the promulgation of the Code in 1918.

Nonetheless, the codifiers of the present law have introduced some notable changes in the legal norms which govern the application of the principle *"si preces veritate nitantur."* The present law has for the most part, for instance, abolished the more severe doctrine enunciated by Pope Innocent III concerning the effect which maliciously false *preces* had upon the validity of rescripts.[5] It has clearly defined the meaning of subreption and obreption. It has made the invalidity caused by false *preces* to be effected *ipso iure* for rescripts of justice, as well as for rescripts of favor.

In treating the norms which govern the principle *"si preces veritate nitantur,"* the writer proposes to offer a commentary that begins with an analysis of canon 40 in the light of canon 39. He then proceeds to a consideration of the prescriptions of the three paragraphs of canon 42. Upon this consideration there follows a study of the norms contained in canons 45 and 1054 respectively. After that the principle of canon 41 is examined. Then there follows a discussion of the decision concerning the presence or absence of truth in the petitions. This discussion involves an analysis of the investigation that executors are to make in order to reach a decision concerning the truthfulness of the *preces*, together with a consideration of the basis for the aforesaid decision. There is included also the presentation of a practical solution to the problem caused by the presence of doubtful subreption and obreption, and a consideration of the remedies that are available for the sanating of the falsified *preces* and the rescripts vitiated because of untruthfulness in the petitions for them.

[5] Cf. *supra*, pp. 65-66.

CHAPTER IV

COMMENTARY ON CANON 40—THE TRUTH

Canon 40 of the Code of Canon Law is merely a cryptic rewording of the statement made by Pope Alexander III (1159-1181) when he officially and formally introduced the Roman Law principle *"si preces veritate nitantur"* into the Church's law on rescripts.[1] Canon 40 reads as follows:

> In omnibus rescriptis subintelligenda est, etsi non expressa, conditio: *Si preces veritate nitantur,* salvo praescripto can. 45, 1054.[2]

Abbo-Hannan, as a part of their commentary, translate this canon in the following manner:

> In all rescripts this condition must be understood even when not expressly stated: if the request be founded in truth, without prejudice however to canons 45 and 1054.[3]

Article 1. The Significance of the Condition "si preces veritate nitantur"

It has already been noted that the term *"preces"* in the clause *"si preces veritate nitantur"* signifies the formal petition that is presented for rescripts.[4] Such a petition is composed of three distinct parts, namely, the *pars narrativa,* the *pars postulativa,* and the *pars motiva.*[5] Hence, whatever is said in this article concerning the truth that is required in the *preces* must be applied to each of these three parts of petitions.[6]

[1] Cf. *supra,* p. 38.

[2] Cans. 36 to 62 are found in *Titulus IV, De rescriptis,* of *Liber I* of the Code of Canon Law. This title contains the Church's general legislation on rescripts.

[3] *The Sacred Canons* (2 vols., St. Louis and London: B. Herder Book Co., 1952), I, 73. The translated text is used with the permission of the publisher.

[4] Cf. *supra,* p. 17.

[5] For a description of these three parts, cf. *supra,* pp. 16-19.

[6] Michiels, *Normae Generales,* II, 353.

A. The Meaning of the Word "Truth"

What, then, is the "truth" on which the *preces* must be founded? The lawgiver does not define what he means by the term "truth" as it is used in the clause under consideration. Nonetheless, from the context in which he has placed this word, there can be no doubt that he intends to convey by it a general philosophical concept which is made specific by his own legal norms.

The general philosophical concept which the word "truth," as it is used in this condition, conveys is that of ontological or transcendental truth. Ontological truth is the conformity of a thing to the mind and will of God.[7] It is designated by philosophers as *"veritas rei"* or the truth of things.[8] This truth measures an essence by its conformity to the actual existence of a thing faced or related to all being and to God. Hence, it may be said that *the fact of existence* is the ultimate principle of ontological truth.[9]

Fundamental to the proper understanding of this description of ontological truth is the following consideration. St. Thomas Aquinas (1225-1274) defined truth as the equation of thought and thing, insofar as the intellect asserts that to be which is, and that not to be which is not.[10] Although truth always refers to an intellect, nevertheless its ultimate foundation is *res*, reality, actual existence, for truth is merely an affirmation or denial that things as stated by the mind are the same as they are in reality. Moreover, and this point is of the utmost importance here, truth, considered ontologically, is a transcendental aspect of being.

[7] Wilhelmsen, *Man's Knowledge of Reality* (Englewood Cliffs, N. J.: Prentice-Hall, Inc., 1956), p. 135.

[8] Gredt (1863-1940), *Elementa Philosophiae Aristotelico-Thomisticae* (2 vols., Vol. II, 10. ed., Friburgi Brisgoviae-Barcinone: Herder, 1953), II, 19.

[9] Wilhelmsen, *ibid.*, pp. 135 and 139.

[10] "Cum enim veritas intellectus sit adaequatio intellectus et rei, secundum quod intellectus dicit esse quod est, vel non esse quod non est. . . ."—*Quaestiones Disputatae De Veritate,* I, 1 c (ed. R. Spiazzi, Romae: Marietti, 1953). Cf. also Hoenen, *Reality and Judgment according to St. Thomas* (translated by H. Tiblier, Chicago: Henry Regnery Co., 1952), p. 313.

Hence, it can be identified with being. Ontological truth may be said, therefore, to be the truth of being, the truth of objective reality.

This truth of being, then, is what the lawgiver demands for the *preces;* that is, they must represent objective reality. This statement is substantiated by the fact that nowhere in his law does he admit good faith as a valid and sanating excuse in the face of nullifying false petitions. For the most part, in regard to the validity of rescripts, it makes little difference to him whether the lack of truth in the *preces* is due to good or to bad faith.[11] His primary interest is to have the *preces,* which represent an expression of the mind of the petitioner, in accord with objective reality. Ontological truth is the truth of objective reality.

Hence the legislator is not focusing canon 40 on the truth of judgment or logical truth. When he states in his law that a petition must be true, he is not interested so much in the subjective attitudes of the petitioner as he is in the objective existence or non-existence of the facts and causes alleged in the *preces.* That is to say, the lawgiver requires an account of the prospective beneficiary's case as it exists objectively. He wants recitals that are objectively true.[12]

This general concept of ontological truth is the substratum which the lawgiver demands for the *preces* if they are to be truthful. In making this demand a part of his law, however, he specifies the subject matter which ontological truth must represent in the petitions. This specification is effected by the norms of canon 42, §§ 1 and 2. Canon 42, § 1, confines the necessity of truthful *preces* to the expression of truth in those matters the mention of which is demanded for validity by the *stylus Curiae.*[13] Paragraph two of this canon limits the need for truth in the reasons or causes presented in the petitions to the motivating

[11] Cf. Van Hove, *De Rescriptis,* p. 136. Cf. cans. 991, § 1, and 2249, § 2, however, for instances in which bad faith does make a difference in this regard. Cf. *infra,* pp. 134-137.

[12] Bouscaren-Ellis, *Canon Law, A Text and Commentary* (2. ed., Milwaukee: Bruce, 1951), p. 58 (hereafter cited as *Canon Law*).

[13] Cf. *infra,* pp. 137-147.

reasons. More precisely, it calls for truth in the single final cause if only one such reason is offered, or in at least one of the motivating reasons if more than one final cause is alleged.[14]

Hence, when it is understood properly, the word "truth" in the clause *"si preces veritate nitantur"* denotes ontological truth concerning the subject matter that is prescribed by the Church's law on rescripts. Rodrigo states this conclusion in these words: "VERITAS PRECUM *intelligitur earum obiectiva conformitas cum realitate de iure exprimenda in negotio circa quod preces versantur."* [15]

Since the subject matter of the ontological truth that is required in the *preces* for rescripts is carefully specified by the lawgiver himself, it follows that the condition under consideration here is not vitiated by any and every lack of truth in petitions. Only when there is absent all or part of the truth that is required by law to be present does this condition go unfulfilled.

In practice, then, the truth that is required by law in the *preces* can be violated in two ways, one negative, the other positive. It is violated in a negative manner by subreption or the *"reticentia veri."* [16] It is transgressed in a positive way by obreption or the *"expositio falsi."* [17]

B. The Import of the Verb *"nitantur"*

It is noteworthy that the only verb expressed in the condition *"si preces veritate nitantur"* is *"nitantur."* This word is a form of the verb *"nitor, niti,"* meaning to be founded on, to rest upon, to depend upon.[18] Accordingly, by using only this verb in the

[14] Cf. *infra*, pp. 168-171.

[15] *Tractatus de Legibus*, p. 558.

[16] The matter of subreption is the content of can. 42, § 1, and it will be treated fully in the commentary on that canon. Cf. *infra*, pp. 126-132, 137-168.

[17] The matter of obreption is the content of can. 42, § 2, and it will be treated fully in the commentary on that canon. Cf. *infra*, pp. 126-132, 168-173.

[18] *Cassell's Latin Dictionary*, p. 365.

stated condition, the legislator shows that he is demanding simply the *existence* of truthful petitions. He does not, therefore, make the validity of rescripts depend upon an investigation into the truthfulness of their *preces,* unless such an investigation is called for by a special or distinct clause attached to them.[19]

C. The Force of the Particle *"si"*

The particle *"si"* also deserves attention in this consideration of the significance of the clause *"si preces veritate nitantur,"* for in the light of canon 39 this particle establishes the exact nature of this condition. Canon 39 reads as follows:

> Conditiones in rescriptis tunc tantum essentiales pro eorumdem validitate censentur, cum per particulas *si, dummodo,* vel aliam eiusdem significationis exprimuntur.

Accordingly, since the condition in question, a necessary condition in the text of every rescript, is introduced by means of the particle *"si,"* it must be considered to be a condition that is, as a rule, essential to the validity of rescripts.[20] Consequently, if the

[19] Cf. Van Hove, *op. cit.*, p. 134, and O'Neill, *Papal Rescripts of Favor,* p. 117.

[20] Conditions in rescripts may be either essential or accidental. They are essential if the validity of the rescripts depends upon their fulfillment or observance. Hence, the non-fulfillment of such conditions deprives rescripts of all force. Conditions in rescripts are accidental if their fulfillment affects only the lawfulness of the letters, not their validity. That is to say, when conditions are accidental, their non-observance does not prevent the letters from being valid. Their non-fulfillment, however, renders the acts done in virtue of the rescripts unlawful. This same distinction between essential and accidental conditions applies to those conditions in rescripts which concern the execution of the letters.—Cf. Maroto, *Institutiones,* I, n. 284, ad I.

Some may object to the direct mode of argument which the writer has used above to establish that the condition in question is an essential condition. Indeed, there can be some doubt as to whether or not can. 39 can be rightfully interpreted as ruling that all conditions in rescripts which are introduced by means of the particle *"si"* are automatically essential in nature. Before the Code, however, it was the more common opinion that the particle *"si"* did always indicate that the condition which it introduced in rescripts was an essential one. Likewise, such leading present-day canonists as Michiels and Van Hove maintain that can. 39

preces are not founded on truth as required by the law, the rescript for which they have been presented is invalid and completely lacking in force. Hence the necessity of having truthful *preces,* as essential to the validity of rescripts, arises from the will of the legislator.

The basic necessity, however, of having truthful petitions, although it is not always directed to the validity of the rescripts, arises *ex rei natura.*[21] It must be remembered that, in granting a rescript, the superior ordinarily acts only upon the facts, circumstances, and reasons which are offered in the petition to describe and explain the case to be covered by the requested rescript. In a word, the rescript is consequent to the petitioner's *preces.* It is issued precisely to cover the case as it is proposed in the petition. Indeed, the rescript operates only on that basis. When a petitioner introduces falsehood into his *preces,* he defaces the nature of the subject matter to be stated in the rescript. In other words, he presents to the superior a case that, depending on the nature of the falsehood incorporated into the petition, is substantially or accidentally different from his case as it is in objective reality. Consequently, the case which the superior intends to cover with the rescript which he issues is not really the petitioner's case. Needless to say, the factor of having a substantial or an accidental difference between the case as it is in reality and as it is described in the *preces* naturally has an important effect upon the decision concerning whether the rescript involved is valid or invalid.[22]

Furthermore, a consideration which does much to explain the importance of having truthful *preces,* as far as rescripts are concerned, is the presumption that a superior in granting his rescripts intends to act reasonably and truly voluntarily. This

---

can be safely interpreted as enunciating the aforesaid more common pre-Code opinion concerning the force of the particle "*si*" in conditions in rescripts.—Cf. Michiels, *Normae Generales,* II, 348, and Van Hove, *De Rescriptis,* p. 123.

[21] Blat (1870-1943), *Commentarium Textus Codicis Iuris Canonici* (5 vols. in 7, Vol. I, Romae, 1921), I, 134 (hereafter cited as *Commentarium*).

[22] Cf. *infra,* pp. 131-132, 137-141, 170-172.

presumption is not new to canonical thinking, for, besides the teachings of philosophy concerning man's mode of action as a rational being, the Roman Law took definite precautions to enable the Emperor to issue his rescripts in accordance with right reason.[23] There can be no doubt that the Church followed the Roman Law on rescripts until she had formulated her own law.[24]

Moreover, there is certainly nothing in the ecclesiastical law which militates against the presumption under consideration. Rather to the contrary, the following norms have long been fundamental principles in the canonical jurisprudence on rescripts: *"substantia rescripti dependet a voluntate concedentis"* [25] and *"deficiente ea [voluntate concedentis], vires non obtinent [rescripta]."* [26] Yet, only when the *preces* for his rescripts are founded on truth can a superior issue his replies reasonably and truly voluntarily. Otherwise his act of granting rescripts would be neither reasonable nor, indeed, truly voluntary—to say nothing of its being most imprudent.

Toso (d. 1946) drove this point home very forcefully and concisely. For that reason his line of argument is quoted here in its entirety.

> Quare oporteat preces veritate inniti hinc habes, quod Princeps rescripto aut ius singulare constituit contra vel praeter ius commune aut particulare (rescripta gratiae), aut idem ius definit, si controversum, vel, si violatum sit restituit (rescripta iustitiae). Verum, quemadmodum lex non nisi *rationabiliter* ferri potest, ita etiam nonnisi rationabiliter potest a iure statuto discedi aut ius controversum vel violatum definiri vel

[23] "Instrumentorum exempla non prosit precibus adiunxisse, sed necesse sit eorum in supplicatione vim exprimi, ut responsuro principi vera precatio rem aperiat cognoscendam, solis, cum necessitas exegerit, verbis precibus inserendis, quorum de sensu inter partes ita dubitari contigerit, ut etiam merito nostrum expectetur iudicium."—C. (1, 19) 8—*Cod. Iust.*

[24] Cf. *supra*, p. 39.

[25] Fagnanus (d. 1678), *Commentaria,* Lib. I, tit. III, ad c. 20, X, *de rescriptis,* I, 3, n. 62.

[26] Gonzalez-Tellez (d. 1649), *Commentaria,* Lib. I, tit. III, ad c. 20, X, *de rescriptis,* I, 3, n. 17.

> restitui: discedere autem Princeps rationabiliter non potest sine causa, quae et adesse debet et non esse futilis; neque potest rationabiliter definire vel restituere, nisi constet qua de causa ius controvertatur vel quemadmodum sit violatum. Idque ex precibus constare debet: sed constare non potest nisi preces veritate nitantur.[27]
>
> Iamvero, uti [sic] Princeps oratoris preces excipiat, ut nempe eius voluntas ad preces oratoris accedat, sive gratiam concedendo sive ius dicendo, prout oratori est in votis, id faciat oportet, nedum rationabiliter sed etiam et praesertim voluntarie, et ideo non ex ignorantia aut errore, sive id contingat ex dolo sive ex simplicitate oratoris: non enim dicimur velle id, quod per errorem aut ignorantiam nescimus. Oportet igitur preces veritate nitantur. Et quia id verum non est, cui aut aliquid veri sit detractum aut additum falsi, hinc invalidum esse oportet rescriptum, in cuius precibus, ex supplici libello desumptis, aut verum reperiatur esse reticitum (subreptio) aut falsum expositum (obreptio); quemadmodum enim subreptio ignorantiam causat, ita errorem obreptio.[28]

In summary, then, it may be said that the condition *"si preces veritate nitantur"* is an expression of the legislator's will which is directed to the very validity of rescripts. The truth which the lawgiver demands in this essential condition is ontological truth within the bounds that the law itself specifies. The mere existence of such truth is sufficient to satisfy this demand. The necessity of this condition arises from the will of the legislator, which is undoubtedly motivated in this matter by the presumption that a superior, in granting his rescripts, intends to act reasonably and truly voluntarily.

Article 2. The General Principle of Canon 40

Because of the nature of the condition *"si preces veritate nitantur,"* the lawmaker has legislated that, as a general principle or rule, this essential condition must be understood in all rescripts, even if it is not expressly stated therein. Consequently, he has left no room for argument about its presence or absence on the grounds of its not having been set down in so

[27] *Commentaria Minora*, I, 120.

[28] Toso, *ibid.*, p. 125. Cf. also Michiels, *Normae Generales*, II, 355-356; Rodrigo, *Tractatus de Legibus*, pp. 558-559; Cicognani, *Canon Law*, p. 711.

many words in rescripts.[29] Whether it is expressed or not, it is always in effect.[30]

A. The Application of the General Principle of Canon 40

Moreover, there can be no doubt that this general principle of canon 40 is of strict obligation in relation to all rescripts emanating from the Holy See and from ordinaries. All the commentators who give detailed consideration to this matter apply canon 40 to such rescripts *ex rigore iuris*.

There is no such unanimity on the part of the authors, however, when they deal with rescripts which are issued *iure proprio* by superiors who are not included in the expression "Holy See" and who are not ordinaries. The same lack of accord exists among the commentators when they treat of rescripts granted by delegates of the Holy See and of ordinaries. In a word, the problem is this: does canon 40 really apply to these aforesaid rescripts at all, and, if it does, how does it apply to them? A satisfactory solution to this problem is most important because in concrete cases it involves the rescripts issued by such persons as Apostolic Delegates, chancery officials, pastors, and the superiors of non-exempt clerical institutes of pontifical right, all of whom are supposed in this discussion not to be ordinaries.

Actually, the problem in question arises from the general position which the different canonists have assumed in relation to the real ambit of the norms of *Titulus IV, De rescriptis*, in *Liber I* of the Code of Canon Law, for the legislator has placed canon 40 in this title. So, when commentators establish a general stand in reference to the scope of Title IV and make no exceptions to it in regard to canon 40, they must be including this canon in their over-all teaching on the whole title. Accordingly, then, one can discern three different positions which have

29 For the condition *"si preces veritate nitantur"* other conditions with the same meaning are sometimes substituted, e.g., *"si ita est," "si vera sunt exposita,"* and *"veris existentibus narratis."*—O'Neill, *Papal Rescripts of Favor*, p. 117.

30 "Porro, quia expressio clausulae nullam inducit novam conditionem, est habenda ut monitio, quae est intelligenda iuxta regulas generales iuris."—Van Hove, *De Rescriptis*, p. 134.

been subscribed to by canonists in reference to the obligatory application of the canons of Title IV, including canon 40, to rescripts other than those issued by the Holy See and by other ordinaries.

First of all, Van Hove maintained it as a general principle that these canons are to be applied only to rescripts issued directly by the Holy See and by other ordinaries. They have no application whatsoever, therefore, to rescripts issued by other persons. He expressed two reasons for taking this position. His first reason was that in canons 36, § 1, 43, 44, and 61, where the lawgiver refers expressly to authors of rescripts, mention is made only of the Holy See and of other ordinaries. His second reason can be stated in this way: the canons of Title IV, as they appeared in the schema of the Code's Book I that was sent to ordinaries in 1912, dealt solely with papal rescripts; these canons in the Code itself in its present form are extended so as to regulate the rescripts of other ordinaries, but not those of anyone else.[31]

Therefore it must be concluded that, as Van Hove considered it, the norm of canon 40 with its demand for truthful *preces* applies only to rescripts issued directly and immediately by the Holy See or by other ordinaries. For him rescripts other than these are outside the scope of this canon.

Rodrigo holds a different position in this question of the comprehension of the phrase *"in omnibus rescriptis"* in canon 40. He maintains that the norms of Title IV apply inherently (*per se*) and strictly (*ex rigore iuris*) only to rescripts issued directly by

[31] "De ambitu normarum tituli IV, notandum est illas applicandas esse solis rescriptis quibus *gratia* etiam ad lites per *Sedem Apostolicam* vel per *Ordinarium conceditur,* non solutionibus dubiorum iuris, quae dantur ad petitionem alicuius, neque concessionibus gratiarum, in specie dispensationum, quae dantur ab aliis personis ex potestate propria aut ex speciali concessione.

"Alii Superiores, gaudentes potestate iurisdictionis, in concedendis gratiis quas *proprio iure* conferre possunt, debent servare regulas a iure statutas, quibus facultates eorum determinantur et circumscribuntur. Dispensatio ab illis concessa sine causa erit invalida (can. 84, §1). Qui utuntur potestate *delegata* debent servare formam mandati ad normam can. 203, §§ 1 et 2, ad licite et interdum ad valide agendum."—Van Hove, *De Rescriptis,* pp. 81-82.

the Holy See and by other ordinaries. These norms regulate the rescripts of other persons only *ex analogia,* unless other provision be made.[32] To defend his position, Rodrigo, like Van Hove, points to "canons 36, § 1, 43 s., and 61," and concludes from their content that there is no solid basis in law for applying *ex rigore iuris* the norms of Title IV to rescripts of persons who are not ordinaries. In the Rule of Law: *"Accessorium naturam sequi congruit principalis,"* [33] however, he does find a basis for applying these norms analogously to such rescripts, especially to such as are issued by delegates of the Holy See and of ordinaries.

It is to be noted, nonetheless, that Rodrigo qualifies his position on this analagous application by saying: *"dum aliud non constet."* [34] Unfortunately, he does not explain this qualification. Yet, because he does make it, the present writer is not convinced that Rodrigo would not hold that canon 40 is meant to apply to all rescripts by whomever they are issued. It is possible that the role which truthful *preces* have in the reasonable and truly voluntary granting of rescripts is one of the circumstances contemplated by him in the qualification *"dum aliud non constet."* [35]

A third opinion concerning the ambit of the canons of the Code's Title IV in Book I is that expressed by Michiels. This author states very clearly that the legislator's general norms on rescripts apply *ex rigore iuris* to all rescripts, no matter who their author may be.[36] The present writer subscribes to this opinion because of the line of argument which Michiels presents to support his teaching in this matter.

[32] Rodrigo, *Tractatus de Legibus,* pp. 525-526. Coronata (*Institutiones,* I, 72) agrees with Rodrigo on this point.

[33] Reg. 42, R. J., in VI°.

[34] "Ex analogia recte adhuc eaedem normae [i.e., eae Tituli IV] applicandae videntur, dum aliud non constet. . . ."—Rodrigo, *op. cit.,* p. 525. Coronata does not qualify his position in this matter.

[35] Cf. Rodrigo, *op. cit.,* p. 558, where he states: *"Ratio necessitatis* huius [i.e., precum verarum] est tum ut Superior cum scientia ac prudentia necessaria dispenset, tum ubi mala fides intercesserit, quia ut aiebat *Dictum* Grat. C. 25, q. 2, c. 16: 'mendax precator carere debet impetratis.'" Cf. also *supra,* pp. 116-118.

[36] Michiels, *Normae Generales,* II, 292-293.

His reasoning follows this line of thought. First, in regard to rescripts issued by delegates of the Holy See and of other ordinaries, he maintains that the very nature of their commission as delegates demands that their acts as delegates be governed by the same rules as are the acts of those who commissioned them.[37] Secondly, in relation to rescripts granted *iure proprio* by superiors who are not included in the expression "Holy See" and who are not ordinaries, he makes the following observations. Title IV in Book I of the Code contains dispositions

> quae fundantur in ipsa rei natura quibusve determinantur aut circumscribuntur cujuslibet Superioris ecclesiastici vel speciatim ejus, de quo in concreto agitur, facultates et jura.[38]

Moreover, even the purely positive norms of this title are used by the lawmaker to legislate in an absolute manner about rescripts in general. The fact that in several canons the legislator makes mention only of the Holy See and of other ordinaries as authors of rescripts does not necessarily mean that he is restricting this whole title in Book I of the Code to rescripts that are granted by these authorities.

From this line of reasoning Michiels draws two conclusions. On the one hand, he holds that it has not been shown that it is the positive will of the lawmaker to restrict the canons to rescripts granted directly by the Holy See and by ordinaries. On the other hand, he concludes that there is no juridic reason why the legislator should have made such a restriction.

According to Michiels, then, canon 40 with its demand for truthful *preces* must be applied *ex rigore iuris* to all rescripts by whomever they may be granted.

B. Canons 45 and 1054

Immediately after laying down his general rule concerning the necessity of having truthful *preces* for all rescripts, the legislator qualifies it with the clause *"salvo praescripto can. 45, 1054."*[39]

[37] This reasoning certainly seems to be supported by the Rule of Law which states: "Qui facit per alium est perinde ac si faciat per seipsum."—Reg. 72, R. J., in VI°.

[38] Michiels, *ibid.*, p. 292.

[39] Cf. can. 40, and *supra*, p. 111.

The content of canon 45 is that whenever the clause *"motu proprio"* is appended to rescripts which are granted upon someone's petition, these are valid even though in the petition there is withheld some truth which otherwise must necessarily be expressed; but they are not valid if their final cause, when only one is proposed, is false, without prejudice to the provision of canon 1054. Hence, the effect of this canon is to protect *motu proprio* issued rescripts from the invalidating force of subreption and obreption which is indirectly equivalent to subreption, as that invalidation is prescribed in canon 42, § 1.[40] It does not, however, exclude such rescripts from the nullifying effect of obreption, as that effect is set down in canon 42, § 2. In this latter respect rescripts issued *motu proprio* differ from those which convey dispensations from the minor matrimonial impediments.

Rescripts conveying those dispensations are dealt with in canon 1054. This canon provides that a dispensation granted from a minor matrimonial impediment is not invalidated by any defect of subreption or obreption as envisioned in canon 42, §§ 1 and 2, respectively. So the lawgiver has explicitly excepted these rescripts from the invalidating effect of canon 42.[41]

There can be no doubt, therefore, that the clause *"salvo praescripto can. 45, 1054"* in canon 40 does effect a notable qualification upon the general rule which is therein expressed. The question, however, is this: are canons 45 and 1054, besides being exceptions to canon 42, also true exceptions to the general rule of canon 40? [42]

The vast majority of the present-day commentators answer this question in the affirmative.[43] Vlaming (d. 1935)-Bender

[40] Cf. *infra*, pp. 180-187. The sanating force of can. 45 does not extend to subreption or obreption in the *pars postulativa* of the *preces*.—Cf. *infra* p. 187.

[41] The sanating force of can. 1054, however, does not extend to subreption or obreption in the *pars postulativa* of the *preces* for the above-mentioned dispensations.—Cf. *infra*, pp. 194-196.

[42] Cans. 45 and 1054 are treated in this place only in their relationship to can. 40. For a more detailed commentary on them, cf. *infra*, pp. 180-187, 188-199, respectively.

[43] Cf. e.g., Regatillo, *Institutiones Iuris Canonici*, I, 110; Toso, *Commentaria Minora*, I, 120; Rodrigo, *Tractatus de Legibus*, p. 558; Chelodi,

state in so many words that the condition *"si preces veritate nitantur"* is not understood in rescripts conveying dispensations from minor matrimonial impediments.[44]

Michiels, however, maintains that canons 45 and 1054 are really not true exceptions to the principle expressed in canon 40. Rather, canon 45 is an exception to the invalidating effect of canon 42, § 1, and canon 1054 is an exception to the nullifying force of canon 42, §§ 1 and 2. Michiels expresses his position thus:

> Notetur autem, in can. 45 et 1054 non haberi veram exceptionem a principio canonis 40, sed potius a principio in can. 42 § 1 et 2 statuto; quoad omnia enim rescripta, etiam illa quae in can. 45 et 1054 considerantur, subintelligitur conditio "si preces veritate nitantur", saltem qua *praeceptiva* servanda; quoad ultima tamen, vel partialiter (in casu can. 45) vel totaliter (in casu can. 1054) tollitur effectus *irritativus* vi can. 42 § 1 et 2 regulariter huic conditioni adnexus.[45]

This writer cannot agree with the position of Vlaming-Bender on the question under consideration here; nor can he agree completely with that taken by Michiels. First of all, in the light of canon 2361 he believes that canon 40 is intended to establish a norm that affects not only the validity of rescripts but also their lawfulness. Secondly, he submits that in order to reach an entirely correct conclusion concerning whether or not canons 45 and 1054 are true exceptions to the general principle of canon 40, a distinction must be drawn between that which canon 40 demands for the validity of rescripts and that which it requires for their lawfulness. On the one hand, there can be no doubt that the condition *"si preces veritate nitantur,"* as it is stated in the general rule of canon 40, is an essential condition.[46] This rule establishes the aforesaid condition as one the observance of which is necessary for the validity of rescripts *in general.* Canon 45, however, derogates from this general rule insofar as it

---

Ius Canonicum de Personis, p. 132; Maroto, *Institutiones,* I, n. 284, ad II; Van Hove, *De Rescriptis,* p. 135; Blat, *Commentarium* I, 134.

44 *Praelectiones,* p. 368.

45 *Normae Generales,* II, 356.

46 Cf. *supra,* pp. 115-118.

indicates that the condition in question is not essential as far as the *pars narrativa* of the *preces* for *motu proprio* granted rescripts is concerned.[47] Canon 1054 puts aside the essential necessity of having the truth in the *pars narrativa* and the *pars motiva* of the petitions for the rescripts which it treats.[48] It seems to the writer, therefore, that these two canons must be regarded as true exceptions to the general rule which canon 40 expresses concerning the absolute necessity of having truthful *preces* for the *validity* of *all* rescripts.

On the other hand, it is likewise not to be doubted that it is the intention of the lawgiver that the truth always be expressed in the petitions for rescripts, even though he does not demand its presence in every case under pain of invalidity. Truth is a fundamental and expected basis for all serious transactions carried on by men. What is more, in canon 2361 the legislator has authorized appropriate punishment for *all* petitioners who commit wilful deceit in their *preces* to the Holy See and to local ordinaries. He in no way excepts from the provisions of that canon petitioners either of rescripts that are later issued *motu proprio* or of rescripts that convey dispensations from the minor matrimonial impediments. Accordingly, since it is in canon 40 that the lawmaker lays down his general requirement for truth in the *preces* for rescripts, this writer agrees with Michiels when he says that the condition *"si preces veritate nitantur"* is established in that canon as a requirement for the *lawfulness* of *all* rescripts without exception. Hence, this condition is to be understood for lawfulness in all rescripts, even in those that are issued *motu proprio* and in those that convey dispensations from minor matrimonial impediments.[49]

[47] Cf. *infra*, pp. 181-183.

[48] Cf. *infra*, p. 194.

[49] Apropos of the foregoing discussion, the problem arises of reconciling the prescriptions of cans. 45 and 1054 with what has already been said on pp. 116-118 concerning the important role which truthful *preces* have in the reasonable and truly voluntary granting of rescripts. This problem is considered below on pp. 183, 192-194.

CHAPTER V

COMMENTARY ON CANON 42—SUBREPTION, OBREPTION

Canon 42 is a most basic law in the Church's general legislation on the truth that is required in the *preces* for rescripts. Its importance lies in the fact that its norms bring into focus the exact meaning and the precise extent of the invalidating force of the condition *"si preces veritate nitantur."* [1]

The text of canon 42 reads as follows:

> § 1. Reticentia veri, seu subreptio, in precibus non obstat quominus rescriptum vim habeat ratumque sit, dummodo expressa fuerint quae de stylo Curiae sunt ad validitatem exprimenda.
>
> § 2. Nec obstat expositio falsi, seu obreptio, dummodo vel unica causa proposita vel ex pluribus propositis una saltem motiva vera sit.
>
> § 3. Vitium obreptionis vel subreptionis in una tantum parte rescripti aliam non infirmat, si una simul plures gratiae per rescriptum concedantur.

Article 1. General Commentary

There can be little doubt that the legislator, in wording this canon as he did, had a twofold purpose in mind. First of all, he must have intended to lay down a single rule that would be so clear as to remove, as far as possible, all anxieties and abuses that might become connected with the application of canon 40.[2] Secondly, he must have wanted to settle, once and for all, many of the controversies which had arisen among pre-Code canonists apropos of the application of the principle *"si preces veritate nitantur."* [3] That the lawgiver has accomplished this twofold

[1] Cf. Cicognani, *Canon Law,* p. 714, and Toso, *Commentaria Minora,* I, 122.

[2] Cf. Van Hove, *De Rescriptis,* p. 144, and Michiels, *Normae Generales,* II, 360.

[3] Cf. Van Hove, *loc. cit.*

purpose with canon 42 can be seen, it is hoped, from the following remarks which are offered by way of general commentary upon this canon.

A. Subreption and Obreption in General [4]

In canon 42, §§ 1 and 2, the legislator draws a clear distinction between subreption and obreption, the two defects that can violate the truth that is required in the *preces* for rescripts. In the light of the history of this part of the Church's law on rescripts this distinction represents a step forward in ecclesiastical jurisprudence. Until the Code the lawgiver himself had never reserved either term to signify exclusively either a falsehood which originated through a suppression of the truth or that which came about through a positive statement of an untruth.[5] In the Code,

[4] Before offering his general remarks upon subreption and obreption, the writer wishes to make it clear that in this particular part of his work, that is, under A., he will consider these defects as they are in themselves. More precisely, he proposes in this place to examine solely the nature of subreption and obreption, especially as that nature is defined by the definitions which the lawmaker himself has given of these two defects, and as it is described through the elaborations which the commentators have made upon the legislator's definitions. He intends to prescind, as far as possible, from the effects which the lawmaker has attached to these defects. These effects will be examined and explained later in the more particular commentary on the first two paragraphs of can. 42.—Cf. *infra*, pp. 137-144, 168-173. The writer has two reasons for adopting this plan. The first is the fact that the lawgiver himself in can. 42, §§ 1 and 2, treats not only the effects of subreption and obreption but also the nature of these defects. His second reason is the fact that he has found that some authors tend to be confusing in their treatment of subreption and obreption simply because they do not always indicate when they are talking about these defects in themselves and when they are speaking of them as invalidating forces upon rescripts.

[5] Several pre-Code commentators noted that the reason why the legislator himself made no distinction between subreption and obreption was that both defects produced the same effect upon rescripts. Following the example of the lawgiver, not a few of the authors who wrote before the promulgation of the Code used these terms indiscriminately to signify the presence of falsehood in rescripts, no matter how the falsehood had arisen. Nonetheless, many of the pre-Code commentators, especially the later ones, understood the two terms to mean what they now do in the present law of the Church. Cf. *supra*, pp. 58-60.

however, subreption means a *"reticentia veri,"* that is, a suppression, a concealment, or a non-exposition of the truth. Obreption signifies an *"expositio falsi,"* that is, the positive statement of a falsehood.

In defining subreption as a *"reticentia veri"* and obreption as an *"expositio falsi,"* the lawgiver is adhering to the basic notions conveyed by the literal meanings of these two words. Both are derived from the same root, namely, *repere,* meaning to creep or crawl.[6] The specific literal meanings of these words come from the prefixes which are attached to this common root. These prefixes, namely, *sub* or *subtus* meaning under, and *ob* meaning, in this instance, over or against, when joined to *repere,* give a graphic description of the manner in which subreption and obreption, respectively, violate the truth that is required in the *preces.* That is to say, subreption, on the one hand, connotes a creeping under the truth. Hence, it indicates a *negative* violation of the truth, precisely through a concealment or suppression of the truth. Obreption, on the other hand, connotes a creeping over or against the truth. It indicates, therefore, a *positive* violation of the truth through the expression of a falsehood that is contrary to objective reality.[7] Hence, the literal meanings of the terms "subreption" and "obreption" lend themselves to the definitions which the legislator has given to these words in canon 42, §§ 1 and 2.

The authors have elaborated upon the cryptic definitions of subreption and obreption which the lawgiver himself has given. In regard to subreption their elaboration is centered upon the word *"veri."* Vlaming-Bender sum up the results of this elaboration by defining subreption in this way: *"Subreptio est reticentia veri, quod ex rei natura vel ex lege aut de stylo Curiae exprimendum erat. . . ."* [8] Hence, in present-day terminology a sur-

[6] *Cassell's Latin Dictionary,* p. 482.

[7] "Subreptio est actus subrependi (a *subtus* et *repo*) et proprie significat *subtus* et clam serpere, significatione quadam negativa."—Toso, *Commentaria Minora,* I, 122. "Obreptio est actus obrependi (ab *ob* et *repo*) et proprie significat *contra* et clam serpere, significatione quadam positiva contrarietatis."—Toso, *ibid.,* p. 123. Cf. also Cicognani, *Canon Law,* p. 710.

[8] *Praelectiones,* p. 285.

reptitious petition is one which is marred by the suppression or the concealment of some fact or circumstance about the petitioner, about the prospective beneficiary if he is not the petitioner, and/or about the relevant case, the mentioning of which fact or circumstance is needed in order to make the *preces* correspond faithfully to reality.[9] Therefore, not every act of subreption alluded to in canon 42, § 1, begets the invalidity of rescripts.[10]

In reference to obreption, the commentators enlarge upon the legislator's definition of this term by specifying the possible objects of false statements in the petitions. Rodrigo presents their doctrine in this matter by stating:

> alter [defectus est] positivus, qui dicitur *obreptio,* atque stat in expositione falsi, circa ea quae ex natura rei aut ex Curiae stylo sunt in dato negotio aperienda ne rescribens graviter erret aut decipiatur.[11]

Thus, today an obreptitious petition is one which contains the allegation or suggestion in the *preces* of some fact, circumstance, or cause which is positively false and altogether contrary to reality.[12] Accordingly, not every act of obreption referred to in canon 42 begets the invalidity of rescripts.[13]

Because of the nature of subreption, as it appears from the foregoing definition, it may be stated as a general rule that this defect will be found only in the *pars narrativa* and the *pars postulativa* of the petitions.[14] A petitioner is most likely to conceal the truth concerning some circumstance which should be set down in either of these parts, especially when that circumstance is known to stand in the way of his obtaining the rescript that he is requesting.[15]

It is difficult to see, however, how the *pars motiva* of the *preces*

[9] Michiels, *Normae Generales,* II, 353.

[10] Cf. *infra,* pp. 137-141.

[11] *Tractatus de Legibus,* p. 558.

[12] Michiels, *loc. cit.*

[13] Cf. *infra,* pp. 168-173.

[14] For a description of these two parts of the *preces,* cf. *supra,* pp. 16-19.

[15] Cf. Toso, *Commentaria Minora,* I, 125.

can be infected with subreption. It must be remembered that, aside from the positive legislation of the Church, the presence of a reason or a cause for the granting of a rescript is demanded if a superior is at all to issue his reply reasonably. Nonetheless, the validity of rescripts does not inherently (*per se*) depend on whether or not the petitioner mentions such a cause. That is to say, in the last analysis and as far as the validity of rescripts is concerned, the burden of having a sufficient reason for which to grant rescripts rests primarily upon the superior who issues them, not upon the petitioner.[16] Hence, a petitioner is not guilty of subreption if he conceals either the motivating or the impelling reasons which he can truthfully offer to obtain the rescript that he seeks. If such concealment takes place, the petitioner is running the risk in most cases that the superior will refuse to accede to his request.[17] Indeed, even if the superior does grant the rescript without having any sufficient cause whatsoever for doing so, it is true that the rescript thus issued may be invalid. Its invalidity, however, is not due intrinsically (*per se*) to the fact that the petitioner has not offered a true final cause in his *preces*. Rather it arises from the will of the legislator himself, as is the case whenever there are involved dispensations from the law of the Church, granted by superiors subordinate to the supreme ecclesiastical lawgiver.[18] Or else the invalidity of the rescript is due to a *defectus voluntatis* on the part of the superior to issue rescripts without a sufficient reason for so doing.[19] *"Deficiente ea*

[16] Cf. Michiels who states: "Dum *subreptio,* juridice loquendo, generatim verificatur in sola petitionis parte expositiva,—quippe cum subreptio audiatur reticentia veri necessario exprimendi et causae, etsi ad rationabilem rescripti concessionem ex parte rescribentis sint necessariae, ex parte oratoris tamen non sint ad validitatem exprimendae. . . ."—*Ibid.,* p. 364. Cf. also can. 84, § 1.

[17] Cf., however, can. 1054. Apropos of rescripts conveying dispensations from minor matrimonial impediments, it must be noted that such dispensations are granted *"ex rationabilibus causis a S. Sede probatis"* and not necessarily because of the reason or reasons which the petitioner alleges. Cf. *infra,* pp. 192-194.

[18] "A lege ecclesiastica ne dispensatur sine iusta et rationabili causa, habita ratione gravitatis legis a qua dispensatur; alias dispensatio ab inferiore data illicita et invalida est."—Can. 84, § 1.

[19] Cf. Michiels, *ibid.,* p. 741, and Toso, *loc. cit.*

[*i.e., voluntate concedentis*], *vires non obtinent* [*rescripta*]."[20]

Unlike subreption, obreption is of its very nature such that one may find this defect in any of the three parts of the *preces*. Obreption is most likely to appear, however, in the *pars motiva* of the petitions.[21] The fact that obreption occurs most frequently in the causes which petitioners allege in their *preces* undoubtedly explains why the lawgiver has explicitly related this defect only to those reasons when he legislates concerning the effect of obreption upon rescripts.[22]

It would be erroneous, however, for one to conclude that, inasmuch as the legislator speaks of obreption only in relation to the *pars motiva* of the petitions, he has made no provision for the defect of positive untruthfulness when it appears in the other two parts of the *preces*. Actually the statement of a falsehood can indirectly amount to a suppression of the truth that should be expressed. For instance, if a non-Catholic petitioner falsely asserts that he is a Catholic, he is concealing or suppressing the fact that he is a non-Catholic. Likewise, a baptized person who erroneously asserts that he has never been baptized is concealing the true fact of his baptism. Hence, there are times when obreption can be correctly reduced to subreption. In such instances the resulting lack of truth in the *preces* is governed by the principles which the lawgiver has made explicitly for subreption in canon 42, § 1.[23] For all practical purposes, the legislator in canon 42, § 1, has combined obreption and subreption of the necessary circumstances under the single term of subreption of the necessary circumstances.[24]

A final consideration in this general treatment of subreption

[20] Gonzalez-Tellez, *Commentaria,* Lib. I, tit. III, ad c. 20, X, *de rescriptis,* I, 3, n. 17.

[21] Sipos (1875-1949), *Enchiridion Iuris Canonici, ad usum scholarum et privatorum* (6. ed., recognovit L. Gálos, Romae: Orbis Catholicus—Herder, 1954), p. 31; Michiels, *ibid.,* p. 364.

[22] Cf. can. 42, § 2.

[23] "Subreptio autem fieri potest vel reticendo simpliciter veritatem exprimendam, vel allegando falsitatem circa ea quae ad validitatem sunt alleganda."—Van Hove, *De Rescriptis,* p. 145.

[24] O'Neill, *Papal Rescripts of Favor,* p. 133.

and obreption concerns the distinction which the authors draw between *substantial* and *accidental* subreption and obreption. These defects are substantial when their presence invalidates the rescript that is affected by them. They are accidental when they do not affect the validity of the rescript in which they occur.[25]

According to the norm of canon 42, § 1, then, subreption is substantial only when there is the suppression of those facts and circumstances the mention of which is required for the validity of rescripts by the *stylus Curiae*. In virtue of the principle of canon 42, § 2, obreption is substantial only when *all* the motivating causes alleged in the petitions are false.[26]

B. The *ipso iure* Derived Effect of Substantial Subreption and Obreption

Canon 42, §§ 1 and 2, attaches to substantial subreption and obreption an invalidating effect upon rescripts. Moreover, the language, which the lawgiver uses in this canon indicates that he intends this effect to take place *ipso iure*. That is to say, the Code itself decrees the invalidity of rescripts obtained through substantial subreption or obreption, for canon 42 states clearly that such rescripts are void, and not simply that they are voidable.[27]

What is more, the lawgiver, in ascribing this *ipso iure* derived effect to these defects, makes no distinction between rescripts of justice and rescripts of favor. *Ubi lex non distinguit, nec nos distinguere debemus.* Hence, it must be concluded that the legislator intends the same principle in this matter to apply to both types of rescripts.[28] Accordingly, under the present law it is no longer necessary to await an exception or objection on the part of the petitioner's opponent in order to see a rescript of justice nullified.[29] Likewise, a judge who has received his juris-

[25] Cf. Rodrigo, *Tractatus de Legibus,* p. 558.

[26] Cf. Regatillo, *Institutiones Iuris Canonici,* I, 110.

[27] Cf. Cicognani, *Canon Law,* p. 718, and Maroto, *Institutiones,* I, n. 284, ad II, d, 2°.

[28] Cf. Van Hove, *op. cit.*, p. 144.

[29] According to the pre-Code jurisprudence, when a rescript of justice had been obtained through substantial subreption or obreption, it became invalidated only by means of a successful exception raised upon these

diction through a rescript which is vitiated by substantial subreption or obreption is bound *ex officio* to declare his incompetence, for in such a situation there is question of his absolute incompetence.[30]

C. Good and Bad Faith in Relation to Subreption and Obreption

It has already been noted that under the present law the legislator demands that the recitals in the *preces* for rescripts be in conformity with objective reality.[31] Hence, it is not surprising to find that in canon 42, or also in any of the other canons in Title IV of Book I of the Code, no distinction is made between good and bad faith as far as the invalidating effect of subreption and obreption is concerned. That is to say, when substantial subreption and obreption occur in the *preces*, it makes little difference to the lawgiver, in respect to invalidity, whether these defects are due to the petitioner's simplicity, ignorance, or error, or whether they arise from his malicious, deceitful, or fraudulent intentions.[32] In other words, the existence of subrep-

---

grounds by the beneficiary's opponent. A rescript of favor when thus obtained was nullified *ipso iure*. Cf. *supra*, pp. 99-105.

30 Cf. can. 1611, and Van Hove, *loc. cit.* Cf. also cans. 1679 and 1682. The foregoing consideration is of practical importance in the case of a *ratum et non consummatum* marriage, as well as in all other cases in which a judge receives his jurisdiction or delegation through a rescript of justice.

Ojetti (1862-1932) maintained that in the case contemplated in the preceeding text the judge is not bound *ex officio* to declare his incompetence.—*Commentarium in Codicem Iuris Canonici* (4 vols., Vol. I, Romae, 1927), I, 227 (hereafter cited as *Commentarium*). Van Hove answered Ojetti's argument on this point by saying: "Ratio, quam laudatus commentator affert, legislatorem nempe rem committere arbitrio partis, non valet sub iure Codicis, quia iam non conceditur iurisdictio necessaria ad processum instituendum. Partes autem non possunt pro suo arbitrio iudicem constituere cum debita iurisdictione. Tamen applicandum est principium c. 209: in errore communi aut in dubio positivo et probabili, sive iuris sive facti, iurisdictionem supplet Ecclesia pro foro tam externo quam interno. Cf. c. 1606, remittens ad c. 199-207 servandos a iudice delegato."—*Ibid.*, nota 1.

31 Cf. *supra*, pp. 112-114.

32 Cf. Cicognani, *op. cit.*, p. 717.

tion and obreption in the *preces* for rescripts is to be judged objectively. Their cause is immaterial as far as their invalidating effect is concerned. This demand for an objective judgment concerning the presence of these defects is a very logical one for the lawgiver to make, for the value and force of rescripts ultimately depends upon the intention of the superior who grants them, and not upon the dispositions of the petitioner.[33]

Nonetheless, the Church has not eliminated altogether the distinction between good and bad faith where rescripts are concerned. On the one hand, while the legislator no longer prescribes the sanction of a rescript's invalidity precisely because of bad faith as such in its petition, yet, he does provide for some appropriate punishment to be meted out upon a person who deceitfully falsifies the *preces*. In a word, under the present law a petitioner who fraudulently or deceitfully falsifies his *preces* commits an ecclesiastical crime which is punishable by the ordinary according to the gravity of the offense.[34] Moreover, it is to be noted that this penalty can be incurred in connection with any kind of rescript, inclusive of rescripts issued *motu proprio* and of such as convey dispensations from minor matrimonial impediments.[35]

On the other hand, there still exist cases, specifically mentioned in the Code, in which the lawgiver makes a special concession in favor of subreption that arises out of good faith. These cases are treated in canon 991, § 1, and canon 2249, § 2, respectively. Canon 991, § 1, states:

> In precibus pro irregularitatum ac impedimentorum [sacrae ordinationis] dispensatione, omnes irregularitates ac impedimenta indicanda sunt; secus dispensatio generalis valebit quidem etiam pro reticitis bona fide, iis exceptis quae in can. 990, § 1 excipiuntur, non autem pro reticitis in mala fide.[36]

33 Michiels, *Normae Generales*, II, 371.

34 Can. 2361.

35 O'Neill, *Papal Rescripts of Favor*, p. 125.

36 The irregularities and impediments which are excepted from the scope of can. 991, § 1, are those which arise from voluntary homicide and abortion, *effectu secuto*, and those which are brought before a judicial tribunal. Cf. cans. 985, n. 4, and 990, § 1.

Canon 2249, § 2, reads as follows:

> Petens absolutionem, debet casus omnes indicare, secus absolutio valet tantum pro casu expresso; quod si absolutio, quamvis particularis petitio facta sit, fuerit generalis, valet quoque pro reticitis bona fide, excepta censura specialissimo modo Sedi Apostolico reservata, non autem pro reticitis mala fide.

Consequently, in these two cases it appears that subreption which arises out of good faith and which should ordinarily be considered substantial is not invalidating. That which involves bad faith, however, carries with itself its usual nullifying effect upon rescripts, and is, therefore, to be considered substantial subreption.

Nevertheless, Cicognani questions whether or not canons 991, § 1, and 2249, §2, represent real exceptions to the general principal that the existence of substantial subreption and obreption, together with their nullifying effect, is to be judged solely on an objective basis. In fact, he argues that real exceptions are not involved in these aforesaid canons. His argument is that what really happens in the cases contemplated in these laws is that the favor involved is not granted precisely because no petition was presented for the removal of the irregularity, impediment, or censure that was concealed in bad faith. Hence, in reality there is no question of a false application's being presented, but rather of no petition's being offered for the suppressed irregularity, impediment, or censure.[37]

This writer cannot agree with Cicognani, however, in his conclusion on this point. Actually, even when good faith is involved in the petitioner's failure to mention all the obstacles involved in the case covered by the general dispensation of canon 991, § 1, and the general absolution of canon 2249, § 2, no petition has been specifically presented for the removal of the suppressed irregularity, impediment, or censure. Still the legislator decrees that the concealed obstacle is removed by the general dispensation or absolution.

Moreover, it seems to the present writer that Cicognani, in reaching his conclusion, considers solely the situation in which, while the petitioner *de facto* requests a rescript to remove only

[37] Cicognani, *Canon Law*, p. 718.

some but not all of the obstacles binding him, a general rescript is actually granted. In such circumstances, it can in truth be said that no petition has really been presented for the removal of the obstacle that is concealed, and, if bad faith is involved, that obstacle is not removed by the superior's grant.

It must be noted, however, that canon 2249, § 2, prescribes that if the petitioner is seeking a general absolution from his censures, he must mention all of them.[38] Furthermore, canon 991, § 1, indicates that a petitioner who is bound by several obstacles to sacred ordination should always seek a general dispensation. It expressly states that in presenting the *preces* for a dispensation from such irregularities and impediments the petitioner should mention all the obstacles which stand in his way.[39] Accordingly, when a petition is presented either for a general dispensation or for a general absolution, subreption will be involved in it if the petitioner fails to mention all the irregularities and impediments, or censures by which he is bound. Nonetheless, the law, as stated in canons 991, § 1, and 2249, § 2, decrees that the general dispensation or absolution, respectively, will be universally effective for a person in good faith, even though he committed subreption concerning some of the obstacles covered by the requested general rescript. A person who is guilty of malicious subreption, however, is released only from what he mentioned in his petition. In a word, his rescript is invalid with reference to all the cases which he wilfully suppressed.

Consequently, this writer believes that the legislator does make an exception in favor of good faith in the cases contemplated in canons 991, § 1, and 2249, § 2. He has been led to this conclusion by the fact that when a general rescript is requested

[38] This is not to say, however, that a person must always request a general absolution every time he asks to be absolved from one of the several censures binding him. Can. 2249, § 1, indicates that a person can be absolved from one of his censures while the others, which bind him, remain in force.

[39] This is not to say, however, that one cannot be dispensed from some of his irregularities or impediments while the others remain in effect. The fact that a general dispensation removes both the obstacles mentioned in the *preces* and those concealed in good faith, while those that are hidden in bad faith remain, substantiates the preceding statement.

in connection with those cases and subreption is committed in the petition for it, the subreption is merely accidental and, therefore, non-invalidating if it arises from good faith. It is substantial and nullifying, however, if it is caused by the petitioner's bad faith.

Article 2. Commentary on Canon 42, § 1—Subreption

The content of paragraph one of canon 42 may be expressed in the following manner: the concealment of truth or subreption in the *preces* for a rescript does not prevent that rescript from being valid and effective, provided mention was made in the petition of whatever is demanded to be expressed for validity by the *stylus Curiae.*[40]

A. The General Principle of Canon 42, § 1

As has already been noted, the legislator intends canon 42 to specify the subject matter of the ontological truth which he demands in the *preces* if rescripts are to be valid.[41] In paragraph one of this canon he lays down a general principle to govern this specification in regard to the facts and circumstances which he requires to be mentioned in the petitions for rescripts. That principle can be stated in these terms: in order that a rescript be not nullified and deprived of its intended force by reason of subreption, it is necessary and sufficient that there be expressed in the petition for it all those facts and circumstances which, by the *stylus Curiae,* must be mentioned for the validity of the rescript.[42]

Hence, what the legislator is demanding under pain of nullity in this paragraph are petitions that are *substantially* true. This is not to say, however, that the lawgiver does not always expect to receive petitions that are completely truthful, for there can be no doubt that he wants the full truth at all times and in all

[40] The text of can. 42, § 1, reads as follows: "Reticentia veri, seu subreptio, in precibus non obstat quominus rescriptum vim habeat ratumque sit, dummodo expressa fuerint quae de stylo Curiae sunt ad validitatem exprimenda."

[41] Cf. *supra,* pp. 113-114.

[42] Michiels, *Normae Generales,* II, 360.

cases. Nonetheless, it is his obvious purpose in this part of his law to define precisely how much truth must be had in the *preces* if the rescripts are to be valid. Thus, he requires that the recitals in the *pars narrativa* and *pars postulativa* of the petitions be substantially true. He does not demand under pain of nullity that they be completely true.[43]

Furthermore, the lawgiver himself describes what he means by substantially true recitals in these two parts of the *preces*. They are those in which everything is truthfully mentioned which, by the *stylus Curiae,* must be expressed for the validity of rescripts.

Conversely, one can say that in this paragraph the legislator draws a clear and concise distinction between what the authors call substantial or invalidating subreption and that which is accidental or non-invalidating. Substantial subreption, then, is had directly only when a petitioner fails to mention all the facts and circumstances the expression of which is demanded for the validity of the rescript in question by the style of the Curia.[44] It occurs indirectly only when a positive statement of falsehood, or obreption, creeps into the expression of these facts and circumstances.[45] Accidental subreption arises directly from the concealment or suppression of matters the mention of which is required by the nature of things, by the law, or by the *stylus Curiae,* but not for the validity of the rescript involved. It comes about indirectly through statements of falsehood in the expression of these matters.

Consequently, the key expression in this paragraph, as far as the invalidating effect of subreption is concerned, is the clause

[43] "*Ratio est,* quia in data hypothesi dicitur tandem substantialiter totum verum, quantum, ex stylo Curiae in occurrente negotio requiritur, etsi exprimatur accidentaliter diminutum, atque etiam forte omittendo quae nota a rescribente eum retraxissent a rescripto favorabili concedendo. In casu igitur adhuc verum est quod preces veritate nitantur, nempe substantiali."—Rodrigo, *Tractatus de Legibus,* p. 559.

[44] For a listing of some of these facts and circumstances, cf. *infra,* pp. 149-168.

[45] Cf. Van Hove, *De Rescriptis,* p. 143, and O'Neill, *Papal Rescripts of Favor,* p. 133. For the discussion of how obreption is sometimes equivalent to subreption, and is, therefore, governed in such instances by the same principles as is subreption, cf. *supra,* p. 131.

"dummodo expressa fuerint quae de stylo Curiae sunt ad validitatem exprimenda." As long as the terms of that clause are complied with, a rescript cannot be adjudged invalid on the grounds of subreption. In other words, once that condition has been fulfilled, any direct or indirect suppression of the truth in the *preces* will not prevent, as Blat puts it:

> *quominus rescriptum* per illas obtentum *vim habeat* etiam impetratum "pro alio praeter eius assensum" (can. 37) *ratumque sit*, vel recognoscatur ut validum in foro quoque externo, quamvis in hoc vitium illud in probatis esset. . . .[46]

The reason why the lawmaker has specified in this manner the subject matter of the objective truth that must be present in the *pars narrativa* and the *pars postulativa* of the *preces* is undoubtedly the *finis legis* of canon 42, § 1. The purpose of this particular part of the Church's law concerning the application of the principle *"si preces veritate nitantur"* is to make sure that the superior will be provided with sufficient information to enable him to judge prudently whether or not he can reasonably grant a petitioner's request.[47] If this purpose is to be accomplished, two things, and, indeed, only two things, have actually to be communicated to the superior through these two parts of the *preces*. These matters are, first, the object of the petitioner's request, and second, an indication as to whether or not that request can be granted, provided there is a sufficient reason for doing so.[48]

Yet, who is better qualified to decide which facts and circumstances convey such information to the superior than the supreme ecclesiastical legislator himself? After all, the vast majority of rescripts are granted by him personally or by others, for example, the various branches of the Roman Curia, who use the power which he has bestowed upon them through his law. Or else they emanate from persons employing the power which the Holy See has delegated to them. Such is the case, for instance, when bishops use their Quinquennial Faculties to grant rescripts.

[46] *Commentarium,* I, 135.

[47] Cf. Michiels, *Normae Generales,* II, 361.

[48] Toso, *Commentaria Minora,* I, 125.

So, by positive legislation the lawmaker has decreed that the facts and circumstances which are required by the style of the Curia to be mentioned for the validity of rescripts are such as to convey to the superior sufficient information to permit him to issue his rescripts reasonably.

Moreover, it is not difficult to understand why the legislator has attached to substantial subreption a nullifying effect upon the rescripts that have been obtained through *preces* infected by it. When a petitioner consciously or unconsciously conceals a fact or circumstance which belongs to the very substance of his case, he presents to the superior not his case as it is in reality, but another and substantially different one. Since the matter in question is not mentioned at all or else is expressed falsely, the superior naturally believes either that it does not exist or that it exists as stated in the petition. As a result, he intends the rescript, which he actually grants, for the case described to him in the petition, not for the prospective beneficiary's case as it really is. Hence, the rescript which he issues not only does not fit the beneficiary's case, but it was never intended to be applied to it. Consequently, the rescript is of no value to the proposed beneficiary.[49]

Furthermore, it is most important in this discussion to emphasize the fact that it is the lawmaker himself who has decided when subreption invalidates rescripts and when it does not. From this consideration, as well as from the general principle enunciated in canon 42, § 1, three conclusions must be drawn. First, not every act of subreption in the *preces* carries with itself an invalidating effect upon rescripts.[50] Second, when a petitioner omits something that, by the style of the Curia, needs not to be mentioned for the validity of the rescript, the rescript

[49] Cf. Rodrigo, *Tractatus de Legibus*, p. 559. In this same place Rodrigo makes this pertinent observation also: "*Eis reticitis,* datur insinceritas substantialis, aequivalens moraliter et iuridice obreptioni itidem substantiali. Reapse, aequivalenter et quoad effectum mentitur decipiendo rescribentem, et vitiat substantiam veritatis necessariae, qui iure interrogatus de tota rei substantia, eius partem dissimulat."

[50] Cappello, *Tractatus Canonico-Moralis de Sacramentis,* Vol. V, *De Matrimonio* (6. ed., Taurini-Romae: Marietti, 1950), p. 276 (hereafter cited as *De Matrimonio*).

remains valid and stands to benefit its recipient. This is true even though the mentioning of the suppressed fact or circumstance would have made the granting of the rescript more difficult or even caused the superior to refuse to issue it at all.[51] Third, if something is concealed which, by the *stylus Curiae*, needs to be expressed for the validity of the rescript, the rescript is invalid, even though the superior would most certainly have granted the very same rescript had the suppressed fact or circumtance been mentioned.[52]

B. The *stylus Curiae*

Since the requirements of the *stylus Curiae* constitute the criterion by which is to be decided whether subreption in the *preces* is substantial or accidental, careful attention must be paid to the expression *"stylus Curiae"* as it appears in canon 42, § 1.[53] Without a clear understanding of the import of this expression in its present context one is likely to form a completely erroneous judgment concerning subreption and its effects upon rescripts.

At the outset, then, what curia does the lawmaker have in mind in canon 42, § 1? There can be no doubt that he is referring primarily to the Roman Curia as it is described in canon 242, for the norms which govern the effect of subreption on rescripts are a part of the Church's universal law. Moreover, the formal style of the Roman Curia, precisely that which has the nature of the *stylus iuris,* alone has a universally binding power. It must be observed not only by the parties to a case handled by the Roman Curia but also by all the lower curiae whenever they deal with matters that come within the scope of the *stylus iuris Curiae Romanae.*[54] On this interpretation of the word *"Curia"* all the authors agree.

[51] O'Neill, *Papal Rescripts of Favor,* p. 126, and Vermeersch-Creusen, *Epitome Iuris Canonici,* I, 155-156.

[52] Michiels, *Normae Generales,* II, 360.

[53] The writer has already considered the *stylus curiae* in a general way. Cf. *supra,* pp. 26-32. In that place he attempted to explain what is meant by the terms *"curia"* and *"stylus."* He likewise tried to indicate there the different kinds of *stylus* and the juridical force which each kind may have.

[54] Michiels, *Normae Generales,* II, 361.

There is a difference of opinion among the commentators, however, on whether or not the term *"Curia"* is meant to apply only to the Roman Curia. In other words, the authors disagree as to the correctness of including in the comprehension of this word as it stands in canon 42, § 1, other curiae that are of lower rank than the Roman Curia. Such curiae are those established by ordinaries beneath the Sovereign Pontiff who have the power and the right to issue rescripts. Diocesan curiae and the curiae of major superiors in exempt clerical institutes are examples of such lower curiae.

Several of the commentators restrict the term *"Curia"* in this canon to signify only the Roman Curia.[55] Their reason for taking this position is that the style of the Roman Curia "alone establishes law."[56] Van Hove called this opinion the more common canonical teaching on this point.[57] Moreover, in stating his own position on this question, he undoubtedly gave an insight into the thinking of the other proponents of the aforesaid opinion. He said:

> Stylus autem Curiae intelligendus est sensu obvio et usitatissimo de stylo Curiae Romanae. Nihil tamen obstat, quin Ordinarii determinent stylum in sua propria curia servandum etiam ad validitatem rescripti, in concedendis favoribus potestate sua ordinaria. Decet saltem ut in elargiendis favoribus quos concurrenter cum Sancta Sede conferre possunt, utantur et ipsi stylo Curiae Romanae.[58]

Other authors maintain, however, that the lawgiver himself intends this term to apply also to other curiae besides the Roman Curia.[59] In other words, it is the opinion of these commentators

[55] This is the opinion, e.g., of Toso, *Commentaria Minora,* I, 122; Vermeersch-Creusen, *Epitome Iuris Canonici,* I, n. 160; Ojetti, *Commentarium,* I, 225; Cappello, *Summa Iuris Canonici* (3 vols., Vol. I, 4. ed., Romae: Apud Aedes Universitatis Gregorianae, 1945), I, n. 151, ad 2; Cicognani, *Canon Law,* p. 716.

[56] Cicognani, *loc. cit.*

[57] *De Rescriptis,* p. 145, nota 2.

[58] *Op. cit.,* p. 145.

[59] Among these commentators are Michiels, *Normae Generales,* II, 361; Maroto, *Institutiones,* I, n. 284, ad II, c; Blat, *Commentarium,* I, 107;

that it is not necessary for ordinaries beneath the Pope to prescribe specifically that substantial subreption is caused by a failure to mention in the *preces* matters the expression of which is required for validity by the style of their own curiae. For these authors that prescription is already contained in canon 42, § 1.

Michiels defends his support of this opinion in the following way:

> Ni fallimur, huic alteri sententiae est subscribendum, quotiescumque agitur de rescriptis ab illis Ordinariis propria auctoritate concessis . . .; ratio videtur aperta, quia in his materiis indubitanter inducere possunt [curiae inferiores] proprium stylum, styli Curiae Romanae magis determinatum vel extensivum; hic autem, semel cum introductus est, incunctanter dicendus est sub culpa, et si ita statutum fuerit, sub poena nullitatis servandus.[60]

The present writer believes that the term *"Curia"* in canon 42, § 1, comprehends both the Roman Curia and the lower curiae. He has two reasons for subscribing to this opinion. First of all, the style of these lower curiae can establish particular customary law, even though it cannot produce universal customary law.[61] Secondly, there can be no doubt that, unless the contrary is obvious, the lawmaker in the Code's Title IV of Book I is legislating for rescripts of both the Holy See and other ordinaries, as is evident from canon 36, § 1. Yet the style of the Roman Curia does not touch many points of particular law which often involve rescripts granted by the lower ordinaries *iure proprio*. Hence, if the legislator himself did not intend the curiae of these ordinaries to be included under the term *"Curia"* of this canon, there would be a serious lacuna in one of the most fundamental laws concerning the truth that is required in the *preces*. He would then be making no positive provision for the determination of the pres-

---

Coronata, *Institutiones*, I, 75; Rodrigo, *Tractatus de Legibus*, pp. 559-560; and Wernz-Vidal, *Ius Canonicum ad Codicis Normam Exactum* (7 vols. in 8, Vol. I, 2. ed., Romae: Apud Aedes Universitatis Gregorianae, 1952), I, 271.

[60] *Loc. cit.*

[61] Cf. cans. 26, 27, and 28.

ence or absence of invalidating subreption in the rescripts of lower ordinaries.

Turning now from this consideration of the comprehension of the term *"Curia"* to an examination of the significance of the word *"stylus"* as it appears in canon 42, § 1, one finds complete unanimity among the authors in describing this style as being a *stylus formalis,* and more precisely a *stylus iuris.*[62] Hence, this style has the force of law. It has also the firmness and stability of law.[63]

In spite of this unanimity, a question arises at this point on whether the expression *"stylus Curiae"* in canon 42, § 1, is to be understood in a strict or in a broad sense. That is to say, is the legislator using this expression in this canon in a strict sense, thereby restricting it to embrace only those requirements which arise from the customary law, instructions, and observances of the different curiae? Or does he intend it to be taken in a broad sense, so that it comprehends not only the *stylus curiae,* strictly so-called, but also norms that are established in the matter of subreption by the written universal and particular law of the Church? [64]

Blat, on the one hand, explicitly states that the *"stylus Curiae"* of canon 42, § 1, is to be understood in a strict sense. For him,

[62] Cf. Van Hove, *op. cit.,* p. 145; Michiels, *loc. cit.;* Rodrigo, *op. cit.,* p. 559.

In the jurisprudence of the Church the expression *"stylus curiae"* signifies the manner or way in which a curia *usually* uses its public power to handle and solve matters within its competence. This expression also points to the norms according to which a curia's *modus agendi* is molded. A *stylus formalis* is concerned with the solemnities or formalities usually employed by a curia in preparing, solving, and executing its transactions, both judicial and nonjudicial. A *stylus iuris* denotes the laws and rules which result from the usage and practice of a curia. Cf. *supra,* pp. 28-29.

[63] Cf. *supra,* p. 31.

[64] "Sumitur [stylus Curiae] autem lato sensu de regulis quae lege universali Ecclesiae determinantur. . . . Ius consuetudinarium, instructiones et observantia stylum Curiae sensu stricto constituunt."—Van Hove, *De Rescriptis,* p. 145. The writer includes the curiae lower than the Roman Curia and also particular law in this discussion because he supports the opinion which maintains that the term *"Curia"* of can. 42, § 1, comprehends also other curiae besides the *Curia Romana.*—Cf. *supra,* pp. 143-144.

then, the rules of the universal law of the Church concerning matters which must be mentioned in petitions for the validity of rescripts are not included. He qualifies his statement, however, by noting that these rules of the universal law are dealt with in canon 42, § 1, if they have become incorporated into the style of the Roman Curia.[65] Van Hove, on the other hand, expressly maintained that the style of the Curia contemplated in this canon is to be taken in a broad sense.[66] Indeed, he seems to have spoken the mind of most present-day canonists in this matter.[67]

This writer also believes that the expression *"stylus Curiae"* should be taken in a broad sense, especially because of the following very logical comment made on this point by Michiels:

> Patet quod in materia nostra stylus Curiae praeprimis determinatur praescriptionibus et ordinationibus *ipso iure* communi, et si de stylo Curiae inferioris Ordinarii agatur, jure insuper particulari, sive circa omnia rescripta, sive circa determinata eorum genera, puta circa rescripta beneficialia aut matrimonialia, statutis; si quis enim juris vigentis statuta adamussim servare censendus sit, est ipsa Curia, rectae negotiorum eccelsiasticorum administrationi praeposita.[68]

Nonetheless, the present writer can also see some probability in the position taken by Blat on this question. It is not unreasonable to suppose that the legsilator has established the re-

[65] "In hoc stylo seu usu Curiae Romanae ab Auctoribus relato, sub hoc Decretalium titulo vel pro diversis materiis, distinguere oportet, quae propter ius scriptum (forte nunc saltem quoad necessitatem huiusmodi mutatum) requirebantur in praxi, et alia 'necessaria exprimenda' solo ex Curiae Romanae stylo. De his enim non de illis intelligenda est paragraphus canonis, excepto casu quod illorum aliquod in stylum futurum transeat."—Blat, *Commentarium,* I, 135.

[66] *Loc. cit.*

[67] Cf., e.g., Michiels (*Normae Generales,* II, 362) who states: "Praeter ipsius *juris statuta* autem ad stylum Curiae quoque pertinent *speciales regulae* in materia rescriptorum a Curia vel Curiae officiis tamquam sibi propriae servari solitae, speciales conditiones ab ipsis in materia rescriptorum stabiliter exigi consuetae." Cf. also Abbo-Hannan, *The Sacred Canons,* I, 74; Beste, *Introductio in Codicem,* p. 112; Berutti, *Institutiones Iuris Canonici* (6 vols., Vol. I, Taurini-Romae, 1936), I, 133 (hereafter cited as *Institutiones*).

[68] *Ibid.,* pp. 361-362.

quirements of the *stylus Curiae* as the criterion of the presence or of the absence of substantial subreption with the understanding that petitioners will heed the demands that he makes in this matter in other parts of the Code. It must be remembered that the canons of Book I, Title IV, are not the only ones that govern rescripts, for depending upon their objects, rescripts are subject to other prescriptions found in different parts of the Code of Canon Law.[69] When there is question of rescripts that are granted *iure proprio* by lower ordinaries, it is obvious that these will be governed by particular laws through which rulings are made in this matter. Hence, the lawmaker in canon 42, § 1, may well be giving the style of the Curia as an added criterion over and above the various prescriptions already found in other parts of the law.

In practice, then, no matter which of these opinions is the correct one, this much is certain: a rescript will be invalid if in the *preces* for it there are not mentioned all the facts and circumstances which, by law and by the *stylus Curiae,* strictly so-called, need to be expressed for the validity of the rescript in question.

Apropos of the requirements of the *stylus Curiae* in this matter, it should be noted that even though these are at least partially introduced by the usage and practice of a curia, nonetheless, they are accurately fixed and determined and, as such, they enjoy considerable permanence. What is more, where the Roman Curia is concerned, they are made known through authentic publications. This is true especially in regard to rescripts that are used relatively more frequently than others. Such, for example, are the rescripts that concern marriages and benefices.[70]

The authentic publications just mentioned which give the regulations and conditions that govern the Holy See's rescripts have appeared more frequently ever since the Vatican Council. At that council many bishops requested that the Apostolic See lay down clearer and, indeed, easier rules to expedite the obtaining of rescripts through the Roman Curia. The bishops were concerned especially with rescripts that affected marriage.[71]

[69] Cf., e.g., can. 62, can. 156, § 3, can. 534, § 2.

[70] Michiels, *loc. cit.*

[71] Van Hove, *De Rescriptis,* p. 145.

Subsequent to this request of the bishops, the Sacred Congregation for the Propagation of the Faith issued on May 9, 1877, an instruction in which it outlined the facts and circumstances which had to be mentioned for the validity of rescripts conveying matrimonial dispensations.[72] Pope Leo XIII (1878-1903) issued on February 20, 1888, an apostolic letter by which he improved and made more stable the practice of the dicasteries of the Roman Curia in the matter of handling rescripts.[73] The reformation of the Roman Curia by Pope St. Pius X in 1908 with its systematic reorganization of the Curia involved an even greater stabilization of the *stylus Curiae* in regard to rescripts.[74]

The *stylus Curiae Romanae* which was publicized in these documents is by and large still the same today, even though the Holy See has issued other instructions which have had a direct bearing precisely on the truth and the subject matter of the truth required in the *preces* for rescripts. Such a document is the one given by the Sacred Congregation of the Sacraments on May 7, 1923, concerning the cases of ratified non-consummated marriages.[75]

C. Matters to Be Mentioned for Validity

The facts and circumstances that must be mentioned in petitions for the validity of the rescripts depend upon the prescriptions of law, the requirements of the *stylus Curiae,* strictly so-called, and the objects or subject matter of the rescripts.

The law that is here involved is any kind of law, universal or particular, that has a bearing on this matter. The requirements of the universal law apply to the *preces* for rescripts of the Holy See, whether they are issued directly by Rome or granted by its delegates. Furthermore, whenever the prescriptions of the universal law are laid down as fundamental norms for all rescripts in general or for all rescripts in a particular class, they are to be

[72] *Collectanea,* II, n. 1470.

[73] *ASS,* XX (1888), 543-544.

[74] *AAS,* I (1909), 63-64, 70-71, 91-92.

[75] *AAS,* XV (1923), 389-436; cf., especially, pp. 389-390, 393. For an English translation of this document, cf. Bouscaren, *The Canon Law Digest,* I, 764-792; cf., especially, pp. 764-765, 767.

observed by whomsoever the rescripts are granted. The demands of the particular law, however, are in and of themselves (*per se*) to be observed only in regard to rescripts which are properly under the scope of the particular law involved in the case.[76]

In reference to the requirements of the *stylus Curiae,* strictly so-called, it must be noted that the demands of both the Roman Curia and the lower curiae in this matter must be considered.[77] The style of the Roman Curia affects all rescripts which are governed by the universal law of the Church. The *stylus* of the lower curiae is binding upon rescripts which fall within the scope of the respective proper competence of these curiae, that is, upon those which have respect to particular law.

As for the subject matter of rescripts, it also has a major role in determining what must be mentioned in the *preces,* for in most instances both the law and the *stylus Curiae,* strictly so-called, are directed in their requirements to cover the various different objects which constitute the subject matter of rescripts. Accordingly, these more specific demands in respect to the particular, special subject matter of rescripts together with those regulations in the law and the *stylus Curiae* which apply to rescripts in general, must be taken into account for a determining of what must be mentioned in *preces* if the subsequent rescripts are to be valid.

It is not the purpose of this study to set down all the facts and circumstances which have to be expressed in the petitions for the hundreds of rescripts that may be requested. In fact, it is almost impossible to compose such a list, especially for cases involving particular law and the style of individual lower curiae, which may vary considerably from one place to another. Consequently, in the pages which follow, the writer plans to present a schema of what the universal law necessitates for mention in the *preces* for the validity of the more commonly used rescripts

[76] This writer, as has already been noted, subscribes to the opinion that the canons of the Code's Book I, Title IV, *De rescriptis,* apply, unless the contrary is apparent, to rescripts by whomever they are issued, and not only to those which are issued directly by the Holy See and by ordinaries. —Cf. *supra,* pp. 121-122.

[77] It has already been indicated that this writer is of the opinion that the term *"Curia"* in can. 42, § 1, comprehends both the Roman Curia and the lower curiae.—Cf. *supra,* pp. 143-144.

that emanate from the Holy See directly or in virtue of its delegation. As far as the *stylus Curiae Romanae,* strictly so-called, is concerned, he proposes to treat of its demands in an explicit manner only in relation to rescripts conveying dispensations from matrimonial impediments.

a) The requirements of the universal law

In this matter the universal law of the Church, as it is contained in the Code of Canon Law, has made some general requirements and others that are directed to rescripts with a particular type of subject matter. (Such rescripts are hereafter designated as particular rescripts.)

1) *Concerning the general requirements of the universal law.* Canonists are not in agreement in specifying which canons of Book I, Title IV, *De rescriptis,* of the Code definitely and directly lay down requirements the transgression of which will always result in substantial subreption in the *preces.* They do agree, however, that one such requirement is present in the first part of canon 44, § 2, that is, in the words *"Gratia . . . invalida est."* This canon rules that a favor once denied by the vicar general and later obtained from the bishop without mention of the vicar general's refusal is invalid. Consequently, if a favor has been denied by the vicar general, mention of this fact must be made in the petition to the bishop for the same favor. Otherwise the subsequent rescript will be invalid, *"nisi forte ipse [Episcopus] eam [recusationem] bene novisse et memorem eiusdem fuisse noscatur."* [78]

Concerning other general canons, however, which at first sight may seem to indicate matters that must be expressed in the *procos* for the validity of the relevant rescripts, some authors list them as offering such indication; others deny that the concealment of the matters treated in them constitutes a substantial subreption, or, indeed, any subreption at all. The canons in question are principally the following: canon 43,[79] the second

[78] Rodrigo, *Tractatus de Legibus,* p. 530. Cf. also Michiels, *Normae Generales,* II, 362-363; Van Hove, *De Rescriptis,* p. 144; Abbo-Hannan, *The Sacred Canons,* I, 74.

[79] Can. 43 states: "Gratia ab una Sacra Congregatione vel Officio Romanae Curiae denegata, invalide ab alia Sacra Congregatione vel

part of canon 44, § 2,[80] canon 46,[81] and canon 48, § 2.[82] To these may be added canon 36, § 2, insofar as it excepts from its general principle canons 2265, § 2, 2275, n. 3, and 2283.[83]

Michiels lists canon 43 and the second part of canon 44, § 2, as referring to matters which must be mentioned in the *preces* for the validity of the relevant rescripts.[84] O'Neill put canon 46 into the same category.[85] Cicognani does likewise with canon 48, § 2.[86] Van Hove, however, had this to say in this matter:

> *Sensu proprio* subreptio non est omissa mentio censurae quae obstet valori rescripti (can. 36, § 2), nec inhabilitatis ad determinatas gratias acquirendas (can. 46), nec refutationis

Officio aut a loci Ordinario, etsi potestatem habente, conceditur sine assensu Sacrae Congregationis vel Officii quocum vel quibuscum agi coeptum fuit, salvo iure S. Poenitentiariae pro foro interno."

80 The second part of can. 44, § 2, reads: "Gratia autem ab Episcopo denegata nequit valide, etiam facta denegationis mentione, a Vicario Generali, non consentiente Episcopo, impetrari."

81 Can. 46 states: "Rescripta etiam *Motu proprio* concessa personae de iure communi inhabili ad consequendam gratiam de qua agitur, itemque edita contra alicuius loci legitimam consuetudinem vel statutum peculiare, vel contra ius alteri iam quaesitum, non sustinentur, nisi expressa derogatoria clausula rescripto apponatur."

82 Can. 48, § 2, reads: "Si sint [de una eademque re duo rescripta inter se contraria] aeque peculiaria aut generalia, prius tempore praevalet posteriori, nisi in altero fiat expressa mentio de priore, aut nisi prior impetrator dolo vel notabili negligentia suo rescripto usus non fuerit."

83 Can. 36, § 2, states: "Gratiae et dispensationes omne genus a Sede Apostolica concessae etiam censura irretitis validae sunt, salvo praescripto can. 2265, § 2, 2275, n. 3, 2283." These last-mentioned canons deal respectively with a person who has been excommunicated, personally interdicted, or suspended. Can. 2265, § 2, the provisions of which are followed in the other two canons for their respective subjects, provides in reference to the matter under consideration: "quod si haec sententia [i.e., declaratoria vel condemnatoria] lata fuerit, excommunicatus nequit praeterea gratiam ullam pontificiam valide consequi, nisi in pontificio rescripto mentio de excommunicatione fiat."

84 *Ibid.*, p. 363. Cf. also Toso, *Commentaria Minora*, I, 125; Chelodi, *Ius Canonicum de Personis*, p. 130; Berutti, *Institutiones*, I, 133.

85 *Papal Rescripts of Favor*, p. 125. Cf. also Toso, *loc. cit.*, and Chelodi, *op. cit.*, p. 131.

86 *Canon Law*, p. 716. Cf. also Toso, *loc. cit.*

precum per S. Congregationem vel Episcopum (can. 43 et 44, § 2), quia earum mentio in precibus non sanaret vitium rescripti. Mentio censurae in ipso rescripto requiritur ut hoc valeat (can. 2265, § 2); clausula in rescripto apponenda est ut derogetur inhabilitati ad obtinendam gratiam determinatam (can. 46); assensus S. Congregationis vel Episcopi, qui gratiam denegaverunt, est obtinendus (can. 43 et 44, § 2). Subrepticium non fit rescriptum propter omissam in precibus mentionem consuetudinis vel statuti particularis vel iuris alteri quaesiti (can. 46), quia vitium non sanatur, nisi expressa derogatoria clausula rescripto apponatur. Vera subreptio non est omissio denegationis gratiae per Ordinarium proprium in precibus ad alium Ordinarium, quia mentio requiritur ad solam liceitatem rescripti." [87]

The present writer subscribes to the position that Van Hove took on this question. A careful examination of the canons under consideration reveals that the invalidity or ineffectiveness which they contemplate for rescripts arises fundamentally (*per se*) and directly not from the fact that the matter treated by them respectively is not mentioned in the petitions involved.[88] Directly this nullity or ineffectiveness is due to the fact that the superior does not or can not effectively remove the obstacles that prevent the recipients of the rescripts from benefiting from the letters.

It is possible, and in some instances most likely, that the su-

[87] *Op. cit.*, pp. 143-144. The last sentence of this text refers to can. 44, § 1, and in it Van Hove expressed the almost unanimous opinion of authors concerning the import of that canon.

Maroto looked upon the mentioning of one superior's previous refusal to grant a favor as another condition in rescripts, besides *"si preces veritate nitantur,"* which must be considered as essential in most instances. He completed his analysis of this factor thus: "Ac procedit quandoque sane per modum subreptionis, ut si gratia, denegata a Vicario Generali, petatur ab Episcopo nulla facta mentione denegationis; sed alias independens est a subreptione, nec sufficit manifestare denegationem ut rescriptum possit valide obtineri; est ergo conditio diversa ab ea quae ex veritate precum desumitur, et habet locum non tantum in rescriptis, sed et in oraculis vivae vocis."—*Institutiones,* I, n. 284 ad B).

[88] The defects enumerated in can. 46 are said to render the rescript ineffective as far as the prospective beneficiary is concerned; they are not said to result in the invalidity of the rescript.—Cf. Abbo-Hannan, *The Sacred Canons,* I, 78. Likewise, can. 48, § 2, seems to be dealing with the ineffectiveness of rescripts rather than with their invalidity.

perior does not include in the rescripts themselves derogatory clauses to remove the obstacles to the validity or effectiveness of the letters, as envisioned in the canons in question. The reason for this is the fact that the *preces* for the rescripts make no mention of these hindrances. The same may be the case regarding the invalidating lack of consent referred to in canons 43 and 44, § 2. Hence, it may be said that a petitioner's failure to express the facts and circumstances mentioned in the canons under consideration is an indirect cause of the nullity or ineffectiveness of his rescript.

Nonetheless, it must be noted that according to these canons if the proposed derogatory clauses are present in the rescripts, or if the consent of the one who first refused to grant the favor is had in order to issue the rescripts the second time they are requested, the rescripts are valid or effective. What is more, the lawgiver seems not to be concerned regarding the reason why the aforesaid clauses and consent are present. In other words, so far as the obstacles in question are concerned, the legislator makes the validity or effectiveness of the rescripts involved depend primarily upon the presence of these clauses or consent. If their validity or effectiveness depends upon the petitioner's mentioning these obstacles, this dependence is at most incidental. Indeed, in some instances there is no such dependence at all. Thus, if the superior would of his own accord effectively remove the obstacles in question without their having actually been brought to his attention by the petitioner, the subsequent rescript would be valid.

Nevertheless, while this writer believes that the obstacles referred to in the canons under consideration need not absolutely (*per se*) be mentioned for the validity of the rescripts requested in their presence, he advises that in practice they be expressed as a precautionary measure. There is always the possibility that the superior will not take the steps noted in these canons to remove these hindrances unless the petitioner informs him of their existence.

2) *Concerning the requirements of the universal law for particular rescripts.* The law of the Code requires for the validity of rescripts conferring offices or benefices that the petition make

mention of any other *incompatible* office or benefice which the prospective recipient may already have. Otherwise the rescript is invalid, unless it contains a clause derogating from the law forbidding the simultaneous holding of incompatible offices or benefices.[89] Moreover, in regard to benefices the Code demands that, if the requested benefice is in the peaceful possession of another person, the petitioner inform the superior of the name of the possessor, the time during which the other person has been in possession, and the particular reason from which it is clear that no right to the benefice belongs to the possessor.[90]

In reference to rescripts granting permission to religious to contract debts and obligations, canon 534, § 2, prescribes as follows:

> In precibus pro obtinendo consensu ad contrahenda debita vel obligationes, exprimi debent alia debita vel obligationes, quibus ipsa persona moralis, religio vel provincia vel domus, ad eum diem gravatur; secus obtenta venia invalida est.

Concerning the *preces* for dispensations from irregularities and impediments to sacred ordination, canon 991, § 2, lays down this rule:

> Si agatur de irregularitate ex homocidio voluntario, etiam numerus delictorum exprimendus est sub poena nullitatis concedendae dispensationis.

In reference to the alienation of ecclesiastical property that is divisible, canon 1532, § 4, makes the following prescription:

> Si agatur de alienanda re divisibili, in petenda licentia aut consensu pro alienatione exprimi debent partes antea alienatae; secus licentia irrita est.

It may be advantageous at this point to consider petitions from dispensations from the matrimonial impediments of mixed religion and disparity of worship in the light of the rulings of

[89] Can. 156, § 3, and can. 1439, § 1. The writer wishes to emphasize that in this instance the invalidity of the rescript involved may be due directly to the petitioner's failure to mention an incompatible office or benefice. Hence, his position here is not contradictory to that taken above under the general requirements.—Cf. *supra*, pp. 151-152.

[90] Can. 1447.

canon 1061, § 1, and canon 1071 respectively regarding the *cautiones* necessary for the validity of these dispensations. Canon 1061, § 1, states as follows:

> Ecclesia super impedimento mixtae religionis non dispensat, nisi: 1°. . . .; 2°. Cautionem praestiterit coniux acatholicus de amovendo a coniuge catholico perversionis periculo, et uterque coniux de universa prole catholice tantum baptizanda et educanda; 3°. Moralis habeatur certitudo de cautionum implemento.

Canon 1071 reads as follows:

> Quae de mixtis nuptiis in canonibus 1060-1064 praescripta sunt, applicari quoque debent matrimoniis quibus obstat impedimentum disparitatis cultus.[91]

In view of the essential importance of the *cautiones* to the validity of these dispensations, it may seem that some reference to these promises should be made in the petitions for the rescripts which convey the dispensations, especially if both the parties or the non-Catholic party involved refuses to make the promises.

[91] Cf. cans. 1043, 1044, and 1045, § 1, which require the *cautiones* even in the cases contemplated therein. Cf. also Vlaming-Bender, *Praelectiones*, p. 148; Van Hove, *De Rescriptis*, p. 145; Oesterle, "De Cautionibus Matrimonialibus," *Jus Pontificium* (Romae, 1921——), XV (1935), 75; Harrington, "The Importance of the *Cautiones* in Disparity of Worship," *The Ecclesiastical Review* (*The American Ecclesiastical Review*), Vols. I-XXXII, Philadelphia, 1889-1905; from 1905: *The Ecclesiastical Review*, Vols. XXXIII-CIX, Philadelphia, 1905-1943; from 1944: *The American Ecclesiastical Review*, Washington, D. C., Vol. CX, 1944-), LXV (1921), 261.

Apropos of the prescriptions of cans. 1061, § 1, nn. 2 and 3, and 1071, it is interesting to note the following remark made by D. Boyle in defending the opinion that insincere *cautiones* do not invalidate the dispensations for which there are required *cautiones* that beget moral certainty: "The *preces* in the application for a dispensation embrace the *cause* for the dispensation and not the *cautiones*, which constitute the condition under which the dispensation is granted."—*The Juridic Effects of Moral Certitude on Pre-Nuptial Guarantees*, p. 105. (For a proposed rebuttal of the aforesaid opinion regarding insincere promises, cf. Kelly, "Insincere '*Cautiones*,' in the Light of Recent Rota Decisions," *The Jurist* (Washington, D. C., 1941-), XIII (1953), 33-56.) Nonetheless, it must be remembered in regard to the *cautiones* that it is the intention of the lawgiver that they be made before the dispensation is granted. Cf. Vlaming-Bender, *op. cit.*, p. 149.

Nonetheless, the writer submits that the mention in the formal *preces* of the fact that the *cautiones* have or have not been made is not necessary for the validity of the subsequent rescript. He takes this position for two reasons. First of all, neither canon 1061, § 1, nor canon 1071 expressly or equivalently demand for the sake of the validity of the relevant rescripts the mention of the *cautiones* in the *preces* for those rescripts.[92] Secondly, he has been able to find no source nor authority for saying that the *stylus Curiae Romanae* requires the mention of the *cautiones* in the petitions for such dispensations in order to preserve the validity of the rescripts conveying them.[93]

As a further clarification of his position on this point of the mention of the *cautiones,* the writer wishes to stress that in this discussion he is referring only to the formal preces.[93a] He does not intend by the position which he has taken to indicate that the superior who is asked to grant the relevant dispensations should not be informed that the *cautiones* have or have not been made. On the contrary, he strongly urges those through whom petitions for rescripts conveying dispensations from the impediments of mixed religion and disparity of worship are presented to relay to the superior the aforementioned information. He maintains, however, that this information is not required to be mentioned in the *pars narrativa* of the formal *preces* in order to fulfill the essential condition *"si preces veritate nitantur"* as specified in canon 42, § 1.

b) The requirements of the stylus Curiae Romanae, strictly so-called [94]

As has already been noted, the writer proposes to treat explicitly of the requirements of the *stylus Curiae Romanae,*

[92] Cf. can. 11 which states: "Irritantes aut inhabilitantes eae tantum leges habendae sunt, quibus aut actum esse nullum aut inhabilem esse personam expresse vel aequivalenter statuitur."

[93] Needless to say, if mention of the *cautiones* should be demanded for validity by the style of another curia, those who are governed by that *stylus* would have to abide by it.

[93a] Cf. *supra,* p. 18.

[94] The *stylus Curiae Romanae,* strictly so-called, consists of the customary law, instructions, and observances of the various dicasteries of the Roman Curia.—Cf. *supra,* p. 144.

strictly so-called, only in relation to petitions for rescripts that convery dispensations from matrimonial impediments.[95]

1) *Concerning rescripts for the external forum.* In this regard the basic document to be considered is the Instruction issued by the Sacred Congregation for the Propagation of the Faith on May 9, 1877.[96] The Sacred Roman Congregations still require for the validity of their rescripts that many of the matters prescribed in this Instruction be mentioned, even though some of its demands no longer bind under pain of nullity.[97]

Accordingly, then, the following matters must be mentioned for the validity of the rescripts under consideration: [98]

1. "The surname and family name of the petitioners, which are to be set down distinctly, clearly, and without abbreviations."

This demand, however, must be understood in the light of canon 47. This canon rules that rescripts are not rendered invalid by an error in the name of the person to whom or by whom they are issued, nor by a mistake in the place of residence of the grantee, nor by an error concerning the subject matter of the rescript, provided that in the judgment of the ordinary there is no doubt as to the identity of the person or the object of the favor.[99]

[95] The relationship between these requirements and the petitions for rescripts conveying dispensations from the minor matrimonial impediments will be considered in the commentary on can. 1054. Cf. *infra*, pp. 188-199.

[96] *Collectanea*, II, n. 1470, pp. 105-106.

[97] Cf. Gasparri, *Tractatus Canonicus de Matrimonio* (ed. nova ad mentem Codicis i.c., 2 vols., Romae, 1932), I, 198-203 (hereafter cited as *De Matrimonio*).

[98] In these pages concerning dispensations in the external forum, the part of the text which is enclosed in quotation marks represents a translation of those sections of the corresponding numbers of the Instruction of May 9, 1877, already cited, that are still in effect. The rest of the text is a brief commentary on the translated quotations of the aforesaid Instruction.

[99] The ordinary here referred to is the ordinary of the person who obtains the rescript, including the superiors of exempt religious, or the ordinary of the place where this person is staying.—Cf. Cicognani, *Canon Law*, p. 731, and Maroto, *Institutiones*, I, n. 284 ad II, c. 1, 3°. Hence, the judgment in this matter is not left to private persons. However, Cappello makes this pertinent observation in this regard: "Iudicium Ordinarii, de

Hence, from the norms of canon 47 it can be concluded that as long as the error which arises in the petitioners' names is simply an accidental one, that is, one which allows the ordinary to be certain of the identity of the persons involved, the rescript is valid.[100] The following are examples of cases in which a purely accidental error is involved: (*a*) when a simple name is substituted for the diminutive form of that name and vice versa, for instance, Ann for Annette, and Annette for Ann; (*b*) when only one part of a person's double name is given, for example, Joan for Joan Marie; (*c*) when either of the petitioners is indicated not by his own surname but by the baptismal name of his or her father or mother respectively, as may happen when a dispensation from consanguinity is requested and a genealogical tree is presented with the petition; for instance, Thomas, the father's name, is given for William, the son's name, or Grace, the mother's name, for Gladys, the daughter's name; (*d*) when one or the other letter or syllable in the names is incorrectly given, for example, for the surname "Frederick" is given Fredrick or Fredrich, and for the family name "Burns" is given Berns or Byrnes.[101]

2. "The diocese of domicile or quasi-domicile," and for *vagi*, of actual residence.[102]

In commenting on this requirement, Gasparri remarked:

> Proinde hodie sufficit clare scribere in instantia dioecesim, cuius Ordinarius dat has litteras testimoniales, vel preces transmittit.[103]

---

quo in c. 47, non requiritur: si error est ita manifestus, ut nulla sit ratio dubitandi; item si agitur de rescripto pro foro sacramentali, et, generatim, de quocumque rescripto pro foro interno; tunc confessarius ipse seu executor diiudicare debet."—*De Matrimonio*, pp. 275-276.

100 Cappello, *op. cit.*, p. 275.

101 Cf. Cappello, *loc. cit.* Vlaming-Bender, in commenting on can. 47, have this to say: "Quare hodie valet rescriptum quod e.g. pro [oratore] *Petro* habet *Paulum,* aut pro Petro *Muller* habet Petrum *Meyer;* dummodo *iudicio Ordinarii* nulla sit de persona oratorum dubitatio."—*Praelectiones*, p. 369.

102 Cf. Gasparri, *ibid.*, p. 200. Cf. also cans. 90-94.

103 *Ibid.*, p. 200, nota 1. Cf. also can. 1055.

If it happens that there are several dioceses by the same name, the difficulty of identifying exactly the one to which reference is made in the petition can be obviated by a noting of the place, that is, of the country or the state in which the diocese in question is situated.[104]

Furthermore, if each of the petitioners is from a different diocese, the names of both dioceses should be mentioned in the *preces*. It is probable, however, that the expression of both of these names is not required under pain of nullity in petitions referred to the Holy See.[105]

If any error occurs in the name of the diocese, one will apply the norms of canon 47 in order to determine whether or not the error is such as to invalidate the rescript.[106] Hence, if the error is a substantial one so that in the judgment of the ordinary there is real doubt regarding the identity of the persons for whom the rescript is intended, then the rescript is invalid. Such could be the case, for instance, if for the Diocese of Harrisburg mention were made of the Diocese of Greensburg.[107] If, however, the error is purely accidental, the rescript remains valid. Such would ordinarily be the case if a letter was omitted or added in the spelling of the name of the diocese, for instance, if the name "Harrisburg" were spelled Harissburg.[108]

[104] Gasparri, *ibid.*, p. 200, nota 1.

[105] Gasparri, *loc. cit.* Apropos of this requirement, if the relevant dispensation is granted by the petitioners' own ordinary, it is sufficient that there is indication in the *preces* that the petitioners have their domicile or quasi-domicile or their actual residence, if they be *vagi*, in the ordinary's diocese. This indication can be given, for instance, by naming the place in the diocese where the domicile or quasi-domicile or actual residence respectively is had.

[106] Cf. *supra*, p. 156.

[107] Cf. Gasparri, *loc. cit.*

[108] Cappello, *loc. cit.* In this regard Vlaming-Bender make this observation: "Iamvero, dummodo de oratorum personis constet, quis sit eorum verus Ordinarius, non obstante errore in rescripto, pariter facile ac certo cognoscitur; aut saltem facile constabit quis sit Ordinarius qui litteras testimoniales dedit vel preces transmisit ad Sedem Apostolicam, quo hic, quatenus ipse non sit '*oratorum* Ordinarius,' tamen, ad normam can. 1055, rescriptum exsequatur."—*Praelectiones*, p. 369.

There is some question whether it is necessary for the sake of the validity of the rescripts under consideration to mention in the *preces* for them also the names both of the pastor and of the parish in which the petitioners have a domicile, quasi-domicile, or, if they are *vagi,* their actual residence. The Instruction of 1877 does not require the mention of these names. Hence, some commentators have concluded that the mention of the names of the petitioners' pastor and parish is not required for the sake of validity, even if *angustia loci* is given as the cause for the seeking of the dispensation.[109] Yet, the formulas of the Sacred Congregation of the Sacraments, which is competent for the Latin Church, except for missionary lands, to handle all matrimonial dispensations except those from mixed religion and disparity of cult, include these names.[110] Vlaming-Bender, therefore, consider it necessary to mention in the petitions the names in question.[111]

This difference of opinion has apparently arisen on this point because it is not sufficiently clear whether, by including the names in question in its formulas, the Sacred Congregation of the Sacraments has thereby made it a part of its *stylus iuris* that the mention of them is required for the validity of the rescripts involved. Hence, in practice, this writer submits that *post factum* the omission of these names does not invalidate these rescripts.[112] When petitions are being prepared, however, he advises that these names be included in them not only because of the extrinsic probability which the opinion of Vlaming-Bender has from their support of it but also because the inclusion of them in its formulas by the Congregation indicates its desire that they be mentioned.

109 Cappello, *De Matrimonio,* p. 272; Gasparri, *loc. cit.*

110 In the Roman Curia the Holy Office is exclusively competent to grant dispensations from the impediments of mixed religion and disparity of cult.—Cf. can. 247, § 3. Concerning dispensations involving two Orientals or an Oriental and a Latin Catholic, cf. can. 257, § 1.

111 "Hic scilicet ad earum calcem nomen, tum suum tum paroeciae suae, una cum nomine dioecesis, in precum exodio iam indicando, apponat. Ita habent formulae S. C. de Sacr."—Vlaming-Bender, *op. cit.,* p. 339. They qualify this statement, however, by saying: "Si alterutra pars sit *acatholica* de huius [paroeciae] loco non est quod mentio fiat."—*Ibid.,* nota 2.

112 Can. 15.—There seems to be a *dubium iuris.*

3. "The species, and, indeed, the lowest species, of the impediment" from which the dispensation is requested.

The species or kind of impediment is mentioned when the petitioner indicates that he is seeking a dispensation from consanguinity, affinity, disparity of cult, etc. The *lowest* species of the following impediments is made known in this manner:

a) regarding public decency, by the petitioner's mentioning whether it has arisen from an invalid marriage or from public or notorious concubinage;[113]

b) regarding a vow of chastity, by his indicating whether it is a vow of perfect chastity, or of not marrying, or of receiving sacred orders, or of entering the religious state;[114]

c) regarding the perpetration of a qualified crime, by the petitioner's mentioning whether it has arisen

> ex coniugicidio utroque machinante, aut ex coniugicidio cum adulterio, alterutro machinante, vel ex solo adulterio cum promissione aut attentatione matrimonii etiam per actum civilem tantum;[115]

d) regarding spiritual relationship, by his indicating whether the impediment to be dispensed exists between the minister and the person baptized, or between a sponsor and the baptized party.[116]

The lowest species of consanguinity is indicated by way of the statement whether this impediment has arisen through a lawful or through an unlawful sexual union. Under the present canonical discipline, however, it is doubtful that the lowest species of this impediment must be mentioned in the *preces* for a dispensation from it in order to ensure the validity of that dispensation. Vlaming-Bender, on the one hand, indicate that mention of the lowest species in the *preces* is necessary for the validity of the

[113] Gasparri, *De Matrimonio,* I, 200, nota 2.

[114] Gasparri, *loc. cit.*

[115] Gasparri, *loc. cit.*

[116] Wernz-Vidal, *Ius Canonicum ad Codicis Normam Exactum,* Vol. V, *Ius Matrimoniale* (3. ed., a Philippo Aguirre recognita, Romae: Apud Aedes Universitatis Gregorianae, 1946), p. 569 (hereafter cited as *Ius Matrimoniale*).

consequent dispensation.[117] Gasparri, on the other hand, who must be recognized as an eminent authority on the requirements of the *stylus Curiae Romanae,* had this to say on this point: "*Quod attinet ad consanguinitatem, valde proderit in precibus adiicere utrum ex copula illicita proveniat, dispensatio enim facilius impetrabitur.*" [118] Accordingly, since a *dubium iuris* seems to have arisen in respect to the *stylus Curiae* in this matter, the present writer submits on the basis of canon 15 that the fact of whether consanguinity has arisen through a lawful or through an unlawful sexual union needs not to be mentioned in the *preces* for the validity of a dispensation from this impediment.

It is important to note, in regard to this requirement of mentioning the *species infima* of impediments, that its purpose is to forewarn a petitioner against indicating in his *preces* an impediment different from the one which really exists. If he does so, the subsequent rescript will be invalid.[119]

4. "The degree of consanguinity or affinity or public decency . . . ; the line, that is [in regard to consanguinity and affinity], whether the line is direct or collateral . . . ; whether the petitioners are joined through a double bond of consanguinity . . ." [120]

[117] *Op. cit.,* p. 339.

[118] *Ibid.,* p. 201, nota 1.

[119] Cf. *infra,* pp. 187, 194-196. Cf. also Gasparri, *ibid.,* nota 2, and Vlaming-Bender, *op. cit.,* p. 369. Gasparri stated that the rescript is not invalid if the erroneous designation occurs only in the rescript itself, and not in the *preces* for the relevant rescript.—*Loc. cit.* Vlaming-Bender, however, have this to say on this point: "Verba autem canonis citati [i.e., can. 47]: '. . . aut *rei* de qua agitur' non possunt applicari ipsi *impedimento* erronee designato e.g. si pro *affinitate* haberetur *consanguinitas,* aut vice versa. Hic enim non foret error 'in *nomine* . . . rei de qua agitur' sed error quoad *rem ipsam,* seu quoad ipsius gratiae substantiam."—*Loc. cit.*

[120] In reference to the multiplication of the bond of consanguinity, the Instruction of 1877 described a basis of multiplication which is no longer recognized under the present canonical discipline, viz., the fact that the consanguinity arises both from the side of the father and from the side of the mother. Under the law of the Code, the impediment of consanguinity is multiplied only when the common ancestor is multiplied.—Can. 1076, § 2. The impediment of affinity is multiplied: a) as often as the impediment

Accordingly, if a petitioner incorrectly mentions a more distant degree than that in which he is bound by these impediments, his rescript will be invalid. When the impediment is one of consanguinity or affinity, however, and the degree stated in the petition is less distant than that in which the persons are actually bound, the consequent rescript will be valid, even if the misstatement is due to bad faith.[121] Such would be the case, for example, if the petitioner who finds himself under either of these impediments would mention that he is bound in the second degree, whereas he is, in fact, bound only in the third degree.

If the degrees of the impediment involved are unequal or mixed, it is not necessary for the validity of the dispensation and the rescript to indicate the less distant degree.[122] An exception must be made to the last statement when the less distant degree that is involved happens to be the first degree of consanguinity.[123]

---

of consanguinity from which it arises is multiplied; b) whenever marriage is successively repeated with a blood relative of a deceased spouse.—Can. 1077, § 2, 1° and 2°. Furthermore, while the Instruction spoke only of multiplied consanguinity, the obligation to mention the existence of a multiplied bond extends to any impediment that is *de facto* multiplied in the case for which a dispensation is sought. Cf. *infra,* p. 163, no. 5.

[121] Cf. can. 1052 and Pontificia Commissio ad Codicis Canones Authentice Interpretandos, 8 iul. 1948—*AAS,* XL (1948), 386. "Haec regula non videtur applicanda publicae honestati, tum ob silentium Codicis, tum propter difficultatem aeque gravem dispensandi in primo et secundo gradu lineae rectae."—Cappello, *op. cit.,* p. 277. The impediment of public decency does not exist in the collateral line.—Can. 1078.

[122] Cf. can. 96, § 3. Cf. also Cappello, *op. cit.,* p. 272. Gasparri agreed with Cappello on this point; he made this observation, however: "Attamen cum in forma rescriptorum S. C. de Sacramentis semper exprimantur ambo gradus lineae inaequalis, ideo etiam in supplici libello erunt declarandi."—*De Matrimonio,* I, 201, nota 1. Cf. the statement of Wernz-Vidal that is quoted in the footnote immediately below.

[123] "Utrum haec [i.e., in linea collaterali inaequali, licet exprimendus sit uterque gradus, id non videtur pertinere ad valorem] extendenda sint ad casum, quo omissa fuerit mentio gradus primi: affirmat *De Smet,* n. 846, cui videtur consentire *Cappello,* saltem in quantum exceptionem non facit n. 275, 4°; negat *Ferreres,* Theol. moral. II, n. 960, pro casu secundi gradus attingentis primum. Stilus Datariae erat habere dispensationem ut invalidam ad normam Const. S. Pii V, *'Sanctissimus'* 20 aug. 1566 (Collect.

Accordingly, one can see the prudence in attaching to the *preces* for dispensations from consanguinity and affinity a genealogical tree. Such a schema of the exact relationship existing between the parties can often give the superior more clear and accurate knowledge of the case presented to him. In fact, if a petitioner would make a mistake in naming the degree of his impediment, but the true degree would be shown in the genealogical tree attached to his petition, the subsequent rescript would be valid.[124]

5. "The number of impediments, for example, double or multiple consanguinity or affinity, or relationship by blood and affinity, if such be the case, or any other impediment whatsoever, whether it be diriment or impedient." [125]

Canon 1052 makes an important qualification in regard to this general demand of the *stylus Curiae* against the invalidating

n. 1452²). Si pro sententia affirmante allegatur c. 96, § 3, iure merito observat *Vlaming,* II, n. 453, 4°, hoc Codicis praescriptum non esse novum, sed iam contineri in Decretalibus *Gregorii IX,* cap. 9, de consang. IV, 14, quo supposito S. Pius V dedit suam Constitutionem et Dataria in suo stilo ipsi inhaesit. Pariter S. Paenitentiaria habebat invalidas dispensationes, si primus gradus non fuisset expressus; S. C. de d. Sacr. iam immutasse illum stilum non constat et certe pro immutatione iam facta aut facienda non peti potest argumentum ex c. 96, § 3. Interim ergo, ut consulatur valori, opportunum est non omittere expressionem primi gradus.

"Haec sententia confirmatur iis quae in Instr. S. C. de Sacr. d. 1 aug. 1931 continentur. Dicitur enim ibi haud sufficere ad dispensationem huius impedimenti obtinendam suetas, quae pro ceteris impedimentis etiam maioris gradus adducuntur, causas. Monentur praeterea Episcopi de obligatione saltem subscribendi propria manu et speciali modo commendandi huiusmodi preces, quotiescumque litteras ipsas commendatitias suis manibus integre exarare non valeant. Ex his verbis elucet S. Congregationem in dispensando impedimento consanguinitatis magnum discrimen facere inter secundum gradum lineae collateralis simpliciter et secundum gradum attingentem primum in eadem linea; qua de re dubitare iam non licet hanc circumstantiam debere exprimi in precibus ad validitatem dispensationis obtinendae."—Wernz-Vidal, *op. cit.,* p. 569, nota 132. For the text of the Instruction of Aug. 1, 1931, cf. *AAS,* XXIII (1931), 413-415; Bouscaren, *The Canon Law Digest,* I, 514-516.

[124] Cf. Cappello, *op. cit.,* p. 272, ad n. 5°, a). Cf. also S. C. de Sacramentis, instructio, 29 iun. 1941—*AAS,* XXXIII (1941), 302; Bouscaren, *The Canon Law Digest,* II, 258.

[125] Cf. also can. 1050.

effect of subreption set down in canon 42, § 1. Concerning dispensations from consanguinity and affinity this canon states:

> Dispensatio ab impedimento consanguinitatis vel affinitatis, concessa in alieno impedimenti gradu, valet . . . licet reticitum [in petitione aut in concessione] fuerit aliud impedimentum eiusdem speciei in aequali vel inferiore gradu.[126]

On the basis of other norms of the *stylus Curiae,* it may be concluded that a petitioner may omit mention of the following facts and circumstances without laying his rescript open to invalidity:

a) the fact that the relevant marriage is to be contracted or has already been attempted; [127]

b) in the case of the validation of a marriage, the fact that one or both of the parties were in good or bad faith concerning the impediment which has invalidated their marriage, the fact that the banns were announced prior to the marriage, the fact that the canonical form was observed by the parties in attempting their invalid marriage; [127a]

c) the fact that his invalid marriage has been consummated or that he had a malicious intention in consummating it—which fact may be omitted whether or not the invalid marriage is given as the motivating reason for the dispensation; [128]

d) the fact that a *civil* marriage has taken place, unless this is presented as the motivating cause for obtaining the requested rescript; [129]

e) The circumstance of *copula* or *copula incestuosa,* even if

[126] Cf. Gasparri, *ibid.,* p. 202, nota 1. This provision of can. 1052 is applicable even if the misstatement of the degree involved and the suppression of *"aliud impedimentum eiusdem speciei in aequali vel inferiore gradu"* is due to bad faith.—Cf. *supra,* p. 162, note 121.

[127] Cf. Gasparri, *ibid.,* p. 202, n. 342 and nota 2.

[127a] Cf. Gasparri, *loc. cit.*

[128] "Dispensationes matrimoniales super quovis impedimento, sive agatur de matrimoniis invalide contractis, sive de contrahendis esse validas, etiamsi copula, vel consilium et intentio per eam facilius gratiam impetrandi reticita fuerint."—S. C. S. Off., decretum, 18 mart. 1891—*Collectanea,* II, n. 1749. Cf. also Gasparri, *ibid.,* p. 202, nota 2.

[129] Cappello, *op. cit.,* p. 274.

the parties intended or hoped that by committing these acts they would obtain the desired dispensation more easily;[130]

f) the circumstance of the parties' having contracted an invalid marriage with the hope of thereby more easily obtaining the needed dispensation;[131]

g) the circumstance of *raptus "qui praecesserat et purgatus fuerat"*;[132]

h) other circumstances which affect the parties, for example, their family background, their condition of life, their age, their character, and so forth, unless, of course, these circumstances constitute an integral part of the impediment involved, as may happen in the case of age, or they are advanced as the reasons for the rescript, as would be the case if the cause for the dispensation would be the fact that the woman is a widow.[133]

Besides the matters referred to in numbers 1 to 5 above, the authors maintain that the religion of the petitioners must also be mentioned for validity, at least if one of them is a non-Catholic.[134] As far as this writer could ascertain, however, they do not indicate whether it is required to mention simply the fact that one of the parties is a non-Catholic, or whether the particular sect or religious body to which the non-Catholic belongs must also be noted. In view of the purpose of mentioning the religion of the petitioners,[135] the writer submits that it is sufficient simply to express the fact that one of the parties is a non-Catholic.

[130] Cf. the encyclical letter of the Holy Office, issued on June 25, 1885, and approved by Pope Leo XIII. This letter stated that dispensations from matrimonial impediments will be valid "etiamsi copula incestuosa, vel consilium et intentio per eam facilius dispensationem impetrandi reticita fuerint. . . ."—*Collectanea,* II, n. 1635, p. 208.

[131] Gasparri, *loc. cit.*, and Cappello, *loc. cit.*

[132] Gasparri, *ibid.*, p. 204, and Cappello, *loc. cit.*

[133] Cappello, *De Matrimonio,* p. 275.

[134] Cappello, *op. cit.*, p. 273; Gasparri, *loc. cit.* Vlaming-Bender express their mind on this point by saying: "Circumstantiae *aetatis, religionis* . . . eatenus tantum exprimendae veniunt, quatenus postulat . . . ipsius impedimenti (e.g. mixtae religionis) . . . natura. Si de religione nihil exprimatur, uterque orator supponitur catholicus."—*Praelectiones,* p. 341.

[135] Cf. *infra,* p. 166.

The commentators have arrived at their conclusion concerning the necessity of indicating the religion of the petitioners because of the negative response that was issued by the Sacred Congregation for the Propagation of the Faith on November 24, 1902, to the following question:

> Se i Vescovi ed i Vicari Apostolici nei regni Britannici possano, in virtù delle facoltà ordinarie e straordinarie loro accordate dalla S. Sede, dispensare negl'impedimenti di consanguinità e di affinità coi loro diocesani o sudditi quando una parte dei contraenti sia cattolica, l'altra acattolica.[136]

Cappello, while he holds that this requirement must be observed for validity, notes that the force of this demand is not absolutely certain under the law of the Code, since the response of the Holy See upon which it is based does not contain expressly a *"clausula irritans."* [137] Yet it must be remembered that only the Holy Office is competent to grant matrimonial dispensations which involve a non-Catholic.[138] Accordingly, if a rescript conveying a dispensation for a case involving a non-Catholic would be granted, knowingly or unknowingly, by another Congregation, the rescript would be invalid. Hence, the obvious purpose of mentioning the fact that one of the parties is a non-Catholic is to make sure that the petition will be directed to the Holy Office so that it may grant the requested dispensation and rescript.[139]

As this writer sees this matter, if a Congregation other than the Holy Office would grant a rescript conveying a dispensation for a case involving a non-Catholic, the rescript would be certainly invalid. Its invalidity, however, would be due directly to the fact that the superior who granted it would have lacked the necessary power and competence to do so. The nullity of the rescript would arise only indirectly and accidentally from the concealment of the fact that one of the parties is not a Catholic. Actually, since it is not absolutely clear that the style of the Curia demands the mention of the parties' religion under

[136] *Collectanea,* I, n. 664.

[137] *Op. cit.,* pp. 273-274. Cf. can. 11.

[138] Cf. can. 247, § 3. Cf. also Gasparri, *loc. cit.*

[139] Cf. Gasparri, *loc. cit.*

pain of invalidity, one can, in arguing altogether theoretically, say that even though the non-Catholic's religion were not mentioned, the rescript in question when granted by the Holy Office would be valid. The reason for this conclusion is that in such a grant the Holy Office would obviously intend to apply the jurisdiction which in full competence it possesses. Contrariwise, even if the non-Catholic's religion were mentioned, but another Congregation granted the dispensation, the rescript would be invalid.

Viewing this problem practically, however, this writer believes that the religion of the parties should be mentioned in the petitions, at least if one of them is a non-Catholic. Even though in itself (*per se*) the concealment of this fact does not appear to imply a substantial subreption, nevertheless there seems to be no other practical way of fulfilling the purpose which this requirement, as noted by the authors, is meant to serve. Moreover, in such an important matter as making sure that each of the branches of the Roman Curia acts within its own competence and therefore validly, it is most likely that, whenever there is any doubt about the religion of the petitioners, the request will not be granted until the doubt is solved. Nonetheless, *post factum*, if the *only* reason for attacking the validity of the rescripts here discussed is the fact that the religion of the parties was not mentioned in the *preces*, the present writer submits that the rescripts must be adjudged valid if they were granted by the Congregation which was competent in the case.

2) *Concerning rescripts for the internal forum.* If a rescript is intended for the internal *sacramental* forum, there are to be omitted in the *preces* all those matters which will divulge the identity of the petitioners. Accordingly, in place of their real names there should be used fictitious names, such as *Titius* and *Titia*. Their diocese and parish likewise should not be named. The same requirements, however, that have been mentioned for rescripts in the external forum in reference to the species of the impediments in question, their degree and line, and the number of impediments, apply also to the *preces* for rescripts in the internal sacramental forum.[140]

[140] Cappello, *op. cit.*, p. 277. Cf. *supra*, pp. 160-164.

When, however, the requested rescript serves for the internal *non-sacramental* forum, there must be mentioned in the petition for it the same matters that are required when a rescript for the external forum is involved.[141] This statement is based upon the fact that canon 1047 prescribes that there is to be kept in the secret archives of the curia a record of the dispensation from occult impediments that were granted in the internal non-sacramental forum. The same canon also provides that such dispensations are valid and effective in the external forum if the occult impediments become public.[142]

Article 3. Commentary on Canon 42, § 2—Obreption

The content of paragraph two of canon 42 may be expressed in the following manner: as far as the causes proposed for rescripts are concerned, rescripts are not invalidated by obreption, that is, by the allegation of a falsehood, provided that either the single final cause as presented be true, or at least one of several motivating reasons as proposed be true.[143]

A. The General Principle of Canon 42, § 2

In accordance with the lawgiver's intention to use canon 42 to bring into focus the exact meaning and the precise extent of the invalidating force of the condition *"si preces veritate nitantur,"* the wording of paragraph two in this canon clearly indicates that in it the legislator is concerned solely with the truth in relation to the *pars motiva* of the *preces*. More precisely, he is occupied exclusively with the juridic effect which obreption has upon rescripts when it is found in the causes alleged in the petitions for them.[144]

[141] Cf. *supra*, pp. 156-164.

[142] Cappello, *op. cit.*, p. 278.

[143] The text of can. 42, § 2, reads as follows: "Nec obstat expositio falsi, seu obreptio, dummodo vel unica causa proposita vel ex pluribus propositis una saltem motiva vera sit."

For a discussion of the nature of obreption, cf. *supra*, pp. 127-132.

[144] Rodrigo, *Tractatus de Legibus*, p. 560. In this regard it must be remembered that the grantor of a rescript can supply of his own knowledge causes in addition to those alleged in the *preces*. Cf. Bouscaren, *The Canon Law Digest*, Vol. IV, 85-86. Unless there is an indication of such an addition, however, it is not to be presumed. Nonetheless, if the grantor actually

As already indicated, in canon 42 the lawgiver treats *obreption* explicitly only in relation to the causes set down in the *preces*. Yet, this provision should not lead one to conclude that the allegation of a positive falsehood in the petitions never invalidates a rescript as long as at least one of the final causes as presented is true. Obreption in the *pars narrativa* and *postulativa* of the petitions is indirectly equivalent to subreption. Consequently, when a positive allegation of a falsehood appears in those two parts of the *preces*, its effect upon the validity of the subsequent rescripts is governed by the same principles that apply to subreption, that is, the norms of canon 42, § 1.[145]

Accordingly, the second paragraph of this canon sets forth an additional specification in regard to the application of the condition *"si preces veritate nitantur,"* precisely insofar as it affects the causes that are proposed for the rescripts.[146] This added specification may be expressed, by way of a general principle, in this manner: as far as the *pars motiva* of the *preces* is concerned, for the fulfillment of the essential condition *"si preces veritate nitantur"* it is required but it also suffices that there be present one true final cause. In other words, in regard to this part of the *preces* the lawgiver is satisfied to extend his demand for objective truth only to the final cause, or to one of the final causes if several are set down. He does not require under pain of invalidity that the impulsive causes be truthful, unless a petitioner fails to present a truly motivating reason, and the superior accepts the proposed impelling causes in the aggregate as constituting the single final cause for the granting of the rescript.[147]

---

adds a true final cause to the reasons alleged in the petition, all of which reasons are false, the consequent rescript must be adjuged to be valid.

[145] Cf. *supra*, p. 131.

[146] In his commentary on can. 42, § 2, Rodrigo states: *"Supponenda sunt etiam rite expressa* quae de stylo Curiae sunt ad validitatem exprimenda, scil. non quovis modo, sed prout in rei veritate sunt: nam si earum reticentia obest validitati rescripti, a fortiori vel saltem aequo iure praeiudicabit earum falsa expositio."—*Loc. cit.*

[147] Cf. Michiels, *Normae Generales,* II, 366. Cf. *supra*, pp. 20-21, for a description of final and impulsive causes; cf. pp. 21-26, for a discussion of how the exact nature of these causes is determined.

Among the many truly motivating causes that have been accepted by

The juridic reasoning underlying this general principle is undoubtedly based upon the nature of motivating and impelling causes. On the one hand, a truly motivating cause so efficaciously moves the superior to grant the requested rescript that other reasons in the petition may actually be looked upon as being superfluous.[148] Accordingly, following the Roman Law principle: *"Non solent, quae abundant, vitiare scripturas,"* [149] and abandoning the pre-Code discipline that called for the invalidation of rescripts obtained through reasons falsified in bad faith, the legislator has clearly indicated in this law that he considers one truthful motivating cause in a petition as sufficient for the granting of a valid favor.[150] Consequently, the presence of one

---

the Holy See for dispensations from the various matrimonial impediments, the following may be noted: 1) the poverty of a widow; 2) the limitations of the neighborhood; 3) the advanced age of the woman; 4) the lack or the inadequacy of a dowry; 5) public or notorious intercourse; 6) scandal or the woman's loss of reputation; 7) pregnancy and therefore the legitimation of offspring; 8) the validation of a marriage; 9) the danger of an attempted marriage; 10) the cessation of public concubinage; 11) the danger of incestuous concubinage; 12) the removal of serious scandals; 13) the avoidance of lawsuits concerning inheritance; 14) the restoration of peace; 15) a well founded hope for the conversion of a non-Catholic family or even of the non-Catholic party to the marriage; 16) the danger of the defection of the Catholic party; 17) the Catholic training of children born out of wedlock or in a previous marriage, and 18) the promotion of the public interests of the Church.—Abbo-Hannan, *The Sacred Canons,* II, 233-236. Cf. S. C. de Prop. Fide, instructio, 9 maii 1877—*Collectanea,* II, n. 1470. For a discussion of these aforementioned causes and a list of other causes that may be presented for matrimonial dispensations, cf. Abbo-Hannan, *ibid.,* pp. 233-238, and O'Mara, *Canonical Causes for Matrimonial Dispensations,* The Catholic University of America Canon Law Studies, n. 96 (Washington, D. C., 1935), *passim.* It should be noted that numbers 1 to 4 of the causes mentioned above do not ordinarily suffice for the granting of dispensations from the impediments of mixed religion and disparity of cult.—Benedictus XIV, *De Synodo Dioecesana* (2. ed., 2 vols., Parmae, 1764), I, lib. IX, c. 3, n. 3. Numbers 2 to 4 are not motivating causes for dispensations from the impediment of consanguinity in the first degree touching the second degree of the collateral line.—S. C. de Sacramentis, instructio, 1 aug. 1931—*AAS,* XXIII (1931), 415; cf. Bouscaren, *The Canon Law Digest,* I, 514-516.

[148] Michiels, *ibid.,* pp. 366-367.

[149] D. (50, 17) 94.—*Digesta.*

[150] For the pre-Code discipline in this matter, cf. *supra,* pp. 66-68, 72-74, 91-93.

true final cause now suffices to fulfill the condition *"si preces veritate nitantur"* as far as the *pars motiva* of the *preces* is concerned. On the other hand, a merely impelling reason of itself is not sufficient to move the superior to grant the petitioner's request. It merely prompts him, in the presence of a final cause, arising *aliunde,* to accede to the petition with more readiness, that is, more easily. Hence, even if the impulsive cause or causes as presented were completely truthful, in the absence of a truly final cause the superior would have no sufficient reason for granting the rescript. Therefore, at least one true motivating reason is required as a *conditio sine qua non* in the *pars motiva* of the *preces,*[151] unless, of course, the true impelling causes found therein effect in the aggregate a motivating cause.

B. Deductions from the General Principle of Canon 42, § 2

By means of the general principle which he enunciates in canon 42, § 2, the lawgiver has established, as far as the *pars motiva* of the *preces* is concerned, a clear distinction between obreption that is substantial or nullifying and that which is accidental or non-invalidating.[152] Therefore, it is obvious that not every act of obreption in the *pars motiva* of the *preces* invalidates a rescript. As long as there is one true final cause in it, the legislator considers this part of the petition to be substantially truthful. Hence, the consequent rescript will be valid, as far as the *pars motiva* of the *preces* is concerned, even though all the other causes therein, be they final or impelling, are false. Needless to say, however, by describing the required substantially truthful *pars motiva* in this fashion, the lawgiver does not thereby intend to occasion in other causes the allegation of a falsehood along with the truth. Rather, it seems that by establishing the aforesaid general principle he is urging truthfulness, pure and simple, in the petitions, and a disregard for other oftentimes *uselessly* abundant reasons, which merely waste his time.[153] Yet, this is not to say that a petitioner should always be satisfied with proposing only one true reason in his *preces.* As has been noted before, in the last analysis it lies with the superior

[151] Michiels, *ibid.,* p. 367.

[152] Cf. *supra,* pp. 131-132.

[153] Cicognani, *Canon Law,* pp. 716-717.

to decide in a given case whether the cause alleged in the petition is actually motivating or merely impelling. Hence, a reason that was considered to be a final cause in one case may be judged to be only impulsive in another situation because of different circumstances.[154]

Furthermore, it follows as a general rule from the principle of canon 42, § 2, that, when a petitioner presents only several merely impelling causes which are taken in the aggregate to constitute simultaneously the single final cause for the granting of the rescript, each of these impulsive reasons must be true in itself. Otherwise the single motivating reason proposed for the rescript will be false. Some authors make no mention of any exceptions to this general rule.[155] There is good reason to believe, however, that it does not necessarily bind in cases in which, among the several impelling causes proposed, one or the other *relatively insignificant* reason is found to be false. It must be remembered that the *pars motiva* of the *preces* is the cause or causes that are proposed for the rescripts. The substantial part of it is the final cause or causes which are alleged therein. What is more, as far as this part of the petitions and the validity of the consequent rescripts are concerned, the legislator demands only that it be substantially truthful. As canon 42, § 2, indicates, the *pars motiva* is such when it consists of at least one true motivating reason. Hence, since the lawmaker demands only a substantially truthful *pars motiva* in the petitions, he likewise requires only a substantial truthfulness in at least one final cause in the *preces*. In the cases in question, the substantial truthfulness of the single motivating reason must be derived from the truthfulness of the various impelling causes which, when taken together, constitute this one final cause. Rodrigo seems, therefore, to argue convincingly on the side of those who admit exceptions to the aforesaid general rule when he says:

> *Plures causae impulsivae,* seu seorsim insufficientes, possunt conflare unam motivam, quae non vitiabitur substantialiter ob falsitatem in una alterve quae relate ad cumulum leviores

[154] Cf. *supra*, p. 21.

[155] Among these authors are Chelodi, *Ius Canonicum de Personis*, p. 131; Cicognani, *op. cit.*, p. 716; Cocchi, *Commentarium*, I, 248; and Maroto, *Institutiones*, I, n. 284, ad II, A, c, 2°.

> putentur, nam parum pro nihilo reputatur; vel etiam, si iis seclusis, quae verae adhuc remanent causam gravem adhuc constituant.[156]

Consequently, in practice when a rescript is obtained in the circumstances considered in this discussion, it may safely be adjudged valid.

Article 4. Commentary on Canon 42, § 3—Independent Grants

Paragraph three of canon 42 states that subreption or obreption when it occurs in only one part of a rescript does not invalidate another part of the document if several favors are granted simultaneously by the same rescript.[157] In this particular law on rescripts the legislator is concerned only with letters that contain more than one favor, that is, with multiple rescripts. More precisely, the lawmaker is here dealing with rescripts which convey several favors, the natures of which are really different one from another. Consequently, the favors themselves are actually distinct and separable from, and intrinsically mutually independent of, one another. He is also concerned with rescripts which contain several favors that actually have the same nature but are virtually distinct insofar as they are intended for different individuals. Thus, when a single rescript contains a dispensation from the law of fast which has

156 *Tractatus de Legibus*, p. 560. Cf. also Cappello who makes the following statement concerning the universal application of the rule in question: "Quod semper et necessario verum non est. Ex gr. si *decem* causae propositae fuerint, et *una tantum* ex iisdem sit falsa, quisnam dicet rescribentem noluisse propterea concedere gratiam aut dispensationem? Neque ex textu iuris, neque ex stylo Curiae constat *certo* rescriptum irritari. Igitur standum est pro eius valore."—*Summa Iuris Canonici*, I, 120. Among the other authors who support this view are Coronata, *Institutiones*, I, 78, nota 7; Michiels, *Normae Generales*, II, 367; O'Neill, *Papal Rescripts of Favor*, p. 129; Sipos, *Enchiridion Iuris Canonici*, p. 31; and Van Hove, *De Rescriptis*, p. 147.

157 The text of can. 42, § 3, is as follows: "Vitium obreptionis vel subreptionis in una tantum parte rescripti aliam non infirmat, si una simul plures gratiae per rescriptum concedantur." No doubt the reader recognizes immediately that the legislator, in using the word "*pars*" in this canon, is not referring to the *pars narrativa*, etc., of rescripts. Rather, he has reference to the various favors that a single rescript may contain. For that reason the word "part" should be taken here as a synonym of "favor."

been granted not only to one but to several persons, the rescript virtually conveys not just one dispensation but as many dispensations as there are persons for whom the grant has been made.[158] Furthermore, the lawmaker is here legislating for multiple rescripts, only one or the other of the several parts of which is vitiated by subreption or obreption.

He is, therefore, not dealing with rescripts that contain only a single favor meant for one person alone. Nor is he here concerned with rescripts which in each and every part are vitiated by subreption or obreption.[159] He has already sufficiently indicated in paragraphs one and two of canon 42 that the presence of substantial subreption and obreption in the *preces* for such rescripts automatically nullifies the letters themselves and all their contents.[160]

A. The General Principle of Canon 42, § 3

In paragraph three of this canon it is the purpose of the legislator to specify precisely to what extent the invalidating force of subreption and obreption affects the various essentially or virtually distinct favors that a superior may grant in one and the same rescript.[161] The principle which he enunciates in fulfilling this purpose applies both to the cases in which subreption *or* obreption appears in the rescript involved and also to the case in which both defects are found together in the same rescript. This is so because the term *"vel"* in the expression

158 Coronata, *Institutiones*, I, 78-79.

159 An example of such rescripts is had in the case in which the rescript that is involved and all its contents depend as a single unit directly and immediately either upon the entire petition, itself taken as an indivisible unit in reference to the contents of the rescript, or upon the single final cause proposed for the rescript. In this situation substantial subreption or obreption in the *preces*, or obreption in the single motivating reason on account of which the rescript has been granted, results in the complete vitiation of the entire letter. What is more, in this case it makes no difference whether or not the several favors in the rescript are separable and mutually independent of each other.

160 This is said without prejudice to the provisions of cans. 45 and 1054. —Cf. *infra*, pp. 180-199.

161 Rodrigo, *Tractatus de Legibus*, p. 560.

"vitium obreptionis vel subreptionis" of paragraph three of canon 42 can be understood in both a conjunctive and a disjunctive sense, that is, in the sense of and/or.[162]

The general principle itself may be set down in this way: when a petition requesting several truly separable and mutually independent favors is *partially* infected with substantial subreption and/or obreption, there is invalidated only that favor in the consequent rescript which is directly attributable to and immediately dependent upon the nullifying untruthfulness in the *preces*.[163]

It is noteworthy that in the present canonical discipline the force of this principle is not affected by the presence of good or bad faith as the cause of the subreption or obreption in the rescripts in question. As is evident from the wording of canon 42, § 3, the lawmaker propounds this principle without any reference whatsoever to good and bad faith.[164] Nonetheless, it must be remembered that canon 2361 empowers an ordinary to inflict suitable penalties upon anyone who fraudulently or deceitfully commits subreption or obreption in the *preces* for rescripts from the Holy See or from the local ordinary. Hence, even though untruthfulness from bad faith, as such and in itself (*per se*), no longer causes a complete invalidation of the entire rescripts being considered here, it does lay open anyone guilty of it to appropriate punishment.[165]

One can adduce three reasons for explaining the legislator's mind in setting up the general principle that is contained in this part of his law on rescripts. The first is the fact that in the circumstances in which this principle preserves partially the validity of rescripts containing more than one favor, the rescript, like the petition for it, is one only materially. Virtually there are as many distinct *preces* and rescripts as there are separable

162 Blat, *Commentarium,* I, 136.

163 Cf. Michiels, *Normae Generales,* II, 371, and O'Neill, *Papal Rescripts of Favor,* p. 130.

164 For a discussion of the pre-Code discipline regarding the effect of subreption and obreption, when arising from bad faith, on rescripts containing more than one grant, cf. *supra,* pp. 66-68, 73-74, 91-94.

165 Cf. Van Hove, *De Rescriptis,* pp. 150-151.

and mutually independent favors. What is more, because of the separability and mutual independence of the various favors requested in the petition and contained in the rescript, both the petition and the rescript can be envisioned as being divided into several corresponding parts that have exclusive and independent reference to the respective favors themselves. These parts in turn are judged separately as distinct units, and the validity or nullity of each of them is decided independently of the other parts.[166] Hence, because of the virtual divisibility of the *preces* and the consequent rescript, which is based on the separability of the favors involved, the legislator has very logically restricted the nullifying effect of subreption and obreption to that part or to those parts of the rescript which are directly affected by these defects.

The second and third reasons, which underlie the general principle of canon 42, § 3, find expression, respectively, in the following principles of law: *"Utile non debet per inutile vitiari"* [167] and *"Non solent, quae abundant, vitiare scripturas."* [168] Actually, the applicability of these two norms to the general principle under consideration here seems clear from what has been said above regarding the virtual divisibility of the rescript involved. A favor that is nullified is useless, and its being mentioned in the rescript is superfluous, as far as its prospective beneficiary is concerned.

B. The Application of the General Principle of Canon 42, § 3

The general principle of canon 42, § 3, finds application in the following two cases which are of considerable practical importance.

Case I—There is, first of all, the case in which someone uses a single petition to request several mutually independent and separable favors. One or the other of the favors, however, is

[166] "In casu, siquidem, rescriptum non est unum nisi materialiter, sed virtualiter in ipso tot rescripta continentur quot gratiae conçeduntur: vis autem uniuscuique eorum in se tantum, seu independenter ab aliis, considerari potest."—Berutti, *Institutiones,* I, 132-133.

[167] Reg. 37, R. J., in VI°.

[168] D. (50, 17) 94.—*Digesta.*

infected with invalidating subreption or obreption which is directly attributable to some falsehood that is found in the *preces* for the rescript involved. An example of such a case is that in which two distinct dispensations from matrimonial impediments are sought in one and the same petition, with *angustia loci* being offered as the motivating reason for one of the dispensations, and *periculum incontinentiae* as the final cause for the other. Actually, *angustia loci* is not present in the case in question and is, therefore, a false cause. *Periculum incontinentiae,* however, does exist for the petitioner and, consequently, constitutes a true reason for the dispensation for which it is offered. Under these circumstances only that favor in the subsequent rescript which is immediately dependent upon the vitiating falsehood in the *preces* for the letter will be invalidated. The other favor or favors which are not directly attributable to the untruthfulness involved will stand to benefit their intended recipient because, as far as they are concerned, the petition for the rescript is founded on the truth.

That this case is rightfully brought within the scope of the general principle of canon 42, § 3, can be seen from the following considerations. To begin with, the *preces* which are presented are one only materially. Virtually there are as many petitions as there are mutually independent favors, for in the *pars narrativa* of his *preces* the petitioner presents, as the case requires and permits, different facts and circumstances for each of the favors requested.[169] In the *pars postulativa* he certainly mentions the distinct favors which he is seeking.[170] In the *pars motiva* he may possibly propose different causes or reasons in order to obtain each of the separable favors.[171] Hence, the petition in question must be considered virtually divisible. Moreover, the divisibility of these *preces* is carried over into the subsequent rescript which is likewise one only materially, while virtually there are as many rescripts as there are distinct and separable

[169] For a description of the *pars narrativa* of the *preces,* cf. *supra,* pp. 16-18.

[170] For a description of the *pars postulativa* of the *preces,* cf. *supra,* p. 18.

[171] For a description of the *pars motiva* of the *preces,* cf. *supra,* pp. 18-19.

favors. Consequently, in the circumstances envisioned in this case, both the *preces* and the rescript involved have the virtual divisibility that is required to preserve the validity of part of the rescript.[172]

Case II—Another case to which the general principle of canon 42, § 3, is applicable is that in which one rescript with a single favor is granted to several persons at the same time. The *preces* for the letter, however, are false by subreption or obreption in regard to one or the other of the prospective beneficiaries of the rescript, while in reference to the others they are truthful. Such may be the case, for instance, when several members of some religious institute receive a dispensation from their vows through one and the same rescript. Under these circumstances, it is held that the rescript in question is partially valid insofar as it stands to benefit those persons in reference to whom the *preces* are true. It is partially invalid inasmuch as the favor which it contains is nullified for those in regard to whom the petition is false by subreption or obreption.[173]

The application of the general principle of canon 42, § 3, to the case in question here is justifiable because, even though only one particular species of favor is granted in the single rescript, virtually there are as many favors in the letter as there are petitioners or other persons for whom the document is meant. What is more, these virtually distinct favors must be considered separable because of the mutual independence and individuality of the persons who are to benefit from the grant. Furthermore, because of the virtual multiplication of the favors which are contained in the single rescript involved here, the letter itself, as well as the petition for it, can be correctly said to be one only materially, while virtually there are as many petitions and rescripts as there are persons whom the letter is intended to benefit. Moreover, since the virtually distinct favors are separable, the petition for them and the rescript conveying them can right-

[172] Cf. *supra*, pp. 175-176. Cf. also Rodrigo, *Tractatus de Legibus*, pp. 560-561.

[173] Abbo-Hannan, *The Sacred Canons*, I, 75; Coronata, *Institutiones*, I, 78-79.

fully be considered to be virtually severable. Consequently, in this case also there is had the virtual divisibility which with reference to the *preces* and the subsequent rescript is requisite but also sufficient for conserving the validity of that part of the rescript which is not immediately dependent upon the nullifying untruthfulness in the petition for the letter.[174]

[174] Cf. *supra*, pp. 175-176.

CHAPTER VI

COMMENTARY ON CANON 45—*MOTU PROPRIO* GRANTED RESCRIPTS

Canon 45 states that, whenever the phrase *"motu proprio"* is appended to rescripts which are granted upon someone's petition, these are valid even though in the *preces* for the letters there be withheld the recounting of some truth which otherwise must necessarily be expressed; but they are not valid if there be proposed a false final cause as standing alone, without prejudice to the provisions of canon 1054.[1] This canon contains the special norms that define and govern the effect which substantial subreption and obreption have upon rescripts granted *motu proprio*.[2] These norms constitute a partial exception to the prescriptions of both canon 40 and canon 42, § 1.[3] They do not derogate in any way from the principle of canon 42, § 2.[4]

[1] The text of c. 45 reads as follows: "Cum rescriptis ad preces alicuius impetratis apponitur clausula: *Motu proprio,* valent quidem ea, si in precibus reticeatur veritas alioquin necessario exprimenda, non tamen si falsa causa finalis eaque unica proponatur, salvo praescripto can. 1054."

[2] A rescript granted *motu proprio* is one which a superior issues, not in view of the facts and circumstances set forth in the *pars narrativa* of the petition, but rather spontaneously, that is, from his own free choice and liberality and with him prescinding from the aforesaid facts and circumstances. For a more detailed description of this type of rescript, cf. *supra,* p. 9.

"Rescribere Motu proprio potest qui *suo iure* rescribit in materia de qua libere disponit, quin ligetur conditionibus a iure vel a delegante positis. Illud ius spectat ad Romanum Pontificem, ad Ordinarios quando concedunt rescripta in materiis quae propriis legibus tantum reguntur."—Van Hove, *De Rescriptis,* p. 167.

[3] Cf. *supra,* pp. 122-125. For an explanation of why can. 45 is only a partial exception to can. 42, § 1, cf. *infra,* pp. 186-187.

[4] Cf. *supra,* pp. 184-186.

Article 1. The General Principle of Canon 45

The norms which canon 45 lays down in regard to *motu proprio* granted rescripts are actually a restatement of the pre-Code law on this matter.[5] Thus, under the present law, it may be stated as a general principle that, except for rescripts containing dispensations from minor matrimonial impediments, the only time subreption or obreption invalidates *motu proprio* issued rescripts is when the sole remaining final cause proposed for them is false.[6] If *motu proprio* granted rescripts contain the aforesaid dispensations, even the falsification of the sole remaining motivating reason given for the letters does not nullify them.[7]

Nonetheless, it must be noted here that even when *motu proprio* issued rescripts are involved, petitioners who from fraud or *dolus* falsify their *preces* to the Holy See or to the local ordinary lay themselves open to the appropriate penalties which their ordinary is authorized to impose. The superior's *motu proprio* protects the validity of their rescripts as indicated in canon 45; it does not make immune to the aforementioned punishment the petitioners who are concerned here.[8]

Article 2. The General Principle of Canon 45 in Relation to the Pars Narrativa of the Preces [9]

In order to convey the full and proper import of the general principle of canon 45 in relation to the *pars narrativa* of the *preces*, it is important to emphasize that *motu proprio* granted rescripts are not invalidated either by subreption or by obreption committed in this part of the petitions. In other words, it would be a mistake for one to conclude from the words *"si in precibus reticeatur veritas alioquin necessario exprimenda"* in canon 45 that the legislator is thereby restricting the sanating efficacy of the phrase *"motu proprio"* to subreption alone, so that obreption

5 Cf. *supra*, pp. 87-89.

6 For an exception to this general principle, cf. *infra*, p. 187.

7 Can. 1054. Cf. *infra*, p. 194.

8 Can. 2361.

9 The *pars narrativa* of the *preces* is that part of the petition in which the facts and circumstances of the prospective beneficiary's case are stated.

in any part of the *preces* would invalidate the rescripts in question. Practically all modern-day authors concur in this position.[10]

The basic reason for interpreting canon 45 in such a way as to include both subreption and obreption in the *pars narrativa* within the scope of the sanating force of the phrase *"motu proprio"* is the fact that obreption is indirectly equivalent to subreption. As has been already indicated, the truth can be suppressed either by way of an actual concealment of some existing fact or circumstance, or by way of a direct allegation of a falsehood.[11] Yet, in either of these two ways of falsifying petitions the result is substantially the same, namely, the superior does not learn the objective truth about the petitioner's case. The fact that the vitiation of the truth is effected in a negative manner when subreption is employed, and in a positive way when obreption is used, presents only an accidental aspect of the matter. Moreover, it is to be noted that while the legislator in canon 45 speaks explicitly only of the concealment of the truth, implicitly he indicates in this part of his law that he has chosen to prescind from whether or not the facts and circumstances of the case involved exist objectively as they are presented in the *pars narrativa* of the *preces.*[12] Consequently, there seems to be

[10] Cf., e.g., Van Hove, *De Rescriptis,* p. 167; Michiels, *Normae Generales,* II, 368; Rodrigo, *Tractatus de Legibus,* p. 562; Chelodi, *Ius Canonicum de Personis,* p. 132; Cicognani, *Canon Law,* p. 725; O'Neill, *Papal Rescripts of Favor,* pp. 132-133.

The following authors in their commentaries on this canon do not distinguish between nullifying obreption in the *pars narrativa* and in the *pars motiva* when they state that this defect invalidates the rescripts in question: Coronata, *Institutiones,* I, 75; Vermeersch-Creusen, *Epitome Iuris Canonici,* I, n. 161, ad 3; Toso, *Commentaria Minora,* I, 127; Ojetti, *Commentarium,* I, 232; Cappello, *Summa Iuris Canonici,* I, 120. It is most likely, however, that these commentators are using the term "obreption" solely in the sense in which it is found in can. 42, § 2. Van Hove made this same judgment in regard to Toso, Ojetti, and Cappello.—*Ibid.,* nota 1. Nonetheless, Michiels indicates that these three authors seem to be implying that obreption in any part of the *preces* is not sanated in consequence of the use of the phrase *"motu proprio."*—*Ibid.,* nota 2.

[11] Cf. *supra,* p. 131.

[12] Rodrigo, *loc cit.*

no reason why the notion of the concealment of the truth, as it is related to *motu proprio* granted rescripts, should not be interpreted broadly so as to include the concept not only of subreption but also of obreption.[13]

Furthermore, the underlying reason which the legislator must have had in giving the phrase *"motu proprio"* its sanating force over subreption and obreption in the *pars narrativa* of the petitions is to be found in the very nature of rescripts issued *motu proprio.* When a superior attaches this phrase to his rescript, he is thereby indicating that, even though a petition has been presented for his reply, he intends to grant it spontaneously or as if no request had been made to him. In other words, by a fiction of law the superior is thought to have acted on his own initiative, to have been prompted to issue his rescript *"propria sua scientia meraque sua liberalitate,"* and to have received no information from the petitioner.[14] Chelodi went to the heart of the reasoning in this matter when he said: *"ideoque deficiente per fictionem iuris supplici libello, subreptio non intelligitur."* [15]

Accordingly, then, in the case of *motu proprio* granted rescripts it is conjectured that the superior who grants them makes the petitions for them his own and supplies from his own knowledge whatever truthfulness is lacking in the *pars narrativa* of the *preces* actually presented.[16] Indeed, it is this force of the phrase *"motu proprio,"* when it is attached to rescripts, which explains how the superior can be thought to be acting reasonably in granting such letters.[17]

[13] "Quae lata significatio verborum 'reticentiae veri,' ex rerum natura indubitanter legitima, eo magis suadetur quod principium canonis 45 summopere favorabilis est ideoque late interpretanda."—Michiels, *ibid.*, p. 369.

[14] Michiels, *ibid.*, p. 363.

[15] *Loc. cit.*

[16] This supposition is upheld even when the name of the prospective beneficiary of the rescript is substantially falsified, for in such a case the superior grants the rescript for the person indicated by the fictitious name. For a discussion of what constitutes substantial and accidental falsification of names, cf. *supra*, p. 157.

[17] For a discussion of the importance of truthful *preces* to the reasonable granting of rescripts, cf. *supra*, pp. 116-118.

Article 3. The General Principle of Canon 45 in Relation to the Pars Motiva of the Preces[18]

The legislator is most explicit in excluding from the scope of the sanating efficacy of the phrase *"motu proprio"* rescripts the sole motivating final cause for which is false. It is clearly his intention, as indicated in canon 45, that *motu proprio* granted rescripts are not valid *"si falsa causa finalis eaque unica proponatur, salvo praescripto can. 1054."*

The authors, in commenting on this provision of canon 45, use two somewhat different approaches to explain it. The first approach involves looking upon the fundamental reason for this restriction of the sanating efficacy of the phrase *"motu proprio"* as the legislator's intention that rescripts be not issued at any time without at least one true final cause for doing so.[19] What is more, in this line of juridic reasoning it is assumed that *motu proprio* granted rescripts are not granted for any other final causes than those proposed in the *preces* for these letters, except, of course, when rescripts conveying dispensations from minor matrimonial impediments are involved.[20] With this fact in mind, the commentators attribute the lawmaker's insistence upon the presence of a true final cause in the *preces* for *motu proprio* granted rescripts to two considerations. The first is that, if superiors below the Pope are permitted to grant their rescripts without having a just and sufficient reason from the petitioners for doing so, they may become prodigal in conceding their favors.[21] The second and more important consideration is that, if superiors, inclusive of the Sovereign Pontiff, grant their re-

[18] The *pars motiva* of the *preces* is that part of the petition in which the petitioner states the reasons for his request.

[19] Cf. Van Hove, *De Rescriptis,* p. 167. Among the other authors who follow substantially this line of reasoning are Rodrigo, *Tractatus de Legibus,* pp. 561-562; Michiels, *Normae Generales,* II, 367; Cocchi, *Commentarium,* I, 249; and Maroto, *Institutiones,* n. 285, ad 1°.

For an explanation of the immediately foregoing statement in the text in relation to rescripts containing dispensations from minor matrimonial impediments, cf. *infra,* pp. 192-194.

[20] Cf. *infra,* p. 193.

[21] Cf. Rodrigo, *op. cit.,* p. 561.

scripts because of final causes all of which are untrue, their consent to issue the letters is based on error, and *"errantis autem nullus est consensus."* [22] That is to say, had they known that the motivating reasons for granting their rescripts were false, they would not have intended to issue them at all. Consequently, the rescripts actually granted are issued involuntarily, and are, therefore, null and void,[23] for *"substantia rescripti dependet a voluntate concedentis,"* [24] and *"deficiente ea [voluntate concedentis], vires non obtinent [rescripta]."* [25] Accordingly, even rescripts granted *motu proprio* are invalid when the sole remaining final cause proposed for them is false, since they are then issued erroneously, and indeed involuntarily.

The second approach to explaining the provision of canon 45 concerning substantial obreption in the *pars motiva* of the *preces* is centered on the will of the superior who issues the *motu proprio* granted rescripts. Thus, Cappello, who follows this second line of reasoning, states:

> Rescriptum, cui apponitur clausula: *Motu proprio,* infirmatur propter *obreptionem* (can. 45), quia causa motiva, quae a rescribente indicatur, habetur uti *conditio,* sub qua gratiam concedit, ideoque si illa falsa sit, deest conditio seu voluntas concedentis.[26]

Because of the juridic reasoning which is employed by the commentators who follow the first approach, as mentioned above, in explaining the relationship between the phrase *"motu proprio"* and obreptitious final causes in the *preces,* the present writer submits that in canon 45 the legislator indicates with the words *"non tamen si falsa causa, etc."* that, when a superior's *motu proprio* is attached to rescripts, it applies only to the *pars narrativa* of the *preces* for those letters. That is to say, this phrase

[22] Van Hove, *loc. cit.*

[23] Cf. *supra,* pp. 117-118.

[24] Fagnanus, *Commentaria,* Lib. I, tit. III, ad c. 20, X, *de rescriptis,* I 3, n. 62.

[25] Gonzalez-Tellez, *Commentaria,* Lib. I, tit. III, ad c. 2, X, *de rescriptis,* I, 3, n. 17.

[26] *Summa Iuris Canonici,* I, 120. Chelodi also uses this approach to the question under consideration.—*Ius Canonicum de Personis,* p. 132.

does not imply that the superior has any other motivating reason for granting the rescripts in question except that or those reasons which the petitioners themselves have proposed to him. Otherwise, if even by a fiction of law the superior was considered to have issued his rescripts solely on his own initiative and because of what he knew from his own personal knowledge, there could be no question of his having been deceived by the false motivating reasons alleged in the *preces*. In this supposition he would not have been influenced by what the petitions contained.

Moreover, the writer believes that the foregoing conclusion must be reached also when the second approach to this question is employed. In this latter line of reasoning the existence of at least one true final cause in the *preces* for the rescripts in question is made an essential condition under which the favors are granted. Yet, unless this final cause actually provided the efficacious motivation for the superior to issue the rescripts, there seems to be no reason for the lawmaker's demanding that its truthfulness be a criterion in the evaluation of the validity of the letters. The mind of the legislator in reference to the extraordinarily liberal ruling of canon 1054 on this same question of final causes seems to bear out this last statement.[27]

Now, in giving the reason why the effect of the superior's *motu proprio* is different concerning substantial untruthfulness in the *pars narrativa* of the *preces* and regarding invalidating obreption in the *pars motiva* of the petitions, modern authors repeat substantially the following statement of Schmalzgrueber on this point:

> Ratio disparitatis est, quia quando tacetur veritas, pontifex ab illa ad concessionem non movetur; neque sciri potest, an bene informatus de rei veritate gratiam denegasset: imo cum ea gratia procedat ex mera liberalitate principis, potius praesumi potest, quod etiam veritate cognita, adhuc illam concessurus fuisset. E contrario, quando causa falsa exprimitur, satis apparet, quod concessio ex errore processerit, igitur cum errantis nullus sit consensus.[28]

[27] Cf. *infra*, pp. 192-193.

[28] *Jus Ecclesiasticum*, Lib. I, tit. III, n. 11. Cf. Toso, *Commentaria Minora*, I, 127; Maroto, *Institutiones*, n. 285, ad 1°; Cocchi, *Commentarium*, I, 249.

Article 4. The General Principle of Canon 45 in Relation to the Pars Postulativa of the Preces [29]

The general principle of canon 45 seems at first sight to define in an all-inclusive manner the effect of the phrase "*motu proprio*" in relation to *preces* infected with substantial subreption and obreption respectively. Nonetheless, when that principle is applied to the *pars postulativa* of petitions, an exception to it must be made. A superior's *motu proprio* will not make a rescript effective when subreption, and especially obreption, has been committed concerning the favor which the petitioner wants to receive through the particular rescript involved. That is to say, if the petitioner is bound, for instance, by the impediment of the simple vow of perfect chastity, but he mistakenly requests a dispensation from the simple vow of not marrying, which he has never made, the consequent *motu proprio* granted rescript with the dispensation from perfect chastity is invalid. The reason for the invalidity of such a rescript inheres in the fact that, because of the faulty petition, the superior's reply fails to touch the petitioner's case as it actually is. In other words, the rescript obtained from the superior conveys only the favor that was requested in the *preces*, and that favor is absolutely useless to its prospective beneficiary.[30]

[29] The *pars postulativa* of the *preces* is that part of the petition in which the specifically sought favor is stated.

[30] Cf. Rodrigo, *Tractatus de Legibus*, p. 561.

CHAPTER VII

COMMENTARY ON CANON 1054—MINOR MATRIMONIAL IMPEDIMENTS

Canon 1054 states that a dispensation granted from a minor matrimonial impediment is not invalidated by the flaw either of subreption or of obreption, even though the sole motivating reason expressed in the petition for it is false.[1] The ruling of this canon deserves special consideration in this study, not only because the dispensations with which it is concerned are regularly granted by way of rescripts, but also because it represents a notable exception to the general principles of canons 40, 42, §§ 1 and 2, and 45, as far as the validity of rescripts is concerned.[2]

Despite its extraordinarily liberal ruling, however, canon 1054 should not lead one to conclude that petitioners need not be concerned about telling the truth in the *preces* for the rescripts treated by this law. As has been already indicated, this canon does not constitute an exception to the general ruling of canon 40, which insists that truth is always required in the *preces* for the *lawfulness* of the subsequent rescripts.[3] Hence, even in rescripts conveying dispensations from the minor matrimonial impediments, the condition *"si preces veritate nitantur"* is always at least understood as postulated for the lawfulness of these letters. Moreover, in canon 1054 the lawgiver guards only the validity of the letters in question. He does not protect petitioners from the punishment indicated in canon 2361 if they commit wilful deception in the *preces* which they submit to the Holy See and to local ordinaries for these dispensations.[4]

[1] The text of can. 1054 reads as follows: "Dispensatio a minore impedimento concessa, nullo sive obreptionis sive subreptionis vitio irritatur, etsi unica causa finalis in precibus exposita falsa fuerit."

[2] Cf. *supra*, pp. 122-125.

[3] Cf. *supra*, pp. 124-125.

[4] Can. 2361 authorizes the ordinary of the above-mentioned petitioners to punish them in proportion to the gravity of their crime.

Article 1. The General Principle of Canon 1054

The rule of canon 1054, as applied to rescripts, may be expressed, by way of a general principle, in this manner: the validity of rescripts containing dispensations from the minor matrimonial impediments is in no way affected by the law of subreption and/or obreption, even by obreption in the sole final cause proposed in the *preces* for them.[5]

At the outset it is most important for one to understand what is meant by minor matrimonial impediments. In the Latin Church the following diriment impediments are of minor degree: 1) consanguinity in the third degree of the collateral line; 2) affinity in the second degree of the collateral line; 3) public decency in the second degree; 4) spiritual relationship, and 5) qualified crime arising from adultery with a promise of or an attempt at marriage, even by way of a purely civil contract.[6] In the Oriental Churches the following diriment impediments are of minor degree:[7] 1) consanguinity in the sixth degree of the collateral line; 2) affinity *ex digeneia* in the fourth degree of the collateral line, affinity *ex digeneia inter consanguineos viri et consanguineos mulieris* in any degree whenever this impediment is thus enacted in particular law, and affinity *ex trigeneia* in any degree whenever this impediment arises from particular law;[8]

[5] For an exception to this principle, cf. *infra,* pp. 194-195.

[6] Can. 1042, § 2. "Certam habemus sententiam, qua tenetur quodlibet impedimentum sive consanguinitatis sive affinitatis in linea collaterali inaequali et quidem ita ut habeatur aliquis gradus *mixtus cum primo,* non esse impedimentum minoris gradus sed gradus maioris."—Vlaming-Bender, *Praelectiones,* p. 119.

[7] Can. 31, § 1—Pius XII, motu proprio *Crebrae allatae,* 22 febr. 1949—*AAS,* XLI (1949), 89-117 (hereafter cited as *Crebrae allatae*).

[8] Can. 68 of *Crebrae allatae* states in § 1, 1°: "Affinitas ex digeneia oritur ex matrimonio valido etsi non consummato"; in § 3, 1°: "Iure particulari, affinitas praeterea oritur ex trigeneia seu ex duobus matrimoniis validis, etiam non consummatis, si duae personae matrimonium contrahant: a) cum una eademque tertia persona, soluto matrimonio, una post alteram, aut b) cum duabus personis inter se consanguineis"; in § 3, 2°: "Affinitatem ex trigeneia contrahunt alteruter coniux cum iis qui sunt, ex alio matrimonio, alterius coniugis affines ex digeneia." For the law concerning the computation of affinity *ex digeneia inter consanguineos viri et consan-*

3) public decency in the second degree; 4) spiritual relationship; 5) *tutela* and legal relationship arising from adoption for those *"qui lege civili inhabiles ad nuptias inter se ineundas habentur,"* [9] and 6) qualified crime arising from adultery with a promise of or an attempt at marriage, even by way of a purely civil contract.[10]

---

guineos mulieris and affinity *ex trigencia,* cf. can. 68, § 2, 2°, and § 3, 3° and 4° respectively.

[9] The foregoing quotation is from can. 71 of *Crebrae allatae.*

[10] The reason why the writer mentions the Oriental law in regard to the minor impediments is that in the United States it is not uncommon to have marriages between Latin and Oriental Catholics. These persons may be bound by some minor impediment. Hence, can. 1054 of the Latin Code and its counterpart in *Crebrae allatae,* namely, can. 44, would be applicable to the dispensation received by the aforesaid parties.

In reference to the validity of dispensations from impediments when granted to persons of whom one is a Latin and the other an Oriental Catholic, it must be kept in mind that the manner of computing the various degrees of consanguinity and affinity in the collateral line is different in the two disciplines. In the Latin Church this computation is made according to the number of generations, *stipite dempto,* with the longer line being used as the basis for the reckoning whenever the two lines are unequal. For the law in this matter, cf. can. 96, § 3, and can. 97, § 3, which deal respectively with consanguinity and affinity. In the Oriental discipline the degree of these impediments is computed according to the total number of persons in the two lines, *stipite dempto.* For the law on this point, cf. can. 66, § 4, 3°, and can. 68, § 1, 3°, of *Crebrae allatae,* which are concerned respectively with consanguinity and affinity (i.e., the affinity mentioned in can. 68, § 1, 1°, of *Crebrae allatae*). Hence, the final determination of the degrees of the impediments may differ in the two disciplines. Thus, it sometimes happens that an impediment is one of minor degree according to the Latin system, but one of major degree according to the Oriental computation. At other times the degree of consanguinity or affinity may be such according to the Latin discipline as not to constitute an impediment at all, while in the Oriental system an impediment would exist. When this difference in the determination of the degree arises in a concrete case, it has been decided that the computation which one is to use in deciding whether the involved impediment is one of the major or of minor degree is that of the discipline of the bishop who has granted the dispensation.—Cf. Pontificia Commissio ad Redigendum Codicem Iuris Canonici Orientalis, 3 maii 1953—*AAS,* XLV (1953), 312; Bouscaren, *The Canon Law Digest,* IV, 15-16. The writer submits that, when a person recognizes this difference before he presents his petition for the required dispensation, he should compute the degree of the impediment according to the discipline of the bishop who is being approached for the granting of the dispensation. When it happens, however, that the im-

In both the Latin and the Oriental disciplines all other diriment impediments are of the major degree.[11]

In the Latin discipline there has been considerable controversy among the authors concerning impedient impediments and their place in the division between impediments of major degree and impediments of minor degree. This conflict of opinions has been occasioned by canon 1042, § 3, which states: *"Impedimenta maioris gradus alia sunt omnia."* In the following statement Vlaming-Bender give a clear and concise analysis of this matter, as far as the Latin discipline is concerned, and they indicate also the Oriental law on this question:

> Dissensio viget inter canonistas circa sensum verborum "impedimenta maioris gradus alia sunt omnia" (c. 1042, § 3). Quidam legunt: alia impedimenta *dirimentia,* ita ut divisio ipsa non respiciat impedimenta impedientia, quae tunc sunt neque maioris neque minoris gradus, sed remanent extra hanc divisionem.[12] Alii intelligunt haec verba absque distinctione, ita ut impedimenta impedientia sub § 3 comprehendantur et sint impedimenta maioris gradus.[13] Textus canonis, comprehensus sub titulo generali capitis, favet ultimae interpretationi. Ei usque nunc adhaerendum esse putavimus. Sed *Motu Proprio* de disciplina Sacramenti Matrimonii pro Ecclesia Orientali, die 12 Martii 1949 a Pio Papa XII promulgatum, videtur certum reddere sententiam priorem. In hoc enim documento eadem impedimentorum divisio eiusdemque fere

---

pediment of consanguinity or affinity is present in a case according to the computation of the discipline by which only one of the petitioners is bound, but not according to that by which the dispensing bishop is governed, the reckoning according to that petitioner's discipline is to be followed and not that of the dispensing bishop.—The writer makes this statement on the authority of the Reverend Dr. Meletius Wojnar, O.S.B.M., professor of Oriental Canon Law at the Catholic University of America.

11 Can. 1042, § 3, of the Latin Code of Canon Law, and can. 31, § 2, of *Crebrae allatae.*

12 E.g., Cappello, *De Matrimonio,* p. 207; Gasparri, *De Matrimonio,* p. 129, n. 211; Vermeersch-Creusen, *Epitome Iuris Canonici,* II, n. 302; Wernz-Vidal, *Ius Matrimoniale,* p. 181.

13 E.g., Abbo-Hannan, *The Sacred Canons,* II, 218; Coronata, *Institutiones Iuris Canonici, De Sacramentis Tractatus Canonicus,* Vol. III, *De Matrimonio et de Sacramentalibus* (2. ed., Taurini-Romae: Marietti, 1948), p. 141, n. 120 (hereafter cited as *De Matrimonio*).

> tenoris proponitur. Sed c. 31, § 2 quae correspondet canoni 1042, § 3 nostri codicis aliis utitur verbis, scilicet: "cetera impedimenta *dirimenta* sunt maioris gradus." Insuper impedimentum cognationis legalis comprehendit sub impedimenta minoris gradus solum si sit dirimens; non autem si sit mere impediens.[14]

Accordingly, this writer submits that rescripts which contain dispensations from impedient impediments alone never come within the scope of canon 1054. He bases this conclusion on the fact that, because of the way in which the supreme legislator for the whole Church has expressed his mind on this matter in canon 31, § 2, of *Crebrae allatae,* it seems certain that only specific diriment impediments can properly be considered minor impediments.

Another point which deserves consideration in this analysis of canon 1054 is the fact that the extraordinarily liberal rule which the legislator applies to rescripts that contain dispensations from the minor matrimonial impediments seems at first sight to be repugnant to what has already been said in this work concerning the importance of truthful *preces* for the reasonable and truly voluntary granting of rescripts.[15] It must be admitted that a superior can hardly act reasonably and voluntarily in giving his rescripts when the only facts and reasons known to him for doing so are completely false. This seeming repugnance disappears, however, when one understands the mind of the legislator in regard to the granting of dispensations from the impediments in question. The lawmaker's thinking in this matter can be learned from the ruling found in the *Normae peculiares* for the re-establishment of the Roman Curia, which ruling is the juridical basis of the general principle of canon 1054.[16] This ruling reads as follows:

> Dispensations from minor impediments shall all be granted "for reasonable causes approved by the Holy See (*ex certis rationabilibus causis a Sancta Sede probatis*)"; under this

[14] *Praelectiones,* p. 119, nota 2. Cf. also Coussa, *Epitome Praelectionum de Iure Ecclesiastico Orientali,* Vol. III, *De Matrimonio* (Romae: Apud Custodiam Librariam Pontificii Instituti Utriusque Iuris, 1950), p. 51.

[15] Cf. *supra,* pp. 116-118.

[16] Cf. *supra,* pp. 89-90.

form they will have the same force as if given "in virtue of a *motu proprio* and with certain knowledge (*motu proprio et ex certa scientia*)," and so will not be open to question on the ground either of obreption or of subreption.[17]

Accordingly, as for a superior's acting reasonably in granting the rescripts considered in canon 1054, what has been said in regard to the reasonablenes involved in the issuing of *motu proprio* granted rescripts applies also to the rescripts now under discussion.[18] Moreover, in regard to the truly voluntary granting of these rescripts, it is to be noted that these letters are issued because of reasons supplied by the Holy See itself. This is true whether the rescripts in question are issued directly by the Apostolic See or by duly authorized superiors subject to it.[19] These causes, which are provided by the Holy See, exist altogether independently of any reasons that may be proposed by the petitioner. What is more, they are considered always to be true.[20] Consequently, even though all of the reasons which are proposed in the *preces* for the rescripts under discussion here are false, there is present, nonetheless, a true final cause for acceding to the petitioner's request. As a result of this fact, a superior acts truly voluntarily when he grants the rescript that is sought.[21]

Rodrigo explains in the following manner the reason for the exceptional provisions which the lawmaker has made in regard to rescripts conveying dispensations from the minor matrimonial impediments:

> *Ratio exceptionis est,* quia pro his dispensationibus gradus minoris concedendis, causa sufficiens habetur ipsa petitio: finis enim legis dispensandae sic sufficienter obtinetur, scil. ne haec

[17] Ordo Servandus in S. Congregationibus, Tribunalibus, Officiis Romae Curiae, 29 sept. 1908, Pars II, *Normae peculiares,* cap. VII, art. III, n. 21 —*AAS,* I (1909), 91-92. For the pre-Code commentary on this ruling, cf. *supra,* pp. 89-90.

[18] Cf. *supra,* p. 183.

[19] Cf. c. 20, X, *de rescriptis,* I, 3, in fine. Cf. also *infra,* pp. 196-199.

[20] Cf. Michiels, *Normae Generales,* II, 369.

[21] "In illis dispensationibus nulla requiritur causa ipsi petitioni intrinseca, sed adest causa extrinseca, ut puta bonum commune Ecclesiae, pro quo expedit ut gratia saltem sit petenda, licet sine causa speciali semper concedatur."—Van Hove, *De Rescriptis,* p. 148.

matrimonia ineantur pro lubitu et de facili, sed solummodo de Superioris competentis *positivo* consensu, siquidem ea prorsus libera permissa nimium cum publico damno multiplicarentur.[22]

Article 2. The General Principle of Canon 1054 in Relation to the Three Parts of the Preces[23]

In regard to the *pars narrativa* and the *pars motiva* of the *preces* for the rescripts under discussion in this section, there can be no question that the general principle of canon 1054 sanates completely any subreption and obreption found therein. On the one hand, rescripts containing dispensations from minor matrimonial impediments enjoy the same force as if granted "in virtue of a *motu proprio* and with certain knowledge (*motu proprio et ex certa scientia*)."[24] Hence, what has already been said in reference to the efficacy of the phrase "*motu proprio*" upon a defective *pars narrativa* in the petitions for *motu proprio* granted rescripts applies to this part of the *preces* whenever the rescripts dealt with in canon 1054 are involved.[25] On the other hand, the wording of canon 1054 itself makes it clear that even a completely obreptitious *pars motiva* in the petitions for the rescripts treated by this law does not invalidate these letters.

Nonetheless, the very nature of things demands that an exception be made to the general principle of canon 1054 when subreption or obreption is found in the *pars postulativa* of the *preces* for these rescripts. That is to say, the vitiating effect of subreption and obreption in the *pars postulativa* of the petitions

[22] *Tractatus de Legibus*, p. 562. Rodrigo bases this statement on the ruling contained in the *Normae peculiares* as quoted in this section on pp. 192-193. Hence, although he states here that the petition itself is sufficient reason for a superior to grant a dispensation from a minor impediment, he is not contradicting what this writer has said concerning the Holy See itself supplying the final causes for the issuing of the rescripts that convey such dispensations.—Cf. *supra*, p. 193.

[23] The three parts of the *preces* are the *pars narrativa*, in which the facts and circumstances of the prospective beneficiary's case are mentioned, the *pars postulativa*, in which the sought favor is stated, and the *pars motiva*, in which there are set down the reason or reasons that are intended to prompt the superior to grant the request.

[24] Cf. *supra*, pp. 183, 192-194.

[25] Cf. *supra*, p. 183.

for the dispensations in question is not sanated by the force of this canon.[26] This is so because, in spite of the legislator's liberal ruling in this part of his law, it stands to reason that these rescripts are valid only if they contain a dispensation from an impediment that actually exists. Thus, if a dispensation is asked for and granted from the minor impediment of consanguinity, whereas the only existing impediment is the minor one of affinity, the impediment of affinity remains undispensed. The reason why it remains undispensed is that the dispensation which is actually granted cannot conceivably be construed as relating to the case that actually exists.[27] Consequently, it must be concluded that when subreption or obreption appears in the *pars postulativa* of the *preces*, the consequent rescripts, of whatever type they may be, must be adjudged not only ineffective but also invalid. The juridical basis for the foregoing conclusion may be indicated in the following manner. Using the mentioned case as an example, one can say that the rescript granted therein would be valid and effective, all other things being equal, in a situation in which the minor impediment of consanguinity actually existed. That rescript, however, like all other rescripts, is issued only for the specific case at hand and for the purpose of producing only the effect intended by its grantor. So, as far as the existing case is concerned, the rescript lacks intrinsically the force to remove the impediment of affinity precisely because the grantor, in issu-

[26] Cf. Rodrigo, *op. cit.*, p. 561, and *supra*, p. 187, in reference to an identical situation in regard to *motu proprio* granted rescripts. This position is in harmony with a pre-Code opinion held by De Smet.—Cf. *supra*, p. 90. Needless to say, it is presumed in this discussion that in the *preces* there is no other information which will correct the mistaken notion that is caused by the falsehood in the *pars postulativa*, for, if the superior can learn, e.g., from the genealogical tree that is enclosed with the petition, that the wrong dispensation has been requested, but then proceeds to grant the needed dispensation, the rescript in question will be valid.—Cf. Van Hove, *De Rescriptis*, pp. 188-189.

[27] Bouscaren-Ellis, *Canon Law*, p. 508. These authors state in this place that the impediment of affinity remains undispensed "not because the dispensation is invalidated. . . ." This writer submits, however, that the dispensation, and consequently also the rescript, besides being ineffective, must be considered nullified in the here-contemplated circumstances, as he indicates in the text which immediately follows.

ing the dispensation from consanguinity, intends to cancel out the impediment of consanguinity, not the impediment of affinity. Indeed, it must be remembered that rescripts get all their intrinsic force from the intention or the will of the superior who issues them.[28] In the last analysis, therefore, the rescript in question must be considered invalid and, as a result, ineffective because of a *defectus voluntatis rescribentis* to produce the effect really needed by the intended beneficiary of the letter.[29]

Furthermore, it may be remarked here that not only does canon 1054 not sanate the basic invalidity of the rescripts with which it deals when the *preces* for those letters are surreptitious or obreptitious in their *pars postulativa,* but also canon 47 cannot save the validity of such rescripts. The latter canon is ineffective in the case described above,[30] for the rescript there involved contains *de facto* the dispensation which was requested and which is undoubtedly the only one that the superior intended to grant. Unfortunately, the needed dispensation was not even requested.[31]

Article 3. The General Principle of Canon 1054 in Relation to the Rescripts of the Holy See and of Other Superiors

There can be no doubt that the general principle of canon 1054 applies to the rescripts in question when they have been issued directly by the Holy See. The commentators are divided, however, on whether or not these rescripts are valid when they have been granted without at least one true final cause in the *preces* for them by bishops and other superiors in virtue of power delegated by the Holy See or given by the law itself.[32]

[28] Cf. *supra,* pp. 117-118.

[29] ". . . rescriptum esse *validum* significat illud *potens* esse seu *aptum* ad operandam gratiam quae constituit ejus objectum. . . ."—Michiels, *Normae Generales,* II, 325.

[30] Cf. p. 195.

[31] Bouscaren-Ellis, *loc. cit.*

[32] The local ordinaries of the United States are empowered to grant dispensations from the minor matrimonial impediments through their Quinquennial Faculties. Cf. cans. 1043-1045 for an indication of the

The authors who hold for the invalidity of these rescripts when they are thus issued by subordinates of the Holy See base their argument on canon 84, § 1, which definitely has a place in the law on rescripts because of canon 62.[33] Canon 84, § 1, prescribes that a dispensation from an ecclesiastical law, when granted by a subordinate without a just, reasonable, and proportionate cause is illicit and invalid. These commentators conclude therefore that, when bishops and other superiors as subordinates of the Holy See grant a dispensation from a minor impediment without having at least one true final cause in the *preces* for the rescript, the consequent rescript and dispensation are invalid. In other words, for these authors the ruling of canon 84, § 1, prevails over the general principle of canon 1054.[34]

Other commentators, however, hold that canon 1054 derogates from canon 84, § 1.[35] These authors maintain that when superiors who are subordinate to the Holy See grant the dispensations dealt with in canon 1054, at least one true final cause is required in the *preces* only for the lawfulness of the dispensations, not for their validity. In the following passage Van Hove indicated the juridic reasoning which supports this conclusion:

> At causa videtur requiri ad solam liceitatem dispensationis, non ad eius validitatem, quia can. 1054 modo omnino generali statuit, non tantum rescriptum esse validum, sed et ipsam "dispensationem"; proinde derogat regulae can. 84, § 1, etiam apud inferiorem dispensantem. Confirmatur doctrina in can.

---

circumstances in which the law itself gives to local ordinaries and other persons the aforesaid power.

33 Among the authors who have taken this position are Woywod, "Dispensation in Marriage Impediment May Be Made Invalid by Faulty Petition," *The Homiletic and Pastoral Review* (New York, 1900-), XXI (1920-1921), 319-320.

34 "Huic doctrinae favere videtur praxis Curiae Romanae, quae causam exigit ut vi facultatum habitualium dispensatio concedatur in impedimentis minoribus."—Van Hove, *De Rescriptis,* p. 151.

35 Among these commentators are Cappello, *De Matrimonio,* p. 276; Gasparri, *De Matrimonio,* I, 248; Gougnard, *Tractatus de Matrimonio* (7. ed., Mechliniae, 1931), p. 469; Heylen, *Tractatus de Matrimonio* (9. ed., Mechliniae: H. Dessain, 1945), p. 632; Michiels, *ibid.,* p. 369; Van Hove, *op. cit.,* pp. 151-152.

> 2361, qui a poenis ferendis contra illos qui in precibus dolo vel fraude verum reticuerint aut falsum exposuerint eximunt [sic] preces ad rescriptum obtinendum non tantum a Sede Apostolica sed etiam ab Ordinario loci, in materiis de quibus in can. 45 et 1054 agitur.[36]

The present writer agrees with the authors who support the latter of these opinions, insofar as he is convinced that when superiors who are subordinate to the Holy See and who are empowered to grant dispensations from the minor matrimonial impediments do so without having at least one true final cause in the *preces*, their rescripts are valid. This conclusion seems to be substantiated by the fact that canon 1054 makes no distinction between the rescripts in question when they are granted directly by the Holy See and when they are issued by subordinates of the Apostolic See. *Ubi lex non distinguit, nec nos distinguere debemus.* Moreover, it seems from canon 2361 that the legislator himself intends canon 1054 to include within its sanating force the rescripts not only of the Holy See but also of the local ordinaries.

This writer also agrees with the proponents of this latter opinion that, for the lawfulness of the dispensations in question, it is necessary to have at least one true final cause in the *preces*. He accepts this proposition on the basis of his conclusion that canon 1054 does not constitute an exception to the demand of canon 40 for truthful *preces* for the lawfulness of all rescripts.[36a]

Nonetheless, this writer submits that canon 1054 is not in any respect a derogation from canon 84, § 1. He has reached this conclusion from a consideration of the wording of canon 84, § 1, and of the mind of the lawgiver in regard to the granting of dispensations from minor impediments.[37]

Canon 84, § 1, certainly demands a just, reasonable, and proportionate cause for the validity and lawfulness of a subordinate's dispensations from the ecclesiastical law. There is no indication in this canon, however, that the aforesaid cause must be proposed by the petitioners in their *preces* for the dispensa-

[36] *Loc. cit.*

[36a] Cf. *supra*, pp. 124-125.

[37] Cf. *supra*, pp. 192-194.

tions. Hence, it seems correct to conclude from the wording of canon 84, § 1, that this law requires the *existence* of the aforementioned reason, not its *presentation* by the petitioners.

As for the mind of the lawgiver in regard to the granting of dispensations from minor impediments, it has already been indicated that the legislator intends that these dispensations be given *"ex certis rationabilibus causis a Sancta Sede probatis."* [38] These causes the Holy See itself uses in granting the dispensations under consideration here, and it provides other superiors with the same reasons whenever they grant these dispensations.[39] Such reasons undoubtedly have the qualifications of the kind of cause demanded by canon 84, § 1, for the licit and valid granting of dispensations from the ecclesiastical law by subordinates of the Holy See. What is more, the aforesaid reasons are considered always to be present in cases involving dispensations from the minor impediments for which they are used, because Rome supplies them.[40]

Accordingly, whether the Holy See or subordinate superiors grant the rescripts containing the dispensations to which canon 1054 adverts, a just, reasonable; and proportionate cause for the dispensations is had. Hence, the demands of canon 84, § 1, seem to be fulfilled.

[38] Cf. *supra,* pp. 192-194.

[39] Cf. *supra,* pp. 193-194.

[40] Cf. *supra,* p. 193.

CHAPTER VIII

COMMENTARY ON CANON 41—TIME: VERIFICATION OF THE *PRECES*

Canon 41 states that in rescripts in which no executor is required the *preces* for the letters must be founded on truth at the time at which the rescripts are issued; in other rescripts, at the time of the execution of the letters.[1] The legislator uses this canon to determine precisely and succinctly at what time the condition *"si preces veritate nitantur"* has to be fulfilled if rescripts are to be valid, without prejudice, of course, to the prescriptions of canons 45 and 1054.[2] This is not to say, however, that canon 41 has no bearing on the rulings of canons 45 and 1054, which deal respectively with *motu proprio* granted rescripts and with rescripts containing dispensations from the minor matrimonial impediments. On the one hand, the truth is required for *validity* not only in the *pars postulativa* of the *preces* for the rescripts treated by both these canons,[3] but also in the sole remaining final cause proposed for *motu proprio* granted rescripts. On the other hand, truthful petitions are always demanded in virtue of canon 40 and canon 2361 for the *lawfulness* of the rescripts with which canon 45 and canon 1054 are concerned.[4] Hence, canon 41 fully determines the time at which the *preces* for the rescripts of canons 45 and 1054 have to be truthful if these letters are to be both lawful and valid.

Canon 41 is actually a practical application of the norms of canon 38, which contains the basic principles for the determina-

[1] The text of can. 41 reads as follows: "In rescriptis quorum nullus est exsecutor, preces veritate nitantur oportet tempore quo rescriptum datum est; in ceteris tempore exsecutionis."

[2] This matter was not determined so clearly in the pre-Code law. For the pre-Code discipline in this regard, cf. *supra*, pp. 79-87. For a discussion of the prescriptions of can. 45 and 1054, cf. *supra*, pp. 180-199.

[3] Cf. *supra*, pp. 187, 194-196, respectively.

[4] Cf. *supra*, pp. 124-125.

tion of the time at which rescripts become effective.[5] In other words, it is an accepted doctrine among modern-day commentators that the time which the legislator has set for rescripts to take effect is the basis upon which is prescribed the time when the *preces* must be founded on truth.[6] This doctrine is undoubtedly founded upon the similarity that exists between the structure and the wording of the two laws in question. The practical import of this relationship between canon 41 and canon 38 is that the two norms which the lawmaker has enunciated in canon 41 must be interpreted in the light of the parallel norms set down in canon 38. Accordingly, the writer proposes, first of all, to treat the double norm of canon 41, secondly, to set forth the general principle which may be deduced from this twofold ruling, thirdly, as a commentary on this general principle, to present an explanation of the two norms contained in canon 38, and finally, to note several conclusions that flow logically from the general principle of canon 41.

Article 1. The Norms of Canon 41

The two norms which the legislator has set forth in canon 41 in reference to the time at which the *preces* must be true are intended to govern respectively rescripts issued *in forma gratiosa* and rescripts granted *in forma commissoria.*[7]

A. The First Norm of Canon 41: Concerning Rescripts Issued *in forma gratiosa*

According to the first norm of canon 41, petitions for rescripts issued *in forma gratiosa* have to be truthful at the time when these letters are actually issued. The time of the actual issuance of all types of rescripts is the moment when a competent

[5] Abbo-Hannan, *The Sacred Canons,* I, 73.

[6] Cf., e.g., Chelodi, *Ius Canonicum de Personis,* p. 131; Michiels, *Normae Generales,* II, 357; O'Neill, *Papal Rescripts of Favor,* p. 118.

[7] Rescripts issued *in forma gratiosa* are those in which the superior himself grants the favor *complete et perfecte, de iure et de facto,* and applies it directly to the beneficiary, without using any intermediary as an executor of the grant. Rescripts granted *in forma commissoria* are those in which the request is granted through the medium of an executor. For a discussion of these two types of rescripts, cf. *supra,* pp. 11-13.

superior affixes his signature to the letters after they have been properly confected.[8]

It is possible to conclude from the manner in which this first norm is stated in canon 41 that it applies, without exception, to all rescripts issued *in forma gratiosa.* Nevertheless, the commentators are in general agreement that the ruling in question must be interpreted in the light of the first norm of canon 38 and the exceptions thereto in reference to the initial effectiveness of rescripts of this type.[9] Actually, therefore, the import of the first norm of canon 41 is this: as far as rescripts issued *in forma gratiosa* are concerned, their *preces* have to be truthful at the moment when the letters themselves become effective. Ordinarily rescripts of this kind take effect at the moment when they are properly signed. There are exceptional cases, however, in which such letters become effective either before or after the superior's signature is affixed to them.[10]

B. The Second Norm of Canon 41: Concerning Rescripts Granted *in forma commissoria*

According to the second norm of canon 41, the *preces* for all rescripts granted *in forma commissoria* have to be true at the time when these letters are executed. It is to be noted that the legislator, in establishing this norm, draws no distinction between rescripts granted through the agency of a necessary executor and rescripts granted through the intermediation of a voluntary executor.[11] Hence, this second norm applies indiscriminately to all rescripts that are granted *in forma commissoria.* More-

[8] Cf. Michiels, *Normae Generales,* II, 327; Toso, *Commentaria Minora,* I, 118; Vermeersch-Creusen, *Epitome Iuris Canonici,* I, n. 158. "Confectio litterarum requiritur ad validitatem rescripti dati in forma gratiosa, ut constat ex canone 38, aeque ac rescripti dati in forma commissoria, si quidem exsecutor invalide ad exsecutionem litterarum procedit antequam litteras ipsas receperit (can. 53)."—Van Hove, *De Rescriptis,* p. 116. For a list of those officials in the Roman Congregations who have the power to sign rescripts, cf. Van Hove, *op. cit.,* p. 76, nota 4.

[9] Cf. *infra,* pp. 207-214. Cf. also Chelodi, *loc. cit.;* Michiels, *ibid.,* p. 357; O'Neill, *loc. cit.*

[10] Cf. *infra,* pp. 208-214.

[11] For a description of both the necessary and the voluntary executor, cf. *supra,* pp. 14-15.

over, it makes no difference whether the letters be rescripts of justice or rescripts of favor.[12]

The time of the execution of the rescripts is the moment at which their executors discharge completely the commission given to them by the superior in regard to the application of the letters to their intended beneficiaries.[13] Thus, whenever a *necessary* executor is involved, the time of the execution of the rescript is precisely the moment when the executor *de facto* applies to the beneficiary the grant that is *de iure* contained in the rescript itself. Whenever a *voluntary* executor is employed, this time is the moment at which the executor concedes *de iure* and *de facto* the grant sought by the petitioner in his *preces* for the rescript involved.[14] In a more precise manner, the time of the execution of rescripts may be determined on the basis of whether the letters are executed in writing or orally. That is to say, if the execution is performed in writing, as canon 56 prescribes in relation to rescripts intended for the external forum, the time of execution is the moment at which the executor signs the letters of execution.[15] On the other hand, if the execution of the letters

[12] Cf. Toso, *ibid.*, p. 121. Rescripts of justice are those which contain either statements intended to explain a point of law connected with litigation, or provisions pertaining to legal suits and the administration of justice in judicial and non-judicial procedures. Rescripts of favor are those which contain favors that are in no way connected with matters of justice.—Cf. *supra*, pp. 9-11. A rescript of justice always requires by its very nature an executor, namely, the judge who is conducting the case to which the rescript refers.—Toso, *ibid.*, p. 118. In this regard, however, Maroto made this observation: "Forsan aliquando etiam in rescripto iustitiae concedi continget gratiam minoris momenti in favorem unius partis independenter ab alia parte et a iudice; tunc autem erit in forma gratiosa. . . . Id tamen generatim non eveniet, quoniam ea quae sunt ad lites, perficienda sunt in tribunali."—*Institutiones*, I, n. 283, ad 3°, nota 1.

[13] Cf. Michiels, *ibid.*, p. 330.

[14] Cf. *supra*, pp. 11-13. "Exsecutor autem voluntarius potest gratiam concedere in forma gratiosa et tunc preces veritate nitantur momento quo datae sunt litterae; si ipse in forma commissoria subdelegat suam facultatem, momento exsecutionis."—Van Hove, *op. cit.*, p. 134.

[15] In regard to the voluntary executor who has been appointed directly by the grantor of the rescript involved, if he himself executes his rescript *in forma gratiosa*, the *preces* for the rescript must be true when he signs the letters of execution; if he delegates another to execute the rescript

is performed orally, as regularly happens in the case of rescripts meant for the internal sacramental forum, the time of execution is the moment at which the executor actually concedes the favor to its intended recipient.[16]

Furthermore, as will be seen below, the second norm of canon 38 specifies that the time of the execution of rescripts granted *in forma commissoria* is the moment of the initial effectiveness of these letters.[17] Hence, it must be concluded that the *preces* for such rescripts must be founded on truth precisely at the moment when the letters are to become effective.[18]

Article 2. The General Principle of Canon 41

Since both of the norms enunciated in canon 41 demand in the last analysis that the *preces* for rescripts issued *in forma gratiosa* and *in forma commissoria* respectively be true at the time when the letters take effect, these two norms are usually set forth conjointly by means of a single general principle. This principle may be expressed in the following manner: according to canon 41 it is indeed required but it also suffices that the *preces* for the rescripts be truthful at the time when the letters consequent upon them become effective.[19]

That the moment of the initial effectiveness of rescripts should have been designated as the time when the petitions for them must be founded on truth is easily understood

> quippe cum ad hoc praecise momentum referantur omnia, quae fuerunt in supplicatione expressa et in mandato executionis injuncta.[20]

---

which he originally received, the petition for the aforesaid rescript must be true when the latter executor signs the letters of execution.

16 Cf. Michiels, *loc. cit.*

17 Cf. *infra*, pp. 214-215.

18 In speaking of the time of the initial effectiveness of rescripts granted *in forma commissoria,* the authors mention no exceptions to the general rule that this time is the moment of the execution of the letters in question. This writer submits, however, that if a *conditio de futuro* is effectively attached to the execution of such rescripts, the letters take effect only when that condition is fulfilled.

19 Chelodi, *Ius Canonicum de Personis,* p. 131; Michiels, *Normae Generales,* II, 357; O'Neill, *Papal Rescripts of Favor,* p. 118.

20 Michiels, *loc. cit.*

More particularly, in regard to rescripts issued *in forma gratiosa,* it must be noted that it is only when such letters take effect that their beneficiaries obtain an acquired right to the favor granted by the superior.[21] What is more, since in conceding rescripts of this kind the superior grants the requested favor *complete et perfecte, de iure et de facto,* the *preces* have actually spent their force. No further action upon them is required.[22] In reference to rescripts granted *in forma commissoria,* however, it must be remarked that such rescripts always contain a *gratia facienda,* that is, a favor which is not actually bestowed upon its prospective beneficiary until the letters are duly executed. In other words, the superior himself never completely grants the petitioner's request whenever he employs the services of an executor.[23] Moreover, the execution of the letters is conditioned upon the executor's finding the *preces* for them to be truthful.[24]

Article 3. Canon 38: the Basis of the General Principle of Canon 41

The general principle of canon 41 is focused upon the time when rescripts become effective. The full import of that principle will be understood only through an examination of the prescriptions of canon 38. Therein the legislator has expressed his mind in regard to the time of the initial effectiveness of granted rescripts. By pointing out precisely when the various rescripts take effect, the writer hopes thereby to indicate in a comprehensive manner the time when the *preces* have to be founded on truth.

Canon 38 provides that rescripts by which a favor is granted without the required ministry of an executor take effect from the moment at which the letters are issued; others, from the time of their execution.[25] Thus, in reference to the beginning of

21 Cicognani, *Canon Law,* p. 713.

22 Cf. *supra,* p. 11.

23 Cf. *supra,* pp. 12-13.

24 Cf. can. 54, §§ 1 and 2, and Toso, *Commentaria Minora,* I, 138-139.

25 The text of can. 38 reads thus: "Rescripta quibus gratia conceditur sine interiecto exsecutore, effectum habent a momento quo datae sunt litterae; cetera a tempore exsecutionis."

the effectiveness of granted rescripts, the legislator has set forth in this canon also two norms which govern respectively rescripts issued *in forma gratiosa* and rescripts granted *in forma commissoria.*[26]

It is important to note that in canon 38 the lawmaker is concerned with the time when rescripts actually become effective, and not with the time when they come into possession of the innate power and force in virtue of which they can produce the effect intended by the superior in granting the letters. In other words, he is legislating in this part of his law concerning the moment of the initial effectiveness of the rescripts, and not concerning the moment of their initial validity.[27] Needless to say, rescripts must be valid before they can be effective. All rescripts are valid from the moment at which they are issued, provided, of course, that all the requirements for their validity have been fulfilled.[28]

[26] For an explanation of these two types of rescripts, cf. *supra*, pp. 11-13.

[27] These two moments ordinarily coincide whenever a rescript which is issued *in forma gratiosa* is involved. This result is due to the nature of such rescripts.—Cf. *supra*, pp. 11-12. For exceptions to this rule, cf. *infra*, pp. 208-214. As for the rescript granted *in forma commissoria*, however, such a rescript contains either a mandate for the *necessary* executor to grant *de facto* the favor which the superior has already conceded *de iure* to the prospective beneficiary of the letter or it embodies the required faculties for the *voluntary* executor to bestow upon the intended party the favor which the superior himself has not yet granted either *de iure* or *de facto.*—Cf. *supra*, pp. 12-13. Consequently, the letter actually becomes effective, as far as the beneficiary's receiving his favor is concerned, only when the executor executes his mandate or uses his faculties. Hence, these latter rescripts are valid when they are issued, but they become effective only when they are executed. Michiels explains the difference between the validity or the *"valor"* of rescripts and their effectiveness or their *"efficacia"* in this manner: *"Valor* rescripti respicit ipsum esse ejus, dum *efficacia* respicit ejus operari; rescriptum esse *validum* significat illud *potens* esse seu *aptum* ad operandam gratiam quae constituit ejus objectum; rescriptum *efficax* esse seu *habere* (*sortiri*) *effectum* significat rescriptum in se validum reapse seu *effective operari* gratiam istam. . . ." —*Normae Generales,* II, 325.

[28] Cf. can. 37. Cf. also Van Hove, *De Rescriptis,* p. 118. For an explanation of the expression "at the moment they (rescripts) are issued," cf. *infra*, under A.

A. The First Norm of Canon 38: Concerning Rescripts Issued *in forma gratiosa*

According to the first norm of canon 38, which, like the first norm of canon 41, is to be applied precisely to rescripts issued *in forma gratiosa*, rescripts issued *in forma gratiosa* take effect from the very moment at which they are actually issued.[29] As has already been indicated, the time of the actual issuance of rescripts is the moment when a competent superior affixes his signature to the letters after they have been properly confected.[30] It must be emphasized here that in canon 38 the lawmaker designates the *moment* and not the *day* of the signing of rescripts issued *in forma gratiosa* as the exact time of their initial effectiveness. Unfortunately, however, the precise moment at which rescripts have been duly signed is usually not indicated on the letters. In most cases the letters bear only a specified date, which is presumed to correspond to the day on which the competent superior affixed his signature to the documents.[31] Hence, as a practical general rule, the time one must always consider in determining when rescripts issued *in forma gratiosa* become effective is the date appended to the letters, which indicates the day on which the documents were properly signed.[32]

29 For a description of rescripts issued *in forma gratiosa*, cf. *supra*, p. 201, note 7.

30 Cf. *supra*, pp. 201-202.

31 Abbo-Hannan, *The Sacred Canons*, I, 72.

32 Michiels, *ibid.*, pp. 327-328. "Proinde data litterarum non est illa qua gratia fuit concessa per Congregationem Romanam in congressu vel in plena Congregatione, aut in audientia Sanctissimi, si est diversa ab ea quae in litteris inscribitur. Gratia sane tunc conceditur, sed incomplete, adeo ut litterae exigantur ad valorem concessionis et data rescripti sit illa quae in litteris continetur, nisi exceptio statuatur."—Van Hove, *op. cit.*, p. 118. Among the authors whom this writer could consult, only Vermeersch took a position opposite to that expressed by Van Hove in the foregoing statement.—"A qua die valeant acta S. Sedis?" *Periodica de Re Morali, Canonica, Liturgica* (*Periodica de Religiosis et Missionariis*, Brugis, 1905-1919; *Periodica de Re Canonica et Morali, utilia praesertim Religiosis et Missionariis*, Brugis, 1920-1927; *Periodica de Re Morali, Canonica, Liturgica*, Brugis, 1927-1936, Romae, 1937-), XXI (1932), 52* (hereafter cited as *Periodica*); for Vermeersch's position in this matter, cf. *infra*, p. 212.

The foregoing rule is not applicable, however, to rescripts for which, as far as their initial effectiveness is concerned, another moment of time is otherwise expressly indicated or clearly demanded from the nature of the rescript and the favor involved. Thus, in the following cases the moment or the day of the signing of the rescripts is not the time when the letters become effective. Whenever a rescript is granted with a *conditio de futuro* attached to it either by the grantor or by the law, which condition must be realized before the letter can take effect, the effectiveness of the rescript will begin at the moment at which the condition will have been fulfilled. Hence, if a rescript is issued on the condition that the prospective beneficiary will accept the favor contained in it, the letter becomes effective only when that acceptance is had.[33] This is the case whenever there are involved rescripts conferring ecclesiastical benefices, and rescripts containing an indult of secularization or a dispensation from simple vows that has been granted to a religious. These rescripts do not take effect until the benefice,[34] indult, or dispensation has been accepted.[35] Likewise, if the superior, in

[33] Van Hove, *op. cit.*, p. 119. It may be noted here that, on the basis of the wording of cans. 37 and 38, it can be considered probable that, unless the acceptance of a rescript and, consequently, the notification of the beneficiary of its issuance are clearly made conditions on the fulfillment of which the effectiveness of the letter depends, the aforesaid notification and acceptance are not required in order that the rescript can take effect.—Cf. Michiels, *ibid.*, pp. 331-334.

[34] Can. 1436: "Beneficium ecclesiasticum clerico invito et provisionem non expresse acceptanti valide conferri nequit."

[35] S. C. de Religiosis, 1 aug. 1922—*AAS*, XIV (1922), 501; cf. Bouscaren, *The Canon Law Digest*, I, 326. The acceptance of a dispensation from *solemn* vows by the religious for whom the release has been granted is also necessary in order that the dispensation can take effect.—Rodrigo, *Tractatus de Legibus*, pp. 548-549.

"Ita quoque vi juris ad valide agendum practice necessaria est rescripti *notitia*, quando agitur *de dispensationibus matrimonialibus concessis post nulliter contractum matrimonium*, in ordine ad matrimonium convalidandum, in quantum pars impedimenti conscia post concessam dispensationem debet renovare consensum (can. 1133 § 1 et 1134); idem dicendum est *in sanatione in radice*, quando non datur dispensatio a lege de renovando consensu, una vel utraque parte nullitatis inscia (can. 1138 § 3)."—Michiels, *ibid.*, p. 332. If the needed dispensation or sanation had been granted *in*

issuing his reply to a petitioner, sets a specific time in the future when his rescript is to take effect, that is, if he grants his rescript *ex nunc pro tunc,* the letter becomes effective at the later time, and not when it is actually issued.[36] Moreover, a rescript containing a papal dispensation from a *ratum non consummatum* marriage is always issued *in forma gratiosa* and

> effectum habet a temporis momento quo in die audientiae Summus Pontifex dispensationem concessit, dummodo tamen eo momento preces veritate nitantur, tum quoad matrimonii inconsummationem, tum quoad dispensationis causas.[37]

There are three other cases concerning which the authors have found reason to disagree among themselves regarding the exact time at which rescripts granted apart from the use of an executor become effective.

The first case concerns a rescript through which a *sanatio in radice* is granted for the rectification of an invalid marriage.[38] The source of the disagreement here is the wording of canon 1138, § 2, which provides that the convalidation of the marriage involved takes place *"a momento concessionis gratiae."* Cicognani maintains that the phrase *"a momento concessionis gratiae"* is to be taken literally, so that as soon as the superior indicates that he has granted the sanation, even if this moment does not cor-

---

forma gratiosa, however, and the parties lawfully renewed their marital consent thereafter, their marriage would have to be adjudged valid, even though they were completely ignorant of the issuing of the rescript which contained the dispensation or sanation in question here. When the dispensation or sanation had thus been granted, the obstacle to the validity and effectiveness of the parties' consent was removed. Cf. can. 1081, § 1.

36 In such a case the rescript does not have to be post-dated to the day when it actually goes into effect.—Van Hove, *loc. cit.*

37 Regula 103, *Regulae Servandae in Processibus super Matrimonio Rato et Non Consummato—AAS,* XV (1923), 413; cf. Bouscaren, *ibid.,* p. 791.

38 In this case it is supposed that the *sanatio* carries with itself a dispensation from the law requiring the renewal of marital consent. This dispensation was not present in the case referred to above on p. 208, note 35.

Rescripts granting a *sanatio in radice* are issued both *in forma gratiosa* and *in forma commissoria.*—Cf. Ryan, *The Juridical Effects of the Sanatio in Radice,* The Catholic University of America Canon Law Studies, n. 355 (Washington, D.C.: The Catholic University of America Press, 1955), p. 41.

respond to that at which he signs the rescript, the convalidation is effected.[39] Van Hove, however, held that the aforesaid phrase is to be interpreted as signifying the moment of the confection of the rescript in question, that is, the moment at which the superior signs the letter.[40] He expressed his reason for this interpretation thus:

> Concessio enim hic non opponitur confectioni litterarum sed momento quo matrimonium, nunc sanatum, est contractum. Ad hoc momentum enim retrotrahitur effectus sanationis.[41]

Michiels submits that the opinion of Van Hove in this matter is more probably the correct one.[42] This writer agrees with Michiels, because he does not believe that it can be established with certainty that the legislator in canon 1138, § 2, intends to derogate from the first norm which he lays down in canon 38.[43]

The second case involves rescripts conveying to ordinaries the habitual faculties treated in canon 66.[44] In this instance, the commentators are in disagreement among themselves concerning the aforementioned rescripts when there is no indication in these letters as to when the faculties which they contain are to go into effect.[45] Thus, Vermeersch (1858-1936) maintained that such rescripts take effect only on the day on which they are received by their intended recipients.[46] He based his opinion on two responses from the Holy See, issued in 1640 and 1759 respectively, in which it was definitely stated that, whenever habitual facul-

39 *Commentarium in Librum Primum Codicis Iuris Canonici* (2 vols. in 1, recognitum et auctum a Dino Staffa, Romae: Buona Stampa, 1939-1942), II, 309, nota 2.

40 *De Rescriptis,* p. 118, nota 6.

41 *Loc. cit.*

42 *Normae Generales,* II, 328.

43 Cf. *supra,* p. 207.

44 These faculties include the Quinquennial Faculties of the local ordinaries of the United States.

45 There is no question here of a prorogation or renewal of these faculties. For a discussion of this matter, cf. *infra,* pp. 211-214.

46 *Periodica,* XI (1922), (80)-(81).

ties were granted for a definite period of time, the beginning of that period was to be computed *"a die receptionis, et non a die datae."* [47] Van Hove, however, on the basis of canon 38 submitted that the rescripts in question are effective from the day on which they are actually issued.[48] That is to say, it was the opinion of Van Hove that the first norm of canon 38 prevails over the ruling of the above-mentioned responses of the Holy See. To give added weight to his conclusion on this matter, he cited Cappello, Vromant, and Konings-Putzer as authors who maintained that *"nisi in rescripto determinetur tempus a quo facultates valere incipiant, rescriptum valere a die datae."* [49]

The present writer supports the opinion of Van Hove that the first norm of canon 38 prevails over the aforesaid responses of the Holy See in this matter. His reason is precisely the prescription of canon 6, 1°, which provides that all laws, whether universal or particular, if they are contrary to the norms of the Code are abrogated, unless express provision is made in favor of particular laws. Indeed, the norm set forth by the responses from Rome in the years 1640 and 1759 respectively is clearly contrary to the ruling of canon 38 in regard to rescripts issued *in forma gratiosa*. Moreover, those responses evidently established the pre-Code universal law concerning the time of the initial effectiveness of rescripts containing habitual faculties. Furthermore, it may be remarked here that this writer has not been able to find, for the time that has elapsed from the promulgation of the Code of Canon Law, any declaration from the Holy See which could be regarded as maintaining that pre-Code norm in reference to the rescripts in question under the present canonical discipline. According to canon 6, 1°, therefore, the regulation enunciated in those responses must cede to the prescription of canon 38.

The third case in which the authors find reason for disagree-

[47] S. C. de Prop. Fide, 2 apr. 1640 et 22 ian. 1759—*Collectanea,* I, n. 100 and n. 412.

[48] *Op. cit.,* p. 119.

[49] *Ibid.,* nota 2. Michiels also supports Van Hove's teaching on the point in question.—*Loc. cit.*

ing as to the time when rescripts take effect involves rescripts by which faculties, already granted for a determined period of time, for example, for three years, are prorogued or renewed.[50] More precisely, the disagreement arises when the rescripts in question are issued on a day prior to that on which the previously-granted faculties are due to expire. The question is whether the rescripts involved become effective on the day on which they are actually issued, or on the day on which the original faculties are to terminate. The practical importance of this question is that the answer to it will determine the time at which the prorogued or renewed faculties will expire. Thus, if the prorogation or renewal of these faculties is effective from the date of the issuance of the rescript conveying the new grant, the faculties contained in the letter will expire at the time computed from the date on which the rescript is issued. If the initial effectiveness of the rescript with the prorogation or renewal of the faculties begins on the date of the expiration of the original faculties, the length of the period during which the prorogued or renewed faculties will be valid will be computed according to this latter date.

Van Hove maintained that canon 38 demands that the computation both of the time of the initial effectiveness of the rescript in question and of the expiration of the period of the prorogation or renewal of the original faculties is to be made according to the moment at which the rescript is actually issued.[51] Vermeersch was of the opinion that this computation is to be based on the time previously determined for the expiration of the original faculties. He held to this manner of computation even when the rescript containing the prorogation or renewal of the faculties was issued *after* the date on which the original faculties actually expired.[52] Michiels[53] and Rodrigo[54]

[50] This discussion also concerns any other favors that are to be extended after they have been granted for a specified time.

[51] *Op. cit.*, p. 119.

[52] "A qua die valeant acta S. Sedis," *Periodica*, XXI (1932), 52*.

[53] *Ibid.*, p. 329.

[54] *Tractatus de Legibus*, pp. 551-552.

attempt to solve the problem at hand by drawing the following distinction. First of all, if the original faculties have already expired, the rescript with the prorogation or renewal of those faculties becomes effective at the time at which the letter is actually issued. Michiels explains the reason underlying this proposition thus:

> Ratio prioris est, quia novum rescriptum prorogatorium ex se non potest operari antequam sit, seu non potest habere effectum antequam reapse fuerit concessum, ac proinde non potest dici juridice retrotrahi ad momentum exhaustae prioris concessionis, nisi in eo nominatim caveatur contrarium.[55]

Secondly, if the original faculties have not yet expired, the rescript conveying the prorogation or renewal of them takes effect at the time when they are due to terminate. The reason which Rodrigo offers in support of this conclusion is as follows:

> quia id quod in ipso [rescripto prorogatorio] conceditur est temporis prioris prorogatio; atqui hoc quod adhuc vi propria durat nondum eget prorogari; seu aliter, in secundo rescripto conceditur v. c. novum triennium ad usum facultatum, ultra triennium in priori concessum; ergo quamvis concessio teneat iam *ex nunc,* sed ita ut eius tempus non curat nisi *ex futuro tunc,* quod sit initium novi triennii.[56]

The present writer subscribes to the opinion of Michiels and Rodrigo in this matter. He does so for two reasons. The first is that the reasoning offered by these authors in support of their opinion seems sound to him. His second reason is that he believes that the superior who grants the prorogation or renewal of the faculties in question would not intend his rescript, as issued for this purpose, to be superfluously useless. Yet, the rescript would be such during the time between the date of the issuance of the letter and the date of the expiration of the original faculties. Hence, this writer submits that rescripts which convey a prorogation or renewal of habitual faculties contain implicitly from the nature of their contents an indication

[55] *Loc. cit.* Rodrigo gives substantially the same reason for the foregoing proposition.—*Op. cit.,* p. 552.

[56] *Loc. cit.*

that the letters are to become effective not at the moment at which they are actually issued, but on the day when the original faculties expire.[57]

B. The Second Norm of Canon 38: Concerning Rescripts Granted *in forma commissoria*

According to the second norm enunciated in canon 38, which is to be applied precisely to rescripts of justice and to rescripts of favor granted *in forma commissoria*, rescripts granted *in forma commissoria* become effective at the time of their execution.[58] The authors who have been consulted in the preparation of this study make no mention of any exceptions to the foregoing norm.

[57] Because of the solid probability which supports the above-stated opinion of Michiels and Rodrigo, it is perfectly safe to follow it in practice and to act in virtue of the rescript of prorogation or renewal during the time between the termination of the faculties or favor according to the computation based on the date of the issuance of this rescript and the termination of them according to the reckoning based on the date of the previously-set time for the expiration of the original grant. As far as the lawfulness of the acts performed during this interval is concerned, the rules for the legitimate use of probable opinions are applicable. Moreover, if the question of validity arises in reference to these acts, and if they are of a jurisdictional nature, can. 209 applies to them.

[58] Toso, *Commentaria Minora*, I, 118. The time of the execution of rescripts has been explained above.—Cf. pp. 203-204. The principle applies to all rescripts granted *in forma commissoria*, whether they are granted with the use of a necessary or of a voluntary executor, for the legislator draws no distinction in can. 38 between these two types of executors.

The reason for the designation of two different times for the initial effectiveness of rescripts issued *in forma gratiosa* and of rescripts granted *in forma commissoria* can be traced to the diverse natures of these two types of rescripts. On the one hand, rescripts issued *in forma gratiosa* contain favors which the superior himself, in issuing the letters, grants *complete et perfecte, de iure et de facto*, so that nothing more is ordinarily required for them to take effect. On the other hand, rescripts granted *in forma commissoria* contain either a mandate for the *necessary* executor to grant *de facto* the favor which the superior has already conceded *de iure* to the prospective beneficiaries of the letters or they contain the required faculties for the *voluntary* executor to bestow upon the intended parties favors which the superior himself has not yet effectively granted either *de iure* or *de facto*. Cf. *supra*, pp. 11-13.

The present writer submits, however, that if a *conditio de futuro* is effectively attached to the execution of the rescripts in question here, then the letters take effect only when that condition is fulfilled.

Article 4. Conclusions from the General Principle of Canon 41

From the general principle of canon 41, namely, that indeed it is required but that it also suffices for the petitions for rescripts to be truthful at the time at which the letters consequent upon them become effective, the following conclusions can be logically drawn. First, if the *preces* for a rescript are *de facto* false at the moment when the document is meant to take effect, the resulting invalidity of the rescript is not sanated by the fact that the petition in question was true at some time prior to the moment of the intended initial effectiveness of the letter, nor by the fact that the *preces* become truthful after the aforesaid moment.[59]

Second, if the petitions are actually true at the moment when the rescripts obtained through them take effect, these letters must be adjudged valid even though their *preces* were false previous to the time of the initial effectiveness of the documents, or become untrue after that time.[60]

59 Coronata, *Institutiones,* I, 76. This conclusion has been stated in reference only to the validity of rescripts. It applies, however, also to the lawfulness of the rescripts mentioned in cans. 45 and 1054.—Cf. *supra,* p. 200. The times when rescripts issued *in forma gratiosa* and granted *in forma commissoria* respectively become effective have been indicated above.—Cf. pp. 207-215.

60 Michiels, *Normae Generales,* II, 359. This second conclusion from the general principle of can. 41 explains the efficacy of a matrimonial dispensation, the *preces* for which were truthful indeed when the rescript containing it took effect but became false between that time and the day of the celebration of the marriage in question. The dispensation continued to be valid despite the fate of its petition, for once the relevant rescript became effective, the impediment from which the dispensation had been granted was removed absolutely, that is, once and for all. In other words, the action of the dispensation upon the impediment was then perfectly complete, so that even if the final cause on account of which there was the grant of the dispensation ceased after the time of the initial effectiveness of the rescript, and consequently of the dispensation itself,

It must be emphasized at this point, however, that when this second conclusion is applied to rescripts containing dispensations that permit of successive applications, it must be understood in the light of canon 86.[61] Canon 86 provides that a dispensation which has successive applications ceases through the certain and complete cessation of the motivating cause proposed for it. Hence, if the final causes for rescripts conveying such dispensations should cease to exist, as envisioned in canon 86, after the moment of the initial effectiveness of the letters, then the rescripts themselves, together with the dispensations contained in them, would lose their efficacy with the certain and complete cessation of their motivating reasons.

Furthermore, in applying this second deduction from the general principle of canon 41 to rescripts granted *in forma commissoria,* one must keep in mind the prescription of canon 52, which states:

> Rescripta, quorum praesentationi nullum est definitum tempus, possunt exsecutori exhiberi quovis tempore, modo absit fraus et dolus.[62]

This is not to say that a petitioner's rescript is automatically invalidated if he, knowing from the beginning that the *preces* for it were false, through fraud or deceit delays presenting his letter to its executor until, for instance, the false final cause on

---

the impediment did not arise again. This conclusion is based on the principle of law: "Factum legitime retractari non debet, licet casus postea eveniat a quo non potuit inchoari."—Reg. 73, R. J., in VI°.

[61] An example is that of a dispensation from the law of the Lenten fast.

[62] "De *ambitu* illorum vocabulorm [fraus et dolus] non convenit inter scriptores. *Dolus* definitur deliberatum propositum inducendi aliquem ad agendum vel non agendum, illum decipiendo artificiis illicitis, sive silentio seu dissimulatione, verum tacendo, sive verbis seu mendaciis, sive factis. *Fraudem* quidam intelligunt speciem particularem doli, quae fit verbis, dum dolus fit factis, aut quae fit per actionem quae palam ponitur, dum dolus clam perficitur. Alii fraudem definiunt dolum quo damnum alicui infertur. Denique fraus, sensu magis particulari, relate ad legem, definitur actio ad eludendam legem, actio scilicet quae est quidem vere contra legem, apparenter est secundum legem. Ut fraus legis adsit, requiritur ut id quod fit vel omittitur, fieri omittive aliqua lege saltem sit vetitum. 'Cum quid una via prohibetur alicui, ad id alia non debet admitti' (Regula iuris 85, in VI°)."—Van Hove, *De Rescriptis,* pp. 224-225.

account of which it was granted becomes true.[63] Such delay does not automatically nullify the rescript involved, for, on the one hand, the requirement of canon 41 that the *preces* be truthful at the time of the execution of the rescripts granted *in forma commissoria* is fulfilled in the case in question. On the other hand, as has already been indicated, under the present law bad faith of itself does not result in the nullification of rescripts.[64] What is more, it is neither expressly nor indeed equivalently stated in canon 52 that the rescript under discussion here is invalidated because of the fraud or the deceit one employs in delaying its execution until the petition for it can be verified.[65] Consequently, canon 52 cannot be considered an invalidating law.[66]

Nonetheless, it is still a recognized principle under the present law that fraud and deceit must not procure an advantage for anyone, unless, of course, the legislator clearly indicates that he does not wish to deprive a person of some benefit thus obtained, as he does indicate in canon 45 and 1054.[67] Hence, since it is precisely through fraud or deceit that the petitioner maneuvers to have the *preces* for his rescript truthful at the time of the execution of the document, it is concluded from the expression "*modo absit fraus et dolus*" in canon 52 that this law provides

63 Cf. Michiels, *loc. cit.* Toso has taken the opposite stand on this point, for he states: ". . . rescriptum executore interiecto esse validum, si preces, antea falsae, verae fiant tempore executionis, dum ne id oratoris factum sit fraude vel dolo malo, quae cum nemini debeant suffragare, rescriptum ab origine irritum faciunt."—*Commentaria Minora*, I, 121.

64 Cf. *supra*, pp. 133-137. Cf. also Michiels, *loc. cit.*

65 Cf. Cicognani, *Canon Law*, p. 713.

66 Can. 11.

67 C. 15, X, *de rescriptis*, I, 3. Cf. Cicognani, *loc. cit.* For an analysis of cans. 45 and 1054, cf. *supra*, pp. 180-199.

On the basis of this principle, the present writer submits that the provisions of can. 2361 apply whether or not the *preces* mentioned therein are fraudulently or deceitfully false at the time when the rescripts consequent upon them become effective. He believes that in that canon the legislator is providing punishment precisely for the fraud or the deceit involved in the falsification of the petitions. This conclusion seems to be supported by the fact that can. 2361 is placed in Title XV, *De crimine falsi*, of the third part of Book V of the Code of Canon Law.

that, as a penalty for the fraud or the deceit involved, either the executor may refuse to execute the rescript [68] or the rescript itself may be declared null by the superior who has granted it.[69]

[68] O'Neill, *Papal Rescripts of Favor*, p. 119. Cf. can. 54, § 1: "Si in rescripto committatur merum exsecutionis ministerium, exsecutio rescripti denegari non potest, nisi . . . qui rescriptum impetravit adeo, iudicio exsecutoris, videatur indignus ut aliorum offensioni futura sit gratiae concessio. . . ."

[69] Cicognani, *loc. cit.* and Michiels, *loc. cit.*

CHAPTER IX

THE DECISION CONCERNING THE TRUTHFULNESS OF THE *PRECES*

It has already been indicated that, as far as the legislator's demand for truthful *preces* is concerned, the validity or the invalidity of rescripts depends respectively on the *objective* substantial truthfulness or falseness of the petitions for them.[1] Any decision, therefore, that is reached concerning the presence or the absence of truthful *preces* does not alter the objective condition of the rescripts involved. Nonetheless, sometimes it is helpful, and at other times it is required that such a decision be made. That is to say, in the case of a rescript issued *in forma gratiosa,* it will help the beneficiary of the letter to know that his favor is valid, at least insofar as the petition for it is founded on objective truth. In regard to a rescript granted *in forma commissoria,* the executor is bound not to execute the letter if he is certain that the petition for it is substantially false.[2] Such a rescript is *de facto* invalid and, consequently, incapable of effective execution.[3]

Article 1. The Investigation Required of Executors to Reach a Decision Concerning the Truthfulness of the Preces [4]

Rescripts granted *in forma commissoria* deserve special consideration in this discussion in reference to the decision concern-

[1] Cf. *supra,* pp. 112-114. Cans. 45 and 1054 represent exceptions to this statement.—Cf. *supra,* pp. 122-125.

[2] Cf. can. 54, § 1, and *infra,* pp. 219-225. For a description of rescripts issued *in forma gratiosa* and granted *in forma commissoria,* cf. *supra,* pp. 11-15.

[3] "Nam irritum rescriptum nihil est, et ideo nihil potest executioni mandari vel, si magis placet, invaliditas rescripti secumfert mandati invaliditatem et inde incapacitatem executoris."—Toso, *Commentaria Minora,* I, 139.

[4] In cases involving rescripts issued *in forma gratiosa,* the law requires no investigation into the veracity of the *preces* for the letters. The petitioner usually knows whether or not his *preces* are *de facto* founded on the truth.

ing the truthfulness of the *preces,* for it may well be that the executors of these letters have to make this decision in carrying out their commissions. Hence, it is of practical importance to consider the manner in which the different types of executors come to a conclusion concerning the veracity of the petitions for the rescripts that are committed to them for execution.

A. The Necessary Executor with a Commission Merely to Execute the Rescript [5]

The first type of executor to be treated here is the necessary executor, who is described in canon 54, § 1. He is the executor who is given a commission merely to execute the rescript involved, without having any *jurisdictional* power either to investigate the truthfulness of the *preces* for the letter or to judge the validity or the invalidity of the rescript itself.[6]

This type of executor does have a certain amount of non-jurisdictional power, however, which he is to use for investigating the veracity of the *preces* for the rescript committed to him for execution. The fact of his possessing this non-jurisdictional power can be seen from the prescription of canon 54, § 1, which provides that he cannot lawfully refuse to execute his rescript, unless, among other reasons, it is *evident* that the letter is void

[5] The term "necessary" in connection with executors is indicative of the fact that such executors are ordered to execute the rescripts committed to them and, indeed, must do so whenever the requirements of the law are fulfilled.

[6] Van Hove, *De Rescriptis,* pp. 237-238. "Merum ministerium executionis sunt Verbi Dei praedicatio, dispensationis applicatio, excommunicationis fulminatio aut simplex absolutio etc. etc. . . ."—Coronata, *Institutiones,* I, 86. In this discussion the writer proposes for the sake of clarity to describe the type of executor about whom he is speaking and thereby to forestall the controversy that exists among present-day commentators in reference to the so-called *mere* and *mixed* executors, who were recognized in the pre-Code discipline.—Cf., e.g., Augustine, *A Commentary on the New Code of Canon Law* (8 vols., Vol. I, 3. ed., St. Louis, 1920), I, pp. 125 and 142; Ayrinhac, *General Legislation in the New Code of Canon Law* (New York, 1923), pp. 158-159; Coronata, *ibid.,* pp. 71-72; Eichmann, *Lehrbuch des katholischen Kirchenrechts* (Paderborn, 1926), p. 55; Ferreres, *Compendium Theologiae Moralis ad Normam Codicis Juris Canonici* (7. ed., 2 vols., Barcinone, 1928), II, n. 979; Michiels, *Normae Generales,* II, 448, nota 2; O'Neill, *Papal Rescripts of Favor,* pp. 169-173.

in consequence of subreption or obreption.[7] Yet, ordinarily the existence of substantial subreption or obreption is not evident to an executor without some kind of inquiry or investigation which he conducts in order to ascertain whether or not the *preces* are actually truthful.[8] Hence, it seems from the very nature of things that, with his mandate merely to execute the rescript given to him, the necessary executor not only obtains the faculty to inquire into the objective veracity of the *preces* involved but has also the obligation to do so whenever he has a serious suspicion about the truthfulness of the petition.[9] His obligation, however, looks only to the lawfulness and not to the validity of the execution of the rescript.[10]

The investigation which is made by the executor under discussion here should be focused upon the veracity of the *preces* precisely at the time of the execution of the rescript in question, because it is at that time that the petition for the letter must be truthful.[11] Moreover, this examination can be at most an extra-

[7] For an explanation of the terms "subreption" and "obreption" cf. *supra*, pp. 127-132.

[8] Michiels, *ibid.*, p. 449.

[9] Michiels, *loc. cit.* Cf. also Van Hove, *op. cit.*, p. 238. Coronata does not agree with the foregoing statement, for he remarks: "Potest [exsecutor necessarius de quo can. 54, § 1, agitur] tamen et debet rescripti exsecutionem denegare si *pateat* seu *clarum sit,* ex se, et sine ullo examine expresse ad hoc instituto, . . . rescriptum nullum . . . esse."—*Ibid.*, p. 86.

This investigation need not be made if an inquiry was made into the truthfulness of the *preces* before they were sent to the superior, and the executor is certain that the circumstances of the case have not changed in the meantime, or if moral certitude concerning the veracity of the petition can be obtained in some other manner.—Chelodi, *Ius Canonicum de Personis*, p. 134, nota 5. The same may be said whenever the *preces* involved are widely known to be true.—Michiels, *ibid.*, nota 6. It does not seem correct to hold, however, that because of the extraordinarily liberal ruling of can. 1054, this investigation may be omitted whenever rescripts conveying dispensations from the minor matrimonial impediments are involved, as do Michiels (*loc. cit.*) and Van Hove (*loc. cit.*). Even in the case of these rescripts it is possible to have an invalidating falsehood in the *pars postulativa* of the *preces* for them.—Cf. *supra*, pp. 194-196.

[10] Michiels, *ibid.*, p. 449.

[11] Cf. *supra*, pp. 202-204.

judicial inquiry that must be understood to be not an act of jurisdiction but merely an act preparatory to the execution of the rescript.[12] In other words, since this type of executor, *qua talis,* does not possess jurisdiction, he cannot conduct a judicial investigation into the truthfulness of the *preces* in question. Rather, his inquiry in connection with rescripts issued for the internal forum is satisfactory if it consists in the questioning of the petitioner concerning the veracity of the *preces.* The petitioner's word may be accepted as true by the executor, unless he should know from some other source that the party is not telling the truth.[13] As for rescripts in the external forum, the investigation into the truthfulness of their *preces* should be such as to let the executor be satisfied in his own conscience that the petition involved is *de facto* founded on truth.[14] It sometimes happens, however, that the word of the petitioner alone is not sufficient in this instance to give the executor the moral certainty which he desires in regard to the veracity of the *preces.* If such be the case, the executor should then proceed to contact witnesses and to examine pertinent documents as a means of discerning the truth about the real condition of the *preces.*[15]

Once his inquiry has been carefully made, the executor will be in a position to decide with moral certainty whether the *preces* in question are substantially true or false, or whether there is still some doubt about their veracity. As far as the truthfulness of the petition is concerned, it is only when the executor who is considered here is morally certain that the *preces* are false that he can lawfully refuse to execute the rescript given to him. That is to say, even when he is doubtful about the fulfillment of the condition "*si preces veritate nitantur.*" in the case with which he is concerned, he must execute his mandate and permit the intended beneficiary of the rescript to enjoy the favor conveyed

[12] Hence, it is not necessary that the executor always conduct this inquiry personally, even if he has been chosen for his personal qualifications. Cf. can. 57, § 2.

[13] Van Hove, *loc. cit.* Needless to say, the seal of the Sacrament of Penance may not be jeopardized through this inquiry.

[14] Ojetti, *Commentarium,* I, 257.

[15] Michiels, *ibid.,* p. 450; Van Hove, *loc. cit.*

thereby.[16] Canon 54, § 1, makes this point clear, for it states explicitly that the nullification of a rescript by subreption or obreption must be *evident* before its execution can be denied on these grounds by the executor under consideration here.[17] Moreover, *in dubio standum est pro valore actus.*

B. The Necessary Executor with a Mandate to Execute a Rescript *"si per informationes preces veritate niti repereris"* [18]

Another type of executor who must be considered here is he who is given a mandate to execute a rescript with a condition like *"si per informationes preces veritate niti repereris"* attached to the letter.[19] The obvious import of such a condition is that, whenever it is invoked, it is not sufficient for the validity of the execution of the relevant rescript that the *preces* for it be objectively true. Rather, an investigation is required into the veracity of the petition. On the basis of canon 39 this condition must be adjudged an essential condition. Hence, unless this inquiry is made, the execution of the rescript is null and void.[20]

[16] Cf. Toso, *Commentaria Minora,* I, 138.

[17] "Exsecutio potest etiam fieri *ex nunc pro tunc,* sub conditione scilicet suspensiva, adeo ut tunc tantum effectum obtineat, cum ex informatione constiterit de veritate precum."—Van Hove, *loc. cit.* This seems, however, to be an act of jurisdiction and, hence, to be *per se ultra mandatum* with respect to the executor being considered here. Cf. can. 203, § 1.

[18] This condition may be attached also to a rescript committed to a voluntary executor.—Coronata, *ibid.,* p. 87. For an explanation of the voluntary executor, cf. *infra,* p. 224 under C.

[19] Before the year 1885 it was customary to find a like condition, namely, *"si preces veritate niti repereris,"* attached to rescripts.—Cf. *supra,* pp. 52-53.

[20] Can. 55: "Exsecutor procedere debet ad mandati normam, et nisi conditiones essentiales in litteris appositas impleverit ac substantialem procedendi formam servaverit, irrita est exsecutio." There are some authors who maintain that the executor under consideration here is given real jurisdiction to make this investigation. Cf. Coronata, *loc. cit.,* and Van Hove, *op. cit.,* p. 238, nota 4. Hence, in this instance the executor can conduct a judicial inquiry into the truthfulness of the *preces,* if he so desires. "Quando autem inquisitio haec facienda est, non debet exsecutor inquirere, servato ordine iuris; sed in foro externo tenetur inquirere summarie tantum et extraiudicialiter. Hinc est, quod, ut ait D'Annibale, non

The investigation in this case may be made in the same manner as has been indicated for the necessary executor who holds a commission merely to execute the rescript.[21] It is to be noted that in the present circumstances the authors advise that, even when the *preces* involved are widely known to be true, it is the safer course to conduct the examination.[22]

C. The Voluntary Executor

The third kind of executor to be considered in the discussion at hand is the voluntary executor. He is so designated because he is not ordered, as the necessary executor is, to execute the rescript committed to him, but is rather given the power, as canon 54, § 2, indicates, to grant or deny the favor involved *"pro suo prudenti arbitrio et conscientia."* The quoted phrase prescribes the manner in which the voluntary executor is to act upon the rescript which he receives. In a word, his decision to grant or to refuse the favor in question should not be based upon mere arbitrariness, but he should be guided by such factors as whether or not he finds the *preces* for the relevant rescript to be founded on truth.[23] Hence, before acting, the voluntary executor should also inquire into the veracity of the petition, unless it is otherwise known to him that the *preces* are *de facto* truthful. What was said concerning the method of making this investiga-

---

est necessaria depositio testium, nec prohibita est subdelegatio eorum, quae pertinent ad cognitionem causae. In foro vero interno adhibenda est fides oratori, nec ipsi deferendum est iuramentum de veritate."—Ojetti, *ibid.*, p. 222.

[21] Cf. *supra*, p. 222. Cf. also Coronata, *loc. cit.*

[22] "Quaestio est, utrum valeret dispensatio in hoc casu, si notorium omnino esset causam subesse et exposita fuisse vera. Ratio dubitandi est, quia notoria inquisitione non indigent. Dicunt tamen generatim in praxi tutius esse ab exsecutore inquiri."—Ojetti, *loc. cit.* Cf. also Michiels, *ibid.*, p. 453, nota 6. *Contra,* O'Neill, *Papal Rescripts of Favor,* p. 175.

[23] "Iuxta hanc rescripti formam [i.e., rescriptum cum exsecutore voluntario] exsecutor non potest pro suo lubitu gratiam concedere vel denegare, sed si pro prudenti suo arbitrio, idest, iudicio et conscientia iudicaverit vera esse, quae narrata sunt, rescriptum exsecutioni demandare debet, secus exsecutionem denegare tenetur."—S. C. Ep. et Reg., 3 sept. 1852—Bizzarri, *Collectanea in usum Secretariae Sacrae Congregationis Episcoporum et Regularium edita* (Romae, 1885), p. 612.

tion when it is conducted by a necessary executor who holds a commission merely to execute the rescript applies also to the inquiry in this case.[24]

Article 2. The Basis for the Decision Concerning the Truthfulness of the Preces

One of the difficulties which can arise in connection with the decision concerning the truthfulness of petitions is the problem of ascertaining whether the condition *"si preces veritate nitantur"* applies (*1*) only to the *preces* which the petitioner himself presents to the superior, or (*2*) only to the summary of the petition that is incorporated into the rescript itself,[25] or (*3*) to both the original *preces* and the summary of them in the rescript. In other words, is it the petitioner's *preces* themselves, or is it the summary of them in the consequent rescript, or is it the two of them together that serve as the basis of the decision concerning the presence or the absence of invalidating subreption or obreption?

Actually, it is most unlikely that this difficulty will present itself very often at the present time. On the one hand, it happens frequently now that superiors grant their rescripts only with a general indication that they are acceding to the petitioner's request in view of the facts and circumstances mentioned in his *preces* and because of the reasons proposed therein. Thus, rescripts, instead of having a summary of the original *preces*, often carry only such expressions as *"Pro gratia, Iuxta preces, Iuxta petita, Pro gratia iuxta petita, Affirmative."*[26] On the other hand, in cases in which rescripts do contain a summary of the *preces* submitted by the petitioners, one can be sure that diligent care was taken by the ones responsible for drawing up the letters to insure a true and adequate reproduction of the facts, circum-

[24] Cf. *supra*, p. 222. Coronata indicates that the voluntary executor has jurisdictional power to conduct this inquiry.—*Loc. cit.*

[25] For an explanation of the structure of rescripts, cf. *supra*, pp. 7-8.

[26] Van Hove, *De Rescriptis*, p. 79. It should be noted, however, that the Sacred Congregation of the Sacraments indicates in many of its rescripts the motivating reason for the concession involved. Hence, it is possible that this reason would differ from that which the petitioner himself presented.—Van Hove, *op. cit.*, p. 190.

stances, and causes listed in the petitions.[27] So, whenever there is no question of any real and substantial divergency between the actual *preces* and the summary of them in the relevant rescripts, there is no need to choose between them as to which of them is to be used as the basis upon which the decision concerning the presence or the absence of falsehood is to be made.[28]

This need does arise, however, in the rather rare instance in which either in the *preces* presented for a rescript or in the summary of the petition incorporated into the letter itself, but not in both of them, substantial untruthfulness is detected.[29] Unfortunately, the authors are not in agreement in their solution of the problem created by such a circumstance.

Michiels, for instance, is of the opinion that only the *preces* submitted by the petitioner need be attended to in the ascertainment of whether or not the relevant rescript is invalidated because of subreption or obreption.[30] In a word, he maintains that only a petitioner can be accurately said to commit subreption or obreption. Hence, only the *preces* of the petitioner are governed by the nullifying norms of canons 40, 42, and 45. He states his position in this way:

> Quapropter, si precibus *a rescribente* (seu rectius, ab amanuensi rescribentis) in rescripto relatis, reticetur aliquid alioquin

[27] Cf. Ordo servandus in S. Congregationibus, Tribunalibus, Officiis Romanae Curiae, 29 sept. 1908, Pars II, *Normae peculiares,* c. VI, n. 6—*AAS,* I (1909), 73-74.

[28] The present writer believes that a real divergency does not exist between the original *preces* and the summary of them when, for instance, the grantor considers all the reasons proposed by the petitioner as insufficient and supplies a motivating cause of his own. In such a case, even though the actual motivating reason for the rescript is mentioned only in the summary of the *preces,* the grantor, at least virtually, makes it a part of the original petition, and, in the opinion of this writer, the cause in question should be looked upon as being a part of the original *preces.*

[29] If the falsehood is found only in the summary of the *preces,* it is usually attributed to the person who was commissioned to draw up the rescript for the signature of the grantor. Cf., however, *supra,* p. 225, note 26. For a treatment of the procedure that is followed in the Roman Curia in the matter of the composition of rescripts, cf. Van Hove, *op. cit.,* pp. 74-76.

[30] *Normae Generales,* II, 354-355.

> necessario exprimendum vel affirmatur aliquid positive falsum, *vera subreptio vel obreptio,* cum effectibus juridicis in can. 42 statutis, *non habetur, nisi* reticentia veri vel expositio falsi fuerit ex supplici libello desumpta ideoque ipsi oratori sit adscribenda; si vero reticentia veri vel expositio falsi sit soli rescribenti ejusve officiali adscribenda, habetur merus *error,* de cujus sequelis juridicis ad normam can. 47 dijudicare debemus.[31]

To support his stand in this matter, Michiels argues that only his position on this question is in harmony with right reason, the canons of the Code, and the *stylus Curiae Romanae.* Thus, in reference to right reason, he maintains that the word *"preces"* in its obvious meaning can refer only to petitions as they are presented by petitioners. In regard to the canons of the Code which have a bearing on this question, he holds that the expres-

[31] *Ibid.,* p. 355. Michiels cites several modern-day authors as proponents of his opinion.—Cf. *ibid.,* p. 354, nota 3. This writer has found, however, that the commentators who are so cited and whom he could consult do not expressly, if at all, support Michiels' doctrine in this matter. While they warn against the commission of subreption or obreption in the *preces* submitted for rescripts, they are not concerned with the problem under discussion here. They do not even mention, in one way or another, the summary of the *preces.* Cf. Cappello, *Summa Iuris Canonici,* I, 119; Cicognani-Staffa, *Commentarium in Librum Primum Codicis Iuris Canonici,* II, 333-334; Gasparri, *De Matrimonio,* I, 198, nota 1; Ojetti, *Commentarium,* I, 224; Wernz-Vidal, *Ius Matrimoniale,* p. 572. Vermeersch-Creusen took up the question at hand and they had this to say about it: "Quaeres *quaenam preces* attendendae sint: preces quales ab oratore missae sint, an preces quales in diplomate referantur. Fit enim, ut officialis scriptor in hac relatione erret. Arbitramur sic distinguendum esse. Liquet formalem subreptionem vel obreptionem a solo oratore committi posse eaque plerumque a Codice respicitur; sed mutatio ab officiali inducta errorem efficit, cuius effectus variat ad normam can. 47, non can. 42. Sic dicimus cum Leithner [sic], Haring, Matthaeo Conte, partim tantum cum Michiels."—*Epitome Iuris Canonici,* I, n. 161, ad 1. Rodrigo likewise concerns himself with this matter. He argues as follows: "Attenditur veritas precum, non quidem prout orator eas exaravit, sed prout ipsae Superiori oblatae sunt, forte in Curia reformatae: nam tandem ad sibi oblata Superior rescribit; ambae tamen praesumuntur conformes inter se, saltem in rei substantia. Sed bene accidere potest error Officialis Curiae preces transcribentis aut earum summarium redigentis; quo in casu, minus quidem frequenti in Romana Curia, obtinet non proprie obreptio aut subreptio in precibus, sed merus error, de cuius influxu in valorem rescripti providetur in can. 47. . . ."—*Tractatus de Legibus,* p. 558.

sions *"reticere verum," "exponere falsum,"* and *"proponere causam"* can be properly applied only to petitioners themselves. Moreover, he points out that parallel canons in the Code, for example, canons 156, § 3; 991, § 1; 1055; and 2249, § 2, as well as the *stylus* of the Roman Curia which always refers to the petitioner's *preces,* unless the contrary is expressly stated, clearly indicate that it is the intention of the legislator that the *"preces"* be understood as those *"quae continentur in ipso supplici libello."* Michiels, moreover, does not believe that an argument contrary to his teaching can be rightfully drawn from the wording of canon 42, § 3, which treats of the defect of subreption or obreption in the rescript itself, for, as he puts it:

> verba canonis evidenter intelligenda sunt de vitio obreptionis vel subreptionis *relate ad* unam alteramve partem rescripti.[32]

O'Neill[33] and Van Hove,[34] among other commentators,[35] have taken a position on this question that is contrary to that held by Michiels. It is their contention that the presence or absence of subreption and obreption must ultimately be decided according to the summary of the petition contained in the rescript itself. Their teaching in this matter is based on the following considerations: First, the expressions *"reticentia veri"* and *"expositio falsi"* can certainly be applied to the summary of the *preces* in the rescript, as well as to the petition itself.[36] Second, canon 42, § 3, definitely points to subreption and obreption as existing in the rescript itself.[37] Third, this opinion seems not to be in opposition to right reason, for the presumption holds that the grantor of the favor in question was influenced by the cir-

[32] *Loc. cit.*—Italics are Michiels'.

[33] *Papal Rescripts of Favor,* pp. 130-131.

[34] *Op. cit.,* pp. 190-191.

[35] E.g., Abbo-Hannan, *The Sacred Canons,* I, 73, note 20, and Coronata, *Institutiones,* I, 60, nota 6.

[36] O'Neill, *op. cit.,* p. 131. "Denique obreptio et subreptio esse potest non tantum in libello supplici, sed insuper in 'positio' confecta in rebus gravioribus ad administris Curiae Romanae aut in confectione ipsius rescripti."—Van Hove, *op. cit.,* p. 190.

[37] Van Hove, *loc. cit.*

cumstances and reasons stated in the narrative and motive parts of the rescript.[38] Fourth, canon 47 deals with the errors in rescripts, and not with the subreption or obreption that may be found therein.[39] Last, for the purpose of comparison with the true facts of the case, the circumstances and causes as presumably understood and acted upon by the grantor are available to the executor or the beneficiary in the summary of the *preces* in the rescript. It may happen, however, that a copy of the petition that was sent to the grantor was not retained by the sender.[40]

This writer cannot subscribe to either of the foregoing opinions to the exclusion of the other, because while each of them seems to enjoy a certain amount of juridical merit, neither side solves the problem at hand in a satisfactory manner.[41] In view of this fact the present writer submits that, in deciding concerning the presence or the absence of invalidating untruthfulness, one should consider both the *preces* submitted by the petitioner, when that is possible, and the summary of the petition in the rescript itself.

[38] O'Neill, *loc. cit.* For a description of the narrative and motive parts of rescripts, cf. *supra*, pp. 16-19.

[39] "Denique notandum est, canonem 47 circa errores in rescriptis non agere de subreptione vel obreptione et proinde a stylo Curiae, valde stricto circa errores ante promulgationem Codicis, videtur non esse recedendum." —Van Hove, *op. cit.*, pp. 190-191. Rodrigo comments on this same canon in this way: "Finis huius dispositionis [i.e., c. 47] est providere erroribus subrepentibus praesertim in Curia admissis, dum v.c. Officialis summariam precum relationem in rescriptum inserit; et supponitur error non afficere substantiam ipsam casus et gratiae concessae, aut causam motivam necessariam: error quidem in hac causa per quem omitteretur vera exsistens et adduceretur falsa, rescriptum et gratiae concessionem invalidaret, quia tandem rescriptum subsignatur et conceditur secundum ea quae in ipso cxprimuntur."—*Op. cit.*, p. 565.

[40] O'Neill, *loc. cit.*

[41] Van Hove himself remarked: "Quamvis argumentationi quae opponitur [i.e., Michiels] non omnis valor sit denegandus, opinamur in praxi recurrendum esse ad Sacras Congregationes, ut de valore rescripti constet." —*Op. cit.*, p. 191. "Non tamen crederem absurdum sustinere validum rescriptum si constaret Superiorem annuisse precibus praesentatis absque errore in causa motiva, licet postea in rescriptum subsignatum ab ipso error circa causam concessionis insertam irrepserit: id omnino certum esset si causa iacens in rescripto, quae tamen abfuit a precibus, vera exsistat."—Rodrigo, *loc. cit.*

The truth of the matter is that the difficulty under consideration here has arisen because the law on this point is not clear. This unclearness may perhaps be attributed to the fact that in the canons which deal with truth and falsehood in the petitions for rescripts the legislator may well have in mind only the ordinary and usual circumstances that are regularly encountered in this matter, namely, those in which there is no substantial discrepancy between the *preces* of the petitioner and the summary of the petition in the rescript. Whatever the reason for this unclearness may be, the fact remains, at least in this writer's opinion, that a real *dubium iuris* has been caused by the law's lack of clarity.[42] The doubt centers precisely on whether the invalidating force of canons 40, 42, and 45 extends only to the *preces* submitted by the petitioner, or only to the summary of the petition in the rescript, or to both of them together. Moreover, it seems that this doubt cannot be conclusively settled without an authentic declaration from the legislator himself. Until such a declaration is made, there will be good reason to argue for and against the validity of the rescript in question. Consequently the writer further submits that in the face of the *dubium iuris* involved, such a rescript should be adjudged valid, for on the basis of canon 15, canons 40, 42, and 45, although they are truly invalidating laws, cease to bind because of the doubt of law that is here raised against them.

Article 3. Doubtful Subreption and Obreption

It happens sometimes that, after a rescript has been granted, insoluble doubts arise as to whether or not the *preces* for the letter were actually founded on truth as is required by the law. Needless to say, such doubts can be most frustrating, especially for the intended beneficiary of the rescript. It is the writer's purpose here, therefore, to indicate the proper course of action to be followed in the face of doubtful subreption and obreption.[43]

In seeking a solution to this problem, one must at the outset decide whether these vitiating defects are doubtful through a

[42] For an explanation of a *dubium iuris*, cf. *infra*, p. 231, note 44.

[43] The only subreption or obreption that is being considered in this discussion is that which is substantial or invalidating.—Cf. *supra*, pp. 131-132.

dubium iuris or by way of a *dubium facti.*[44] A *dubium iuris* arises in the matter at hand when, for example, it is doubtful whether or not the *stylus Curiae* requires for the validity of the rescript in question the mention of some particular fact that has *de facto* not been expressed. A *dubium facti* is encountered, for instance, when a doubt arises concerning the existence of the single final cause proposed by the petitioner, or indicated by the grantor, as the sole motivating reason for the issuance of the rescript, or when a doubt appears concerning the existence of some fact which had to be mentioned for the validity of the letter, which fact actually was or was not expressed in the *preces.*[45]

When the presence of nullifying subreption and obreption in a petition is doubtful through a *dubium iuris,* the consequent rescript is certainly valid, for canon 15 provides that laws, even invalidating laws, such as canons 40, 42, and 54 are, have no binding force in the face of a doubt of law. When the doubt involved is a *dubium facti,* it is the almost universal teaching of the commentators that, at least theoretically, the rescript in question is valid, precisely on the basis of the principle: *in dubio standum est pro valore actus.*[46] This doctrine is confirmed by the fact that canon 54, § 1, prescribes that a necessary executor who is commissioned merely to execute a rescript is not to refuse the execution of the letter, unless, among other things, *"manifeste pateat rescriptum vitio subreptionis aut obreptionis nullum esse."* That is to say, even a positive doubt about the truthfulness of the relevant *preces* is not sufficient to justify this executor's not

[44] A *dubium iuris* affects the law itself with respect to its existence, its binding force, its extent, its clauses, its cessation. A *dubium facti* affects the application of the law to a fact, i.e., there is uncertainty whether or not a fact or the circumstances surrounding it possess all the requisite elements to bring it within the compass of the law.

[45] Cf. Michiels, *Normae Generales,* II, 372.

[46] Cf., e.g., Cappello, *Summa Iuris Canonici,* I, 120; Coronata, *Institutiones,* I, 80; Michiels, *loc. cit.;* Ojetti, *Commentarium,* I, 227; Van Hove, *De Rescriptis,* p. 149. To the contrary, Rodrigo remarks in this connection: *"In dubio facti* quod excuti non possit, valor rescripti alligatus manet exsistentiae vel inexsistentiae facti dubii in quo innititur; et inde rescriptum praesumetur validum vel invalidum, prout factum a quo dependet praesumendum sit exsistens vel inexsistens."—*Tractatus de Legibus,* p. 567.

carrying out his mandate.[47] Nonetheless, some of the authors advise that in practice, if time permits, it is better to seek a rescript *perinde valere* to ensure that the letter, the validity of which is merely presumed in the circumstances envisioned in this discussion, is really valid.[48] It must be remembered that the presumption involved here cannot supply the rescript with objective validity if the letter actually rests upon substantially false *preces*. It is more than likely that in proposing this practical course of action these commentators are concerned primarily with those rescripts the validity of which is necessary for the objective validity of the acts that are placed in virtue of the letters in question. Perhaps the reader will better understand the foregoing consideration if he sees the following statement of Rodrigo, in which this author gives a comprehensive but concise juridical appraisal of the use of rescripts the validity of which is doubtful by way of a *dubium facti:*

> Quoad usum rescripti *sic dubii:* si hoc concedat iurisdictionalem potestatem, potestatis defectum supplebit Ecclesia in eius usu, iuxta can, 209;—si ius mere subiectivum tribuat ad aliquid agendum, ut rescriptum oratorii privati concessivum, aut rescriptum dispensativum in irregularitate vel impedimento matrimoniali, licitus erit usus rescripti tamquam validi, nisi requiratur ad ipsum valorem actus, huiusque valor sit a periculo nullitatis omnino tutandus, ut accidit in casu de impedimento dirimente matrimoniali.[49]

This writer proposes, therefore, that at least in those cases in which the validity of non-jurisdictional acts is involved it is prudent to seek a *perinde valere* rescript to ensure the validity of the rescripts in question here.[50]

[47] Cf. *supra*, pp. 222-223.

[48] Cf., e.g., Cappello, *loc. cit.;* Chelodi, *Ius Canonicum de Personis*, p. 131; Michiels, *ibid.*, p. 373. The *perinde valere* rescript is explained below.—Cf. pp. 234-236.

[49] *Loc. cit.*

[50] O'Neill, however, inveighed against this course of action, as the following statement made by him indicates: "Seeking a rescript *'Perinde Valere'* in such circumstances [i.e., those in which a *dubium facti* is present] seems entirely unnecessary, however, since the Code itself [c. 84, § 2] states that a dispensation can be lawfully petitioned and validly and lawfully granted

Article 4. Remedies for the Preces and Rescripts Vitiated by Subreption or Obreption

Because of the essential foundation which objectively truthful petitions must provide for the validity of rescripts, canonists are naturally interested in the remedies that are available for sanating any vitiating falsehood that is found either in the *preces* for rescripts or in rescripts themselves. At the present time a special sanating remedy is provided for both of them. The remedy for defective petitions is called the *decretum reformatorium;* the remedy for vitiated rescripts is known as the *perinde valere* rescript.[51]

A. The *decretum reformatorium*

If substantial subreption or obreption is discovered in a petition after it has been sent to the superior, but before the requested rescript is granted, the petitioner can ask for and obtain

---

even if it is doubtful whether the cause is sufficient, and since the principle *'standum est pro valore actus,'* offered by leading canonists and moralists, was intended not to solve theoretical questions but practical difficulties. Only in case it is certain that there is no true remaining motive cause or that something essential has been omitted or incorrectly stated is there any obligation to seek a rescript *'Perinde Valere.'"—Papal Rescripts of Favor,* pp. 129-130. Cf. also Coronata, *ibid.,* nota 4, and Gasparri, *De Matrimonio,* I, 206. The reasoning that was employed by O'Neill in the foregoing statement is certainly not without merit. The writer wishes to note, however, that nowhere, to his knowledge, does the Code provide for the objective validity of a marriage, which validity, as Rodrigo indicates above on page 232, depends upon rescripts whose intrinsic efficacy is rightfully presumed the while they are *de facto* null and void. Moreover, prudence seems to dictate that, even in the presence of a legitimate presumption, when the validity of an act is jeopardized, one should follow, if possible, a safe way of preventing the act from possibly being invalid.

[51] Cf. Rodrigo, *Tractatus de Legibus,* pp. 573-574. For a discussion of these remedies in reference to rescripts that contain matrimonial dispensations, cf. Gasparri, *De Matrimonio,* I, pp. 204-206. Of course, when a rescript has been nullified because of false *preces,* it is always possible for the petitioner to put aside the vitiated letter and request another rescript. Unlike the *perinde valere* letter, this new rescript will be separate and distinct from the previous defective one, and will have no bearing on it.

the so-called *decretum reformatorium.* The purpose of this decree is to modify the vitiated *preces* which were originally sent to the superior, so that after the proper changes have been made, they will *de facto* be founded on truth, as the law requires.[52] One can obtain the *decretum reformatorium* by sending to the superior to whom the first *preces* were directed a new petition in which the petitioner asks for this decree and indicates the items that must be added, withdrawn, or corrected in the original *preces* to make them conform to the truth. It is not necessary for the petitioner to repeat the contents of his original *preces,* nor is he required to inform the superior whether the defects in the first petition were due to good or bad faith. The superior, upon receiving the second petition, examines it together with the first one and thereby obtains the truth about the facts, circumstances, and reasons for the rescript that were in some way distorted in the original *preces.* He then issues his *decretum reformatorium* to sanate the first *preces* and grants the favor on the basis of the knowledge that he has acquired from both petitions. Of course, it is presumed here that the aforesaid knowledge is such as to dispose the superior to accede to the petitioner's request. It may happen that even though the sanated *preces* are truthful, the superior may find another reason for not granting the rescript that is sought.

B. The *perinde valere* Rescript

The *perinde valere* rescript is a letter through which it is intended to validate or sanate a previous rescript which has been intrinsically nullified because the *preces* for it were substantially false.[53] This type of rescript is always issued after the su-

[52] Van Hove, *De Rescriptis,* p. 168.

[53] The *perinde valere* rescript can be used also in cases in which the nullity of the invalid rescript arises from some other cause than false *preces.* In this regard, however, the following statement of Rodrigo must be kept in mind: "*Obiectum sanationis formale* debet esse defectus, ut dixi, ipsius rescripti; non autem defectus Superioris v.c. incompetentis, aut exsecutoris vel oratoris inhabilis; neque invaliditas ipsius actus ad quem habilitare intendebet rescriptum, v.c. invaliditas matrimonii contracti cum rescripto dispensativo nullo, nam tunc potius est locus revalidandi vel sanandi actum invalide positum."—*Op. cit.,* p. 574.

perior has acted upon the petitioner's initial *preces* by granting the rescript requested of him. It differs from the ordinary rescript insofar as it convalidates the vitiated letter in question. What is more, by a fiction of law its sanative effect is made retroactive to the day on which the invalid rescript had actually been granted. Thus the initial rescript, although null until the time when the *perinde valere* letter was issued, is looked upon, after its sanation, as if it had been valid from the moment of its concession.[54] It must be noted, however, that if the rescript which is validated in this manner was granted *in forma commissoria,* its execution has to be repeated.[55]

To obtain a *perinde valere* rescript one has to submit a new petition. In it the petitioner must state substantially, or at least, summarily, the contents of the *preces* that were presented for the invalid rescript. He must also note the reason for the nullity of the defective rescript. Finally, he must ask the superior to validate the former rescript and the favor which it sought to convey.

The petition for the *perinde valere* rescript should be sent to the superior who granted the vitiated letter, unless he does not have the authority to issue the validating rescript. If the grantor of the initial rescript lacks this authority, then the *preces* for the sanating letter should be presented to him who is the grantor's superior in the hierarchical order. The latter has the power to validate the rescripts of the former. One, however, who is merely equal or even subordinate to the grantor in the hierarchical order does not have such authority, unless he possesses it in virtue of special faculties that have been given to him. This is true even if this person can in his own right grant the same kind of rescript as the one which is to be validated.[56]

If it should happen that the *perinde valere* rescript is itself

[54] Cf. O'Neill, *Papal Rescripts of Favor,* p. 191, and Rodrigo, *loc. cit.*

[55] Michiels, *Normae Generales,* II, 408.

[56] Rodrigo offers the following reason for this statement, which reason he refers only to a subordinate of the grantor, but which is applicable also to the grantor's equal: "etenim ipse nequit se immiscere in Superioris negotia, immo est incompetens ulterius ad ea convalidanda."—*Loc. cit.* Cf. also Michiels, *loc. cit.*

invalidated by way of a substantial subreption or obreption in the *preces* for it, its nullity can be sanated by means of another letter, which is called the *perinde valere super perinde valere* rescript. This sanating rescript is obtained in the same manner as the *perinde valere* letter. Upon its issuance, it validates the *perinde valere* rescript, which in turn produces the same effects as it would have produced had it been valid from the time of its concession.[57]

[57] Cf. O'Neill, *loc. cit.*

CONCLUSIONS

A. Historical Synopsis

1. Substantially truthful *preces* have always been required as an essential basis for the validity of rescripts. (Cf. pp. 38-39, 55, 61)

2. The Popes adopted the Roman Law Institute of Rescript for their own use certainly by the year 385. Before the Church developed her own law concerning the truth that was required in the *preces* for rescripts, she observed the prescriptions of the Roman Law in this regard. The first properly ecclesiastical law in this matter which Gratian recorded in his *Decretum* was that issued in 557 by Pope Pelagius I (556-561). (Cf. pp. 38-39)

3. The first express mention of the essential condition *"si preces veritate nitantur"* as a formal element of the law on rescripts was in a decree of the Emperor Zeno in the year 477. Pope Alexander III (1159-1181) canonized this Roman Law expression seven centuries later. (Cf. p. 38)

4. Until the time of Pope Boniface VIII (1294-1303), this condition was considered essential for all rescripts without exception. Pope Boniface VIII, however, partially excepted *motu proprio* issued rescripts from its invalidating force, inasmuch as he provided that subreption, but not obreption, in petitions for these letters did not lay the rescripts open to invalidity. The only other exception, which was made in pre-Code times to the law's demand for truthful *preces* as an essential basis of the validity of rescripts, was that prescribed by Pope St. Pius X (1903-1914) in 1908 in his reform of the Roman Curia. That exception was in favor of rescripts conveying dispensations from minor matrimonial impediments. The norm in which that exception was set forth stated that the rescripts in question were not invalidated by either subreption or obreption. (Cf. pp. 38, 48, 54)

5. The Church's pre-Code legislation concerning the truth which was required in the *preces* for rescripts was almost com-

pletely crystallized by the time of the Council of Trent (1545-1563). Among the Popes who had laid down the basic principles of that legislation before the Council of Trent were Pope Pelagius I (556-561), Pope Alexander III (1159-1181), Pope Lucius III (1181-1185), Pope Innocent III (1198-1216), Pope Honorius III (1216-1227), Pope Boniface VIII (1294-1303) ; after the Council of Trent, Pope St. Pius X (1903-1914). (Cf. pp. 36, 38-39, 41-50, 54)

6. The practical significance of the papal legislation in reference to the correct application of the essential principle *"si preces veritate nitantur"* was not always clear. The result was that many controversies arose among the commentators in this regard. In some instances these differences of opinion persisted until the time of the Code of Canon Law. (Cf. pp. 55-106)

7. By the seventeenth century there was a definite trend among canonists to reserve the term "obreption" to signify the expression of falsehood, and the word "subreption" to indicate either the actual suppression of some truth that should have been expressed or the concealment of such truth by means of a confusing and indistinct statement of it. This usage seemed to become the more exclusive, the closer the authors came to the promulgation of the Code of Canon Law. (Cf. pp. 59-60)

B. Canonical Commentary

8. The term *"preces"* in the clause *"si preces veritate nitantur"* signifies only the formal petition that is presented for rescripts. It does not comprehend, therefore, statements which are not part of the formal petition, as, for example, the acts that are assembled to prove the petitioner's allegations in *ratum et non consummatum* and *in favorem fidei* marriage cases. (Cf. p. 17)

9. Nowhere in his law does the ecclesiastical legislator give a definition of what he means by the word "truth," as it is used in the condition *"si preces veritate nitantur."* From the context in which he has placed this term, however, there can be no doubt that he intends to convey by it a general philosophical concept which is made specific by his own legal norms in canon 42, §§ 1 and 2. This general philosophical concept is that of ontological

or transcendental truth, that is, the truth of objective reality. (Cf. pp. 112-114)

10. The use of the verb *"nitantur"* in the clause *"si preces veritate nitantur"* is indicative of the fact that, by understanding that condition as inherent in all rescripts, the legislator *per se* demands merely the existence of truthful petitions in regard to the validity of rescripts. He does not by that clause make the validity of rescripts depend upon an investigation into the truthfulness of their *preces*. (Cf. pp. 114-115)

11. The general norms of *Liber I, Titulus IV, De rescriptis,* in the Code of Canon Law apply *ex rigore iuris* to all rescripts, no matter who the grantor of them may be, unless, of course, there is clear indication in one or other of these laws that it governs solely the rescripts of a particular superior. (Cf. pp. 119-122)

12. Canon 45, which deals with rescripts granted *motu proprio,* represents a true exception to the general norm of canon 40, namely, that the *essential* condition *"si preces veritate nitantur"* is at least understood in all rescripts. The exception, established by canon 45, consists in the fact that the aforesaid condition is not considered to be essential in relation to the *pars narrativa* of *preces* for *motu proprio* granted rescripts. Neither the *pars postulativa* nor the *pars motiva* of the *preces* for such rescripts, however, is included within the scope of the exception effected in this regard by canon 45. (Cf. pp. 181-187)

13. Canon 1054, which is concerned with rescripts containing dispensations from minor matrimonial impediments, constitutes a true exception to the above-mentioned norm of canon 40 (cf. number 12), for it puts aside the essential nature and effect of the condition *"si preces veritate nitantur"* in reference to the *pars narrativa* and the *pars motiva* of petitions for the rescripts which it treats. The *pars postulativa* of the *preces* for such rescripts, however, is not included within the scope of the exception established in this regard by canon 1054. (Cf. pp. 194-196)

14. The lawmaker sets forth in canon 40, together with canon 2361, his demand for truthful *preces* as a fundamental basis for the lawfulness of all rescripts. Neither canon 45 nor canon 1054 constitutes an exception to this requirement. (Cf. pp. 122-125)

15. Under the law of the Code no distinction is made between good and bad faith as far as the invalidating effect of subreption and obreption is concerned. In the cases contemplated, respectively, in canons 991, § 1, and 2249, § 2, however, the legislator makes an exception to the foregoing principle in favor of good faith. Thus, a general dispensation, if granted in accord with the provision made in canon 991, § 1, or a general absolution, if given in accordance with canon 2249, § 2, is valid if the subreption contemplated in those canons and committed in the petition for the rescript involved in the case arises from good faith. That is to say, if the subreption is due to good faith, it is merely accidental and, therefore, non-invalidating in respect to the matters suppressed in good faith. If the subreption is caused by bad faith, however, it is substantial and nullifying in reference to the matters thus suppressed. (Cf. pp. 133-137)

16. The general principle of canon 42, § 1, can be stated in these terms: in order that a rescript be not nullified and deprived of its intended force by reason of subreption, it is *necessary* and *sufficient* that there be expressed in the petition for it all those facts and circumstances which, by the *stylus Curiae*, must be mentioned for the validity of the rescript. (Cf. p. 137)

17. The requirements of the *stylus Curiae* constitute the criterion by which is to be decided whether subreption in the *preces* is invalidating or non-invalidating. The term "*Curia*" in the expression "*stylus Curiae*" in canon 42, § 1, comprehends both the Roman Curia and curiae inferior to it. The requirements of the *stylus Curiae,* referred to in the aforesaid canon, include not only those which arise from the custom, instructions, and observances of the different curiae but also the norms that are established in regard to the matter of subreption by the written universal and particular law of the Church. (Cf. pp. 141-147)

18. In reference to the general requirements of the common law as to what must be mentioned in the *preces* for the validity of rescripts, only the prescription of canon 44, § 2, if transgressed, always results directly in substantial subreption in petitions. (Cf. pp. 149-152)

19. In and of itself (*per se*) the mention of the religion of the petitioners for matrimonial dispensations does not seem to be

necessary for the validity of the rescripts involved, even if one of the parties is a non-Catholic. Prudence dictates, however, that whenever a non-Catholic is involved, the fact of his not being a Catholic be indicated. The statement of this fact alone, without mention of the particular sect to which the non-Catholic belongs, is sufficient. (Cf. pp. 165-167)

20. The general principle of canon 42, § 2, may be expressed in this manner: as far as the *pars motiva* of petitions is concerned, for the fulfillment of the essential condition *"si preces veritate nitantur"* it is required and sufficient that one true final cause be present therein. (Cf. p. 169)

21. A petitioner should not always be satisfied with proposing only one true reason in his *preces,* for, in the last analysis, it lies with the superior to decide in a given case whether the cause alleged in the petition is actually motivating or merely impelling. A reason that is considered to be a final cause in one instance may be judged to be only impulsive in another because of the different circumstances in the two cases. (Cf. pp. 171-172)

22. A rescript is sometimes obtained because of several merely impelling reasons which have been taken in the aggregate to constitute the single final cause for the grant. In practice, if it should happen that one of these reasons is found to be false, and if that reason is relatively insignificant in relation to all the other causes taken together, the rescript in question may be safely adjudged valid. (Cf. pp. 172-173)

23. The general principle of canon 42, § 3, may be set down in this way: when a petition requesting several truly separable and mutually independent favors is partially infected with substantial subreption and/or obreption, only that favor in the consequent rescript is invalidated which is directly attributable to, and immediately dependent upon, the nullifying untruthfulness in the *preces.* (Cf. p. 175)

24. In canon 45 the legislator indicates by the words *"non tamen si falsa causa, etc."* that a superior's grant made *motu proprio,* when attached to rescripts, applies only to the *pars narrativa* of the *preces* for the letters. That is to say, this phrase does not imply that the superior had any other motivating reason for granting the rescripts in question except that or those reasons

which the petitioners themselves proposed to him. (Cf. pp. 185-186)

25. Rescripts containing dispensations from impedient matrimonial impediments alone never come within the scope of canon 1054. (Cf. pp. 191-192)

26. Even when the *preces* for the rescripts dealt with in canon 1054 are vitiated by subreption or obreption, a superior acts reasonably in granting these letters inasmuch as they are issued *"motu proprio et ex certa scientia."* Moreover, even in the presence of otherwise invalidating obreption in the causes offered by the petitioners, he acts truly voluntarily in granting the rescripts in question insofar as they are always given *"ex certis rationabilibus causis a Sancta Sede probatis."* (Cf. pp. 192-194)

27. The extraordinarily liberal ruling of canon 1054, in reference to the validity of the rescripts with which it is concerned, is applicable both to rescripts issued by the Holy See and to those granted by duly empowered superiors who are subordinate to the Apostolic See. Only for the lawfulness of the rescripts of the subordinate superiors is it necessary to have at least one true final cause in the *preces* for the letters in question. Nonetheless, canon 1054 is in no way a derogation from canon 84, § 1. (Cf. pp. 196-199)

28. The general principle of canon 41 may be enunciated in this manner: for the validity of rescripts it is required and sufficient that the *preces* involved be truthful at the time when the letters consequent upon them become effective regardless of the status of facts before or after that moment, without prejudice, however, to the prescriptions of canons 52 and 86. (Cf. pp. 204, 215-218)

29. Rescripts through which a *sanatio in radice* is granted for the rectification of an invalid marriage take effect under the terms of canon 1138, § 2, at the moment when the grantor signs them or according to canon 38 when they are executed. The same is true of rescripts which convey the habitual faculties that are dealt with in canon 66. Rescripts that contain a prorogation or renewal of habitual faculties, which previously were granted for a specified period of time, become effective the moment they are signed if the original faculties have already ex-

pired. If the original faculties have not yet ceased, the rescripts in question take effect on the day that the previous grant is to terminate. (Cf. pp. 209-214)

30. The necessary executor who has simply the commission to execute the rescript given to him has an obligation to investigate the veracity of the *preces* for the rescript whenever he has a serious suspicion about the truthfulness of the petition. This is true even in cases involving the rescripts mentioned in canon 1054 whenever the executor suspects the veracity of the *pars postulativa* of the *preces* for these rescripts. (Cf. pp. 220-221)

31. In the rare instance in which there arises a real and substantial discrepancy between the *preces* presented by the petitioner and the summary of them incorporated into the consequent rescript, one should examine both the original petition and the summary of it in making his decision concerning the presence or absence of invalidating subreption or obreption. In these circumstances, if substantial untruthfulness should be found in either the petitioner's *preces* or in the summary of them in the rescript, but not in both of them, the rescript should be adjudged valid because of the *dubium iuris* which has arisen in this regard. (Cf. pp. 229-230)

32. The validity of rescripts is sometimes called into question because of a *dubium facti* concerning the presence of nullifying subreption or obreption. Whenever the validity of non-jurisdictional acts depends upon such doubtfully valid rescripts, it is prudent to seek *perinde valere* letters to ensure the validity of the rescripts involved. (Cf. pp. 231-232)

BIBLIOGRAPHY

Sources

Acta Apostolicae Sedis, Commentarium Officiale, Romae, 1909-1929; Civitate Vaticana, 1929-

Acta Sanctae Sedis, 41 vols., Romae, 1865-1908.

Bizzarri, Andreas, *Collectanea in usum Secretariae Sacrae Congregationis Episcoporum et Regularium edita,* Romae, 1885.

Canon Law Digest, The, 4 vols., Milwaukee: Bruce Publishing Co., Vol. I, 7. printing, 1950; Vol. II, 5. printing, 1949; Vol. III, 1954, edited by T. Lincoln Bouscaren; Vol. IV, 1958, edited by T. Lincoln Bouscaren and James I. O'Connor.

Codex Iuris Canonici Pii X Pontificis Maximi iussu digestus, Benedicti Papae XV auctoritate promulgatus, Praefatione, Fontium Annotatione et Indice Analytico-Alphabetico ab Emo Petro Card. Gasparri Auctus, Westminster, Md.: The Newman Press, 1949.

Codicis Iuris Canonici Fontes, cura Emi Petri Card. Gasparri editi, 9 vols., Romae (postea Civitate Vaticana): Typis Polyglottis Vaticanis, 1923-1939 (Vols. VII-IX ed. cura et studio Emi Iustiniani Card. Serédi).

Collectanea S. Congregationis de Propaganda Fide, 2 vols., Romae, 1907.

Corpus Iuris Canonici, ed. Lipsiensis II, post Aemilii Ludovici Richteri curas instruxit Aemilius Friedberg, 2 vols., Lipsiae: Ex officina Bernhardi Tauchnitz, 1879-1881; ed. anastatice repetita, 1928.

Corpus Iuris Civilis, 3 vols., Vol. I, *Digesta Iustiniani Augusti,* quem recognovit Theodorus Mommsen et retractavit P. Krueger, ed. stereotypa 15., 1928; Vol. II, *Codex Iustinianus,* quem Paulus Krueger recognovit et retractavit, ed. stereotypa 10., 1929, Berolini.

Decretales D. Gregorii Papae IX, suae integritati, una cum glossis restitutae, cum privilegio Gregorii XIII, Pontif. Max., et aliorum Principum, Romae, 1582.

Decretum Gratiani, emendatum et notationibus illustratum, una cum glossis, 2 vols., Romae, 1582.

Liber Sextus Decretalium D. Bonifatii Papae VIII, suae integritati una cum Clementinis et Extravagantibus, earumque Glossis restitutus, cum privilegio Gregorii XIII, Pont. Max., et aliorum Principum, Romae, 1582.

Jaffé, Philippus, *Regesta Pontificum Romanorum ab condita Ecclesia ad annum post Christum natum MCXCVIII,* ed 2. correctam et auctam auspiciis Gulielmi Wattenbach, curaverunt F. Kaltenbrunner, P. Ewald, S. Loewenfeld, 2 vols., Lipsiae, 1885-1888.

Potthast, Augustus, *Regesta Pontificum Romanorum inde ab anno post Christum natum MCXCVIII ad annum MCCCIV,* 2 vols., Berolini, 1874-1875.

Schroeder, H. J., *Canons and Decrees of the Council of Trent,* Original Text with English Translation, St. Louis: B. Herder Book Co., 1941.

Reference Works

Abbo, John A. - Hannan, Jerome D., *The Sacred Canons,* 2 vols., St. Louis and London: B. Herder Book Co., 1952.

Aichner, Simon, *Compendium Juris Ecclesiastici,* 6. ed., Brixinae, 1887.

Aquinas, S. Thomas, *Quaestiones Disputatae de Veritate,* ed. R. Spiazzi, Romae: Marietti, 1953.

Augustine, Charles, *A Commentary on the New Code of Canon Law,* 8 vols., Vol. I, 3. ed., St. Louis, 1920.

Ayrinhac, Henry A., *General Legislation in the New Code of Canon Law,* New York, 1923.

Baldus de Ubaldis, *Super Decretalibus,* Lugduni, 1547.

Bargilliat, Michael, *Praelectiones Juris Canonici,* 30. ed., 2 vols., Parisiis, 1915.

Bartoccetti, Victorius, *De Regulis Juris Canonici,* Romae: A. Belardetti, 1955.

Benedictus XIV, *Institutiones Ecclesiasticae,* 3. ed., 2 vols., Venetiis, 1788.

———, *De Synodo Dioecesana,* 2. ed., 2 vols., Parmae, 1764.

Berutti, Christophorus, *Institutiones Iuris Canonici,* 6 vols., Vol. I, Taurini-Romae, 1936.

Beste, Udalricus, *Introductio in Codicem,* 3. ed., Collegeville, Minn.: St. John's Abbey Press, 1946.

Blat, Albertus, *Commentarium Textus Codicis Iuris Canonici,* 5 vols. in 7, Vol. I, Romae, 1921.

Bouscaren, T. Lincoln - Ellis, Adam C., *Canon Law, A Text and Commentary,* 2. ed., Milwaukee: Bruce, 1951.

Boyle, David J., *The Juridic Effects of Moral Certitude on Pre-Nuptial Guarantees,* The Catholic University of America Canon Law Studies, n. 150, Washington, D. C.: The Catholic University of America Press, 1942.

Brys, J., *Juris Canonici Compendium,* 2 vols., Vol. I, 10. ed., Brugis: Desclée de Brouwer et Sii., 1947.

Cappello, Felix M., *Summa Iuris Canonici,* 3 vols., Vol. I, 4. ed., Romae: Apud Aedes Universitatis Gregorianae, 1945.

———, *Tractatus Canonico-Moralis de Sacramentis,* Vol. V, *De Matrimonio,* 6. ed., Taurini-Romae: Marietti, 1950.

Cassell's Latin Dictionary, Revised by J. Marchant and J. Charles, New York and London: Funk and Wagnalls Co., 1942.

Chelodi, Ioannes, *Ius Canonicum de Personis,* 3. ed., recognita et aucta a Pio Ciprotti, Vincenza: Società Anonima Tipografica, Trento: A. Ardesi, 1942.

Cicognani, Amleto G., *Canon Law,* 2. ed., authorized English version by Joseph M. O'Hara and Francis J. Brennan, Westminster, Md.: The Newman Press, Reprint, 1949.

———, *Commentarium in Librum Primum Codicis Iuris Canonici,* 2 vols. in 1, recognitum et auctum a Dino Staffa, Romae: Buona Stampa, 1939-1942.

Claeys Boúúaert, F. - Simenon, G., *Manuale Juris Canonici,* 3 vols., Vol. I, 5. ed., Gandae et Leodii: Prostat apud auctores in Seminariis Gandavensi et Leodiensi, 1939.

Cocchi, Guidus, *Commentarium in Codicem iuris canonici ad usum scholarum,* 8 vols., Vol. I, 5. ed., Taurinorum Augustae: Marietti, 1938.

Conte a Coronata, Matthaeus, *Institutiones Iuris Canonici ad usum utriusque cleri et scholarum,* 5 vols., Vol. I, 4. ed., Taurini: Marietti, 1950.

———, *Institutiones Iuris Canonici, De Sacramentis Tractatus Canonicus,* 3 vols., Vol. III, *De Matrimonio et de Sacramentalibus,* 2. ed., Taurini-Romae: Marietti, 1948.

Coussa, Acacius, *Epitome Praelectionum de Iure Ecclesiastico Orientali,* 3 vols., Vol. III, *De Matrimonio,* Romae: Apud Custodiam Librariam Pontificii Instituti Utriusque Iuris, 1950.

D'Annibale, Josephus, *Summula Theologiae Moralis,* 4. ed., 3 vols., Romae, 1896-1897.

De Angelis, Philippus, *Praelectiones Juris Canonici,* 4 toms., Romae-Parisiis, 1877-1878.

De Becker, Julius, *De Sponsalibus et Matrimonio Praelectiones Canonicae,* 2. ed., Lovanii, 1913.

De Justis, Vincentius, *De Dispensationibus Matrimonialibus,* Lucae, 1726.

De Meester, Alphonsus, *Juris Canonici et Juris Canonico-Civilis Compendium,* 3 vols. in 4, Vol. I, nova ed., Brugis, 1921.

De Rosa, Thomas, *De Executoribus Litterarum Apostolicarum,* Aschaffenburci, 1747.

De Smet, Aloysius, *Betrothment and Marriage,* translated from the French Edition of 1912 by the Rev. W. Dobell, 2 vols., St. Louis, 1913.

Eichmann, Eduard, *Lehrbuch des katholischen Kirchenrechts,* Paderborn, 1926.

Engel, Ludovicus, *Collegium Universi Juris Canonici,* Beneventi, 1760.

Fagnanus, Prosper, *Commentaria in Quinque Libros Decretalium,* 5 vols. in 4, Venetiis, 1709.

Feije, Henricus J., *De Impedimentis et Dispensationibus Matrimonialibus,* 3. ed., Lovanii, 1885.

Felinus Sandeus, *Commentaria in Quinque Libros Decretalium,* 3 vols., Venetiis, 1570.

Ferreres, Joannes B., *Compendium Theologiae Moralis ad Normam Codicis Juris Canonici,* 7. ed., 2 vols., Barcinone, 1928.

Gasparri, Petrus Card., *Tractatus Canonicus de Matrimonio,* ed. nova ad mentem Codicis I.C., 2 vols., Romae, 1932.

Giovine, Petrus, *De Dispensationibus Matrimonialibus Consultationes Canonicae,* 2 vols., Neapoli, 1863.

Gonzalez-Tellez, Emmanuel, *Commentaria Perpetua in Quinque Libros Decretalium,* 4 vols., Lugduni, 1673.

Gougnard, Armandus, *Tractatus de Matrimonio,* 7. ed., Mechliniae, 1931.

Gredt, Joseph, *Elementa Philosophiae Aristotelico-Thomisticae,* 10. ed., 2 vols., Friburgi Brisgoviae-Barcinone: Herder, 1953.

Heylen, V., *Tractatus de Matrimonio,* 9 ed., Mechliniae: H. Dessain, 1945.

Hoenen, Peter, *Reality and Judgment according to St. Thomas,* translated by H. Tiblier, Chicago: Henry Regnery Co., 1952.

Hostiensis, Cardinalis (Henricus de Segusio), *Commentaria in Quinque Decretalium Libros,* 6 vols. in 4, Venetiis, 1581.

———, *Summa Aurea,* Venetiis, 1570.

Laymann, Paulus, *Theologia Moralis,* 5 vols. in 1, Duaci, 1635.

Innocentius IV, *In Quinque Libros Decretalium Commentaria,* Venetiis, 1570.

Maroto, Philippus, *Institutiones Iuris Canonici ad normam novi Codicis,* 2 vols., Vol. I, 3. ed., Romae, 1921.

Maschat, Remigius, *Cursus Iuris Canonici,* 2 vols., Romae, 1757.

Michiels, Gommarus, *Normae Generales Juris Canonici,* 2. ed., 2 vols., Parisiis-Tornaci-Romae: Desclée et Socii, 1949.

Monin, Arthur, *De Curia Romana,* Lovanii, 1912.

Ojetti, Benedictus, *Commentarium in Codicem Iuris Canonici,* 4 vols., Vol. I, Romae, 1927.

O'Mara, William A., *Canonical Causes for Matrimonial Dispensations,* The Catholic University of America Canon Law Studies, n. 96, Washington, D. C., 1935.

O'Neill, William, *Papal Rescripts of Favor,* The Catholic University of America Canon Law Studies, n. 57, Washington, D. C., 1930.

Panormitanus, Abbas (Nicholaus de Tudeschis), *Commentaria in Quinque Libros Decretalium,* 5 vols. in 7, Venetiis, 1588.

Pirhing, Ernricus, *Jus Canonicum in Quinque Libros Decretalium,* ed. novissima, 5 vols. in 4, Dilingae, 1722.

Planchard, J., *Dispenses Matrimoniales Règles a Suivre pour les Demander, les Interpréter, les Mettre a Exécution,* Angoulême, 1882.

Pyrrhus, Corradus, *Praxis Dispensationum Apostolicarum,* Venetiis, 1735.

Regatillo, Eduardus, *Institutiones Iuris Canonici,* 2 vols., Vol. I, 2. ed., Santander: Sal Terrae, 1946.

Reiffenstuel, Anacletus, *Jus Canonicum Universum,* 5 vols. in 7, Parisiis, 1864-1870.

Repetitionum in Universas fere Iuris Canonici Partes, Materiasque sane Frequentiores Volumina Sex, cura L. A. Giunta, Venetiis, 1587.

Rodrigo, Lucius, *Praelectiones Theologico-Morales Comillenses,* Vol. II, *Tractatus de Legibus,* Santander: Sal Terrae, 1944.

Ryan, Thomas C., *The Juridical Effects of the Sanatio in Radice,* The Catholic University of America Canon Law Studies, n. 355, Washington, D. C.: The Catholic University of America Press, 1955.

Sanchez, Thomas, *De Sancto Matrimonii Sacramento,* 3 toms., Antverpiae, 1626.

Sanguineti, Sebastianus, *Iuris Ecclesiastici Institutiones,* 3. ed., Romae, 1896.

Santi, Franciscus, *Praelectiones Juris Canonici,* cura M. Leitner, 5 vols. in 2, Ratisbonae-Romae-Neo Eboraci-Cincinnati, 1904.

Schmalzgrueber, Franciscus, *Jus Ecclesiasticum Universum,* 5 vols. in 12, Romae, 1843-1845.

Sebastianelli, Guilelmo, *Praelectiones Iuris Canonici,* 2. ed., 3 vols., Romae, 1905-1906.

Sipos, Stephanus, *Enchiridion Iuris Canonici, ad usum scholarum et privatorum,* 6. ed., recognovit L. Gálos, Romae: Orbis Catholicus-Herder, 1954.

Soglia, Joannes, *Institutiones Juris Publici Ecclesiastici,* 5. ed., Parisiis, 1853.

Suarez, Franciscus, *Opera Omnia,* 26 vols. in 28, Parisiis, 1856-1866; Vol. VI, *Tractatus de Legibus et Legislatore Deo,* ed. nova, a Carolo Berton, 1856.

Toso, Albertus, *Ad Codicem Iuris Canonici Commentaria Minora,* 5 vols. in 2, Vol. I, 2. ed., Taurini, Romae: Marietti, 1921.

Tuschus, Dominicus, *Practicae Conclusiones Iuris in omni foro frequentiores,* 8 toms., Lugduni, 1634; *Additiones,* Tom. IX, Lugduni, 1670.

Van Hove, Alphonsus, *Commentarium Lovaniense in Codicem Iuris Canonici,* Editum a Magistris et Doctoribus Universitatis Lovaniensis, 1 vol. in 5 toms., Tom. II, *De Legibus Ecclesiasticis,* 1930; Tom. IV, *De Rescriptis,* 1936, Mechliniae-Romae.

Vecchiotti, Septimus M., *Institutiones Canonicae,* 16. ed., 3 vols., Augustae Taurinorum, 1875.

Vermeersch, A. - Creusen, J., *Epitome Iuris Canonici cum Commentariis ad Scholas et ad Usum Privatum,* 3 vols., Vol. I, 7. ed., 1949; Vol. II, 6. ed., 1940, Mechliniae-Romae: H. Dessain.

Vlaming, Th. M. - Bender, L., *Praelectiones Iuris Matrimonii ad Normam Codicis Iuris Canonici,* 4. ed., Bussum in Hollandia: Sumptibus Societatis Editricis Anonymae Paulus Brand, 1950.

Wernz, Franciscus X., *Ius Decretalium,* 6 vols., Vol. I, 2. ed., Romae, 1905.

Wernz, Franciscus X. - Vidal, Petrus, *Ius Canonicum ad Codicis Normam Exactum,* 7 vols. in 8, Vol. I, 2. ed., 1952; Vol. V, *Ius Matrimoniale,* 3. ed., a Philippo Aguirre recognita, 1946, Romae: Apud Aedes Universitatis Gregorianae.

Wilhelmsen, Frederick D., *Man's Knowledge of Reality,* Englewood Cliffs, N. J.: Prentice-Hall, Inc., 1956.

Zitelli, Zephyrinus, *De Dispensationibus Matrimonialibus,* Romae, 1884.

Articles

Harrington, J. C., "The Importance of the *Cautiones* in Disparity of Worship," *The Ecclesiastical Review,* LXV (1921), 257-262.

Kelly, J. Norbert, "Insincere *'Cautiones,'* in the Light of Recent Rota Decisions," *The Jurist,* XIII (1953), 33-56.

Oesterle, G., "De Cautionibus Matrimonialibus," *Jus Pontificium,* XV (1935), 64-81.

Vermeersch, A., "Commentaria de Formulis Facultatum Quas S. Cong. de Propaganda Fide Concedere Solet," *Periodica de Re Canonica et Morali, utilia praesertim Religiosis et Missionariis,* XI (1922), (33)-(144).

———, "A qua die valeant acta S. Sedis," *Periodica de Re Morali, Canonica, Liturgica,* XXI (1932), 52*.

Woywod, Stanislaus, "Dispensation in Marriage Impediment May Be Made Invalid by Faulty Petition," *The Homiletic and Pastoral Review,* XXI (1920-1921), 319-320.

PERIODICALS

American Ecclesiastical Review, The, Vols. I-XXXII, Philadelphia, 1889-1905; from 1905: *The Ecclesiastical Review,* Vols. XXXIII-CIX, Philadelphia, 1905-1943; from 1944: *The American Ecclesiastical Review,* Washington, D. C.: Vol. CX, 1944-

Homiletic and Pastoral Review, The, New York, 1900-

Jurist, The, Washington, D. C., 1941-

Jus Pontificium, Romae, 1921-1940.

Periodica de Religiosis et Missionariis, Brugis, 1905-1919; *Periodica de Re Canonica et Morali, utilia praesertim Religiosis et Missionariis,* Brugis, 1920-1927; *Periodica de Re Morali, Canonica, Liturgica,* Brugis, 1927-1936, Romae, 1937-

ABBREVIATIONS

AAS—*Acta Apostolicae Sedis.*
ASS—*Acta Sanctae Sedis.*
Can.—Canon of the *Codex Iuris Canonici.*
Cod. Iust.—*Codex Iustinianus.*
Conc. Trident.—Concilium Tridentinum.
Digesta—*Digesta Iustiniani Augusti.*
Fontes—*Codicis Iuris Canonici Fontes.*
JL—Jaffé, *Regesta Pontificum Romanorum ab condita Ecclesia ad annum post Christum natum MCXCVIII,* ed. curavit S. Loewenfeld.
Potthast—*Regesta Pontificum Romanorum inde ab anno post Christum natum MCXCVIII ad annum MCCCIV.*
S. C. de Prop. Fid.—Sacra Congregatio de Propaganda Fide.
S. C. de Sacramentis—Sacra Congregatio de Disciplina Sacramentorum.
S. C. Ep. et Reg.—Sacra Congregatio Episcoporum et Regularium.
S. C. S. Off.—Sacra Congregatio Sancti Officii.
Schroeder—*Canons and Decrees of the Council of Trent.*

ALPHABETICAL INDEX

BIOGRAPHICAL NOTE

Donald Edward Adams was born on February 24, 1928, in Hanover, Pennsylvania. After completing the primary grades in St. Joseph's School in Hanover, and two years of his high school studies in Delone Catholic High School in McSherrystown, Pennsylvania, he entered St. Charles College High School, Catonsville, Maryland, to begin his studies for the sacred priesthood. He graduated from St. Charles College in June, 1947. In the following September he took up his studies in the Seminary of St. Charles Borromeo, Philadelphia, Pennsylvania, where he received the degree of Bachelor of Arts in 1949. He was ordained to the sacred priesthood on May 30, 1953, by His Excellency, the Most Reverend George L. Leech, D.D., J.C.D., Bishop of Harrisburg. After two years spent in parochial duties in the Diocese of Harrisburg, during eight months of which he also served as Secretary to the Tribunal, he was assigned to the Catholic University of America to pursue the study of Canon Law. He entered the Catholic University of America in September, 1955. He received the degree of Bachelor in Canon Law from that institution in June, 1956, and the degree of Licentiate in Canon Law in June, 1957.

CANON LAW STUDIES *

392. Adams, Rev. Donald E., A.B., J.C.L., The truth required in the *preces* for rescripts.
393. Bégin, Rev. Raymond F., A.B., S.T.L., J.C.L., Natural law and positive law.
394. Clancy, Rev. Walter B., A.B., J.C.L., The rites and ceremonies of sacred ordination.
395. Cox, Rev. Ronald J., S.T.L., J.C.L., A study of the juridic status of laymen in the writing of the medieval canonists.
396. Demers, Rev. Francis L., O.M.I., A.B., J.C.L., Temporal administration of the religious house in a non-exempt clerical pontifical institute.
397. Dziadosz, Rev. Henry J., M.A., S.T.L., J.C.L., The provisions of the Decree "Spiritus Sancti munera": the law for the extraordinary minister of confirmation.
398. Gerhardt, Rev. Bernard C., A.B., S.T.L., J.C.L., Interpretation of rescripts.
399. Hackett, Rev. John H., A.B., J.C.L., The concept of public order.
400. Murphy, Rev. Richard J., O.M.I., S.T.L., J.C.L., The canonico-juridical status of a communist.
401. O'Connor, Rev. David, M.S.SS.T., J.C.L., Parochial relations and co-operation of the religious and secular clergy.

* For a complete list of the available numbers of this series apply to the Catholic University of America Press, 620 Michigan Avenue, N.E., Washington (17), D. C., for a general catalogue.

www.ingramcontent.com/pod-product-compliance
Lightning Source LLC
LaVergne TN
LVHW050255080826
844660LV00012B/641

* 9 7 8 0 8 1 3 2 2 5 5 2 4 *